M LINE

The Seam Line

Arab Workers and Jewish Managers in the Israeli Textile Industry

ISRAEL DRORI

STANFORD UNIVERSITY PRESS

STANFORD, CALIFORNIA

Stanford University Press
Stanford, California

© 2000 by the Board of Trustees of the
Leland Stanford Junior University

Printed in the United States of America

Library of Congress Cataloging-in-Publication Data

Drori, Israel.
    The seam line : Arab workers and Jewish managers in the
Israeli textile industry / Israel Drori.
        p.   cm.
    Includes bibliographical references and index.
        ISBN 0-8047-3785-1 (alk. paper) — ISBN 0-8047-3787-8
(pbk. : alk. paper)
        1. Textile workers—Israel.   2. Palestinian Arabs—
Employment—Israel.   I. Title.
    HD8039.T42 I725   2000
    331.7'677'0095694—dc21   99-086426

♾ This book is printed on acid-free, archival-quality paper.

Original printing 2000

Last figure below indicates year of this printing:
09   08   07   06   05   04   03   02   01   00

Typeset by James P. Brommer in 9.5/12.5 Trump Mediaeval

Acknowledgments

YEARS of study have expanded the layers of people associated with this research. Their empathy, support, and good will have fueled my work and been my main source of intellectual stimulation, creativity, and insight. The interest and openness of the seamstresses and the supervisors, women from the Arab and Druse villages in the Galilee, allowed me to understand and explain their lives at work. The managers, Jewish men with self-awareness, humor, and endless willingness to help, opened for me a window into the intricacies of managing in the textile industry.

During the many years I spent in the field, I witnessed the evolution of the Israeli textile industry and the fate of those who work in it. These were hard times, when the industry was shaken and saw its last resort in relocating plants. These changes strengthened my attachment to all the people whose fate is with the textile industry. I would especially like to express my deep debt to Dov Lautman, Ruti Goldenberg, Tova Shirman, Emad Talachmi, Shmuel Shachak, Yossi Ron, Gadi Shelach, Amos Tamam, Chaim Navon, Chaim Mattas, Moti Mordechai, Shabi Avroya, Oded Brier, David Goldstein, Meir Sarid, Dror Even, Chana Fiksler, Yossi Menachem, Faraj Nizhar, Meir Elkayam, Meir Gabai, and Ahmed Kaskas. I have deep gratitude to the dozens of supervisors in the plants who unconditionally shared with me their knowledge, thinking, and understanding of the craft of work organization and the meaning of their culture.

The research was initially sponsored by the Institute of Israeli-Arab Studies, and I would like to thank its chair, Professor Shaul Mishal. The Golda Meir Institute for Social and Labor Research at Tel Aviv University provided funds that allowed me to extend my research and supported me during the writing. I am very grateful to Professor Moshe Semyonov, who then was the chair of the institute. His deep knowledge of the Arab labor market in Israel was always available to me. At Tel Aviv University, I enjoyed the help, advice, and encouragement of many colleagues and friends. I thank Dr. Itai Sened, Dr. Gad Barzilai, Dr. Gideon Kunda, Professor Dave Nachmias, Professor Yossi Berechman, Professor Epi Ya'ar, and Professor Simcha Ronen.

During my years of the research, I benefited from the commitment, enthusiasm, and help of Michal Fishelson, Amalya Rimalt-Sofer, and Dana Landau. Their work with the seamstresses and their ability to establish intimate and confident relationships is apparent on every page of this book. Special thanks to Ruti Gauchman for help with the revising of the book. I was lucky to have her intellectual stimulation and depth while molding my theoretical framework. I would also like to thank Esther Epstein and Chaya Amir.

At Stanford University Press, I am deeply indebted to Laura Comay, whose encouragement and concern during early revisions of the book directed and focused me. Stacey Lynn was a faithful guide in the intricacies of publishing, and Julie DuSablon was able to connect to the manuscript and improve it. I thank them. I would also like to thank Professor Susan Tiano for insightful comments on earlier drafts, particularly drawing my attention to issues of patriarchy in the workplace.

I would like to mention the unconditional love and support of my family, Nili, Iddo, and Tali, during the years of my anthropological journeys. They are my source of endurance.

This book is dedicated to the Arab and Druse seamstresses who lost their jobs with the relocation of the plants to Egypt and Jordan. As Amal, one of the seamstresses fired in the closing of the sewing plant in Beit Jan, a Druse village in the Galilee mountains, states, "We are the victims of the concern's rushing after lower costs of production, the law of minimum wages, and the peace process."

I. D.

Contents

Figures and Tables

THE SEAM LINE

CHAPTER 1

Introduction

MANY WORKPLACES in contemporary industrial societies are characterized by diverse workforces replete with gender, ethnic, racial, and religious differences. Women and immigrants continue to join the labor market in increasing numbers (Chemers, Oskamp, and Costanzo 1995; Hodson 1997). Implicit in this diversity are differences in cultural values, behavioral patterns, modes of conceptual thinking, and points of view; the multicultural workplace has become one mark of the era of globalization.[1] This organizational ethnography examines one such multicultural workplace. It is set in the sewing plants of a large Israeli textile concern located in the Arab and Druse communities of the Galilee region of northern Israel.[2] The concern, which employs 6,000 workers and has additional plants in Jordan and Egypt, exports the majority of its products (mainly quality undergarments) to prestigious stores in the United States and Europe, such as Marks and Spencer, Donna Karan, Victoria's Secret, Calvin Klein, Structure, Gap, Polo Ralph Lauren, Hugo Boss, and Hemma. On the shop floors, female Arab and Druse seamstresses and supervisors, whose jobs at the plants are their main opportunities for wage employment, work for Jewish male managers.

In many countries, the textile industry has led the process of industrialization. Leiter, Schulman, and Zingraff (1992) state that the textile industry

is the prototype for the analysis of industrialization, modernization, and the development of capitalism. It is also an exemplar for
studies of the socioeconomic consequences of this transformation
at the level of individual worker, family, community, and society.
Textiles are central to an understanding of Western development
and the analysis of many contemporary developing societies in
which the textile industry serves as the base for a transition from
agrarian to industrial economies.

Just as it was a pioneer of the industrial revolution, the textile
industry is now a driving force behind modern industrial development, which dictates a new international division of labor (Robert
1983). In this context, globalization is manifested by relocation of
production facilities to areas that provide plentiful, cheap labor.
Global factories are notorious for poor labor practices in which the
predominantly female employees are restricted to unskilled and
semiskilled jobs and are required to work in strenuous conditions
for little pay (Bradley 1989; Fernandez-Kelly 1983a, 1983b; Fuentes
and Ehrenreich, 1983).

This book is about the process of creating a work culture amid
a ubiquitous structure of domination—the Arab patriarchal tradition of male control over women and the concern's patriarchal capitalism, a system of managerial control over workers.[3] This book is
about generating meaning in the workplace, an arena that embodies tensions and conflict in manager-worker relationships, unequal
male-female relationships, conformity and rebellion, application of
organizational practices that stem from familial ideology, and systems of control and hierarchy. It is also about solidarity, honor, accountability, and friendship.

Lyla, Ali, Adal, and David

On a hot summer evening, the villagers gather for the festive wedding
of Raymonda, a seamstress at the textile plant. None of the guests
suspect the plot that Lyla, one of Raymonda's Druse co-workers, has
hatched with her secret Muslim boyfriend, Ali. In the middle of the
wedding, she slips away, and they elope in his car. Their safe escape is

thwarted, however, by Fuad, the Druse driver of the plant, who sees them driving hurriedly along the winding village streets. When he recognizes the passengers in the car, he begins a chase and blocks their way. He grabs Lyla out of the car and sends her home. Later, he tells Lyla's cousin about the incident and warns him to make sure she behaves.

The next morning, Lyla arrives at work as if nothing has happened. Two hours into the workday, Lyla's parents suddenly buzz the door of the plant and ask for her. When Lyla comes out, her father slaps her hard on the face and drags her away.

Ali's sister Dalal, who works as a supervisor at the plant, sees what has happened and leaves work immediately. Later, she recounts, "I dragged my brother out of bed and slapped him in the face. I told him, 'That's for messing around with one of them.'" When she returns to the plant, she spreads a rumor that Lyla was not alone in Ali's car but was accompanied by Nagla and Neli, two Druse workers from Dalal's department, who were also being driven home from the wedding by Ali. She recalls, "I said that because I didn't want Lyla's brother to give my brother trouble."

The next morning, Lyla's brother, her eldest sister, and the cousin arrive at the plant. They demand to speak with Dalal and the women she claims were with Lyla in Ali's car. David, the manager, refuses their request and blocks Lyla's brother's attempts to get on the production floor and talk to them. Lyla's brother gets hysterical and yells that he will kill Lyla, burn the plant, and commit suicide. David tries to calm him and says forcefully, "*Habibi* [friend], you will not make a mess in my plant. Take yourself and get out of here. If you want to talk to me, come after work hours."

When the brother finally leaves, David comments, "For them, the brothers are born to guard the women. The women are born to work, marry, and suffer."[4]

There is unrest on the production floor. The women are hurt by Lyla's brother's behavior. Shahira says, "Now in the village they'll say we seamstresses are fickle."

At four, after the closing of the plant, Lyla's brother returns. His hands are covered with blood and he is shaking with anger. David sends him to wash his hands and asks Adal, the supervisor, to make coffee. When Lyla's brother returns, he spreads his hands and says, "I beat her until her face swelled." He looks tired and his face is weary. He begs again and again to speak with the women who claimed to be with Lyla in the car. When he realizes that the manager will not let him, he drinks the coffee and leaves angrily.

Adal, Lyla's supervisor, has known about Lyla's and Ali's love affair since its beginning. As a supervisor, she knows her workers well. She is even proud of her involvement in the romance. Lyla had entrusted Adal with Ali's love letters. Later, Adal shows me one of the letters dealing with the decision to elope:

> *My love,*
> *My happiness,*
> *I love you.*
>
> *I am sitting here depressed and many thoughts are running through my head. A feeling of despair has overtaken my body and my mind. Unfortunately I can only reach one conclusion— we must run away together. I am asking you to understand the situation. I love you very much because you have conquered my heart, my mind, my body, and also my soul. You are everything to me. I ask you not to think that our relationship is nothing. It comes from the root of the heart tree. I love you like the drunk loves his glass. I love you like God loved his people. I love you like a bird who likes to perch on a grapevine. Could we not be together? It makes no sense, just like the sun setting and not rising for a week.*
>
> *Your lover, the hero who swears to you in God. I promise you that after Saturday [the wedding] everything will be different.*
>
> *Honorably,*
> *Your love.*
>
> *P.S. I will never look at another woman in my life. You are the one who has captured my heart. Don't give up and think of nothing but me. I promise to be yours forever. Nothing will be able to separate us.*

When Adal finishes reading me the letter, she can't contain her emotions and a tear trickles down her face. She tells me, "I tried to convince Lyla that these secret meetings with Ali are no good. She is Druse and he is Muslim and we Druse are not so free.[5] I explained this to her, but she did not accept it. She is a good person, and pretty too. You sit with her five minutes and you like her. But she lost her head and thought only about her pleasures. There is always trouble when a Muslim fellow is involved with a Druse woman—it's like chasing danger."

The night after Lyla's brother's visit to the plant, a few of her relatives storm Ali's neighborhood and shoot into the air. The next morning, the chief of the local police station decides to remove them from the village.

The next day, massive absenteeism registers at the plant. Thirty-three seamstresses stay at home—all the workers connected with Dalal's family, all those connected with Lyla, and others whose parents do not let them come.

An accusing finger is pointed at the plant. Rumors are spread that women who work at the plant are amoral. The plant's most valuable asset—its impeccable reputation—is badly hurt. During the fifteen years that the plant has been in the village, the managers have been proud that no incidents have threatened the women's honor. In the village, the families hold the managers responsible for the honor and good name of their daughters while they are working in the plant. This means that the sewing plant should not serve as a breeding ground for ideas, opinions, and actions that go against custom and accepted behavior. Awareness and sensitivity to women's honor in Arab society have led the sewing plants to construct a system of stringent managerial control. The plants are physically segregated from their environments, and the entrances are strictly monitored. No strangers are allowed inside. The male workers—managers and machinists who are generally Jewish—all have families. The managers constantly solicit approval from families and community and religious leaders regarding their daughters' safety.

David says bitterly, "I hear that they are blaming the plant for being negligent, for giving the women a bad education, treating us as something foreign. I'm under terrible pressure—everything I've built here might be lost. It's enough that one father doesn't let his daughter go back to work and other parents follow suit. It's a fire in a field of dry weeds. And if I fall, there is a chance that the plants of the concern in other communities will follow suit."

For a few days the village is in turmoil. The village leaders, the mayor, and the chief of police try to arrange a *sulcha* [reconciliation] between the families. Finally, Dalal's family returns to their home with a promise from Lyla's father that nothing will happen to them. Ali does not return; he goes underground.

The sewing plant suffers terribly. In the first few days, there is significant absenteeism and consequently losses in production. The seamstresses who remain are not focused, and the quality of the products suffers.

David says, "I am not doing anything drastic—I don't want to create a total break. I'm not pressuring the women. I try to understand them. But I insist on one thing. I will not have them talk at the plant about the incident. We are trying to create a feeling of 'business as usual.' The seamstresses have returned to work quickly. They know that if they don't produce, their salaries will suffer."

David decides to not let Lyla return to work. "I know that her family will pressure me to take her back. For them and her it would mean that nothing has happened and she is OK. But I won't do it. The whole village is talking about her. If I bring her back, at least 30 women will go home, and we will never restore our reputation in the village. We have a bad reputation today. Our only luck is that most of the girls are from the supervisors' *hamulas* [extended families]."

The supervisors at the plant take initiative and convince the families that Lyla's incident has nothing to do with the plant. Diana says, "We told them that the plant watches over the women. The whole story stemmed from Lyla herself—not from her home and not from the plant. We even convinced the families to let their daughters go on a trip to the Sea of Galilee on Friday. And you should know that someone anonymous called and said that if something will happen to the daughters, he'll cut off my head. In spite of threatening calls like that one, we insisted. It's important that they know in the village that the plant has nothing to do with the affair and that the families show that they trust us and the managers."

Adal does not want Lyla back in her department. On the one hand, she is sympathetic to Lyla—she is her personal friend and confidante and had helped the romance grow. On the other hand, she is afraid that Lyla's return to the department would lead to its collapse. Adal is afraid to keep Ali's letters, so shortly after showing them to me she gives them to David for safekeeping.

A few months after the event, Lyla's father and brother arrive at the plant and request that she be allowed to return to work. David is faced with a dilemma. He does not want to deny them—this would mean that the plant is taking part in the rivalry between Lyla's and Dalal's families. However, it is clear to him that if Lyla returns to work, there will be unrest at the plant. Furthermore, the workers who have learned about Lyla's intention to return have objected. Samia says, "She is a bad example to the women. She has made a big mess. She has no more friends here."

The manager requests that Lyla come to him herself. He justifies this request by saying that he wants to be personally sure that she is willing to return and wants to test her commitment to excellence at work.

Lyla sits in David's office. She is tense and impatient. He says, "You don't really want to come back."

She answers, "But I do want to come back. The whole affair is behind me. I don't want to stay at home. I want to be back here with my friends. I like it here."

David says, "You will leave here and tell your father that I want you back but you don't want to go back to work."

She looks at him surprised, not understanding. He opens his safe and places Ali's love letters on the desk in front of him. Lyla becomes pale, pulls her lips, rises from her chair, and leaves the plant.

A few weeks later, Lyla and Adal stand behind the plant by a barrel for burning papers, throwing letter after letter into the fire.

The Research Context

In the sewing plants of the Galilee's Arab and Druse communities, the world of work intermingles with the local social system and culture. As the case study demonstrates, the plant is not just a place to work; its influence goes beyond its boundaries. It is a social arena. It is a place where Arab seamstresses and Jewish managers constantly redefine the meaning and structure of their positions with regard to the self, the workplace, and society. This occurs within the context of a demanding workplace in which assembly line production and strict divisions of labor are used.

Although imported into the communities, the plants function as acceptable social entities, in addition to their economic functions. As such, they attempt to be "good corporate citizens" within their communities and to the families of the workers. As this book illustrates, this is not a detached, objective position. The plants are an essential component of the workers' renegotiation of gender identity and work and family status. The plants are also vulnerable to the ever-watchful eye of the community and are held accountable for the paramount values of women's honor and chastity.

To understand the dynamics of creating a work culture in the sewing plants, this book integrates two main approaches prevalent in the literature on industrialization of peripheral areas in an era of globalization. First is the feminist approach, a body of knowledge developed extensively during the past two decades that has revealed the impact of female participation in the labor force within the context of capitalist development and patriarchy (Cairoli 1998). This gender-based analysis of industrialization is not unidimensional, and some complexities of the discourse will be elaborated upon later in the book.

The second approach deals with organizational culture. It attempts to understand and map daily life and the essence of shared meaning in the workplace. In the sewing plant, as individuals with different cultural backgrounds interact, workers and managers engage in cultural processing, whereby they develop interpretive structures that enable them to define their own worlds, to express their feelings, and to make sense of their behavior with regard to shared meanings, values, and norms (Geertz 1973, 1983).[6] The various individuals in the plant come to understand what they can expect from the work environment and how to function within it as they attempt to make sense of the organization of production (Denison 1986).[7] By using the cultural approach, this book seeks to address industrial globalization in the context of the local setting and its impact on work culture and processes (Belanger, Edwards, and Haiven 1994; Hofstede 1991; Poster 1998).

The work culture of the sewing plants in the Galilee is shaped by two distinct cultural perspectives: the system of patriarchal domination that is characteristic of traditional Arab society, and the formal management system of the textile concern that dictates the nature of relationships between Jewish managers and Arab workers. I use these two perspectives to construct an operational framework for understanding how the managers and workers in the Israeli textile industry create shared meaning within a context of inequalities. I see both workers and managers as active participants in this process despite their respective positions on the continuum of these inequalities. All who work at the plant create its culture through constant renegotiation, conflict, shared meaning, and shaping of work values.

The cultural content of the women's employment involves a reality of sex segregation, male domination, and the idealization of the domestic role of women. Additionally, structural underdevelopment and discrimination channel them toward wage employment in industry and toward textile-factory work in particular.[8] Furthermore, the structural inequalities between the Arab and the Jewish sectors in Israel accentuate the power relations within the plants. This study shows that despite these inequalities, the culture of the workplace is not solely determined by the managers. It involves cultural processing by all participants—the workers, supervisors, and managers—in a manner that is not mutually exclusive. The seamstresses are not puppetlike workers whose strings are pulled in the interest of the plant. They may interpret their own situations, fight for their rights, and exhibit "the power of the weak" (Ginat 1982, p. 151).

The study of the interaction between managers and workers and the generation of meaning is important for addressing several themes. What is the role of the work culture on the shop floor in satisfying the demands and needs of both the workers and the managers? What is the process that leads to cooperation between these two seemingly opposed interests? Where does this cooperation fail? How do conflicting values, norms, and worldviews influence the industrial setting? What is the outcome of the interaction between the bureaucratic management system and the local worldview? In terms of women's gender roles, how might entry into wage employment indicate a desire to subvert the acceptable framework of family values? How do the workers negotiate patriarchal patterns to their benefit? How do the managers contribute to the workers' liberation in spite of their re-creation of patriarchal patterns? What are the similarities and differences in the ways Jewish managers and Arab workers perceive work culture and values? How are the different perspectives of managers, supervisors, and seamstresses reflected in the organizational culture? All these questions are significant for understanding multicultural workplaces, for evaluating the implications of managing diversity, and for revealing the organizational processes through which male professional managers and minority women adapt to the workplace.

A Minority Within a Minority: Arab Women
in the Israeli Labor Market

The contradiction between the State of Israel's self-definition as the national home of the Jewish people and the existence of a 20 percent Arab minority within its borders has brought about a system of exclusion in all aspects of life (Carmi and Rosenfeld 1992; Lustick 1980; Smoocha 1990). Whereas the modernization approaches describe the Arab minority in Israel as a separate social entity, with its own internal cultural characteristics (Eisenstadt 1967), new research describes their position within society as one characterized by statewide social, political, and economic inequality and bureaucratic and governmental discrimination (Rosenhek 1995). The dependent structural position of the Arab minority in Israel results from the state's prioritizing the development of the Jewish sector, sometimes at the expense of resource allocation to Arabs; from bureaucratic blockage; and from state policies that create social and economic segregation (Zureik 1979).

The participation of Arab women in the Israeli labor force is influenced by socioeconomic changes in the Arab sector and cultural changes in the Arab view of women's employment. Since the 1960s, the Arab sector has undergone a transition from agriculture to wage employment, particularly in public services, construction, transport, communications, and labor-intensive manufacturing. The development of Israel and its economy has been largely responsible for the increase in Arab wage employment and for the growing level of dependency and integration of the Arab sector in the national economy (Rosenfeld 1964). Changes in the Israeli labor market have helped to shape Arab income levels, occupational status and structure, and overall socioeconomic position (Lewin-Epstein and Semyonov 1993). There are three categories of Arab workers in the Israeli labor market. (1) Those who live and work in their villages or towns (a uni-ethnic labor market) comprise 6 percent of the Arab workforce. Their separation affords them a measure of autonomy. Because they do not have to compete with members of the majority labor force, they have a monopoly on certain occupational positions from which they would be barred in a duo-ethnic situation (Miari 1986; Semyonov

1988; Smoocha 1984). (2) Those who live in Arab villages or towns but work outside them (in a duo-ethnic labor market) comprise 62 percent of the Arab labor force (Lewin-Epstein 1989). (3) Those who live and work in Jewish areas or in mixed neighborhoods (Semyonov 1988) make up the remaining 32 percent of the Arab labor force. The Arabs who work in Jewish areas suffer greater occupational inequality than Arabs working in their own towns and villages. Thus, the integration of Arabs into the Jewish-controlled duo-ethnic workforce ultimately diverts Arabs into low-status, low-paid occupations (Semyonov 1988).

These changes in the structural position of the Arab sector have coincided with changes that increased the rate of Arab women's participation in the labor force in particular. Although the rate is still relatively low compared to Jewish women, participation of Arab women in the labor force increased from 6 percent in the 1970s to 16.7 percent in the mid-1990s, constituting nearly 20 percent of the total Arab labor force (Semyonov, Lewin-Epstein, and Brahm 1999). Arab women have become the reserve labor force for industries seeking cheap, disciplined, reliable, and replaceable labor. The entry of Arab women into industry was facilitated by an aspiration to raise the standard of living in the Arab sector that increasingly invited women's wage employment, either to contribute to the family income or for their own well-being (Al Haj 1988). At the same time, factories opened in the northern area of Israel, intending primarily to provide employment to Jewish workers from development towns, but also employing Arabs from the surrounding villages. In addition, a large number of industrial concerns producing for export (especially in the textile industry) established plants in Arab villages, providing work primarily for women (Haidar 1985, 1991; Schnell, Sofer, and Drori 1995).

The entry into wage employment by Arab women in Israel has been shaped and constrained by their gender identity—their roles as mothers and wives—and the social context of women in Arab society.[9] The basic elements of their gender identity play into the attitudes toward the work of both men and women. As this book shows, industrial work is considered temporary, lasting only until marriage. Women use this period of work to help the family financially and to build their dowries. Taking on wage employment does not circumvent women's roles as wives- and mothers-to-be. The workplace fits into the patriarchal structure of the family.

The importance of family as a social institution is superimposed on the world of work. In the textile industry, women's work is still considered secondary to the home and to the ideal of having children and catering to the husband. However, economic needs may require women to remain at work for a few years after marriage, before having children.

The woman stands at the center of the Arab family, and the family stands at the center of Arab society. A woman's status is based mostly on her family functions, which are her main source of power.[10] She is defined in relation to her family, her work redounds upon the family, and her honor both contributes to and is dependent upon the honor of her family.[11] Opposition to work stems from a fear that the workplace may supplant the family as the central source of women's identity.[12] Although women are expected to do all the housework and take care of the family and children, Arab women working in the plants have found ways of strengthening their position relative to men both within and outside the family sphere.

The importance of kinship relationships and the social, economic, and political roles of men define the Arab family as a patriarchal unit (Moghadam 1993). Male dominance is reflected in the accountability of the man for the honor of his family, particularly of its female members, and for his ability to preserve the gender hierarchy (Kandiyoti 1988). It is expected that the man will provide for his family and serve its economic needs. The economic power of men also translates to social domination at home. Having gained earning power, however, women are able to exercise a degree of autonomy (Moghadam 1993).

The requirement of *hijab*, religious modesty, calls for the segregation of men and women and the confinement of women to the private domain (Mernissi 1987). This segregation channels Arab women into particular types of employment, workplaces that are considered "for women only," in which they are secluded and protected. In addition, women are not encouraged to work outside of their communities. The pattern of employment in the textile factories preserves, at least partially, the seclusion of women in Arab society.

The textile plants where most of the women are employed are often located within the Arab communities themselves. The plants are closed to the outside world, and the women are usually transported to and from work. The basic condition for accepting an industrial enterprise in the community is that it employ only women, in accordance with the rules of seclusion and sex segregation, which strengthens the sexual division of labor. As Lewin-Epstein and Semyonov (1993) write:

> Since the overwhelming majority of women are employed in the "women only" textile and clothing industry, seclusion of women is generally maintained. Hence, gender-linked occupational segregation evolves in new directions as the participation of Arab women in the market economy continues to grow. (p. 109)

Although Arab women have adopted wage employment within the context of their traditional roles, tensions within the Arab communities in the Galilee do exist. The traditional role is perceived as being challenged by their increased participation in the labor force. Since the 1960s, social changes in the Arab sector in Israel have been significant for women and have affected the structure of the family by delaying early marriage and offering new opportunities for education and employment (Al Haj 1987, 1988). The workers in the sewing plants face an apparent contradiction between the role of breadwinner and the role of daughter and wife.[13] These tensions are reflected in the sewing plant and shape its work culture.

The Textile Industry in the Galilee

The textile industry, a pioneer of the industrial revolution, shares the legacy of mass production in assembly lines. The textile industry organizes its production according to a "Fordist" system, which perceives the industrial organization as a machine and advocates systematic and hierarchical management (Sabel 1982). In an era of globalization, new technologies, and new organizational forms, the textile industry must confront the mutability and fragility of mass production and the consequences of dependence on assembly line production. The Israeli textile industry is engaged in a process of adjustment, attempting to reconcile the old and the new, the archaic and the modern, the rigid and the flexible.

The Israeli textile industry developed in peripheral areas and development towns during the 1950s, formative years of the country's independence. Textile factories provided employment for unskilled immigrants, mainly from northern Africa and the Middle East. The industry was organized vertically; the headquarters and upper management were located in the center of the country, and the factories were located in development towns in southern and northern Israel. Some of the development towns became company towns, with the textile industry as the main employer. During the 1950s, 1960s, and 1970s the employment share of the textile sector in developing towns increased from approximately 4 percent to more than 40 percent (Gradus, Razin, and Krakover 1993). Since the 1970s, the textile industry has endured severe setbacks, mainly because of high turnover; job openings in other, higher-paying industries; mismanagement; deteriorating labor relations; and decreases in government subsidies. As a consequence, the industry relocated from Jewish development towns to Arab and Druse communities in the Galilee.

The big institutionalized Jewish concerns migrated to the Arab sector for three reasons. First, they were attracted by a cheap and available labor force of village women. Second, they were able to garner the approval of local leaders, both traditional and civil. This cooperation was motivated by high unemployment in the Arab villages and the desire to keep women workers in the villages. Third, the textile industry relocated to the Arab rural sector because of a shift in Israeli industry toward high-tech products (Drori 1996). Between the 1970s and the 1990s, the number of textile plants in the Galilee increased from 12 to 227.[14] Although Arab female employment constituted just over 16 percent of the active Arab labor force in 1990, women working in textile plants constituted 51 percent of the Arab labor force in industrial sectors (Kurzum 1995). In the textile industry in the Galilee, 86 percent of the workers are Arab women, and among production workers, 98 percent are women. A comprehensive survey, mapping industry distribution in the Arab sector in the Galilee, found that textile plants constituted approximately 30 percent of all the industry in the Arab sector (Schnell, Sofer, and Drori 1995).

Three distinct types of organizations form the textile industry in the Arab communities of the Galilee. The first type consists of the large established sewing plants, those employing hundreds of workers, which are usually affiliated with the largest textile concerns. These plants are equipped with the latest technology and are run by professional managers, and they are backed by logistics services in design, cutting, sewing, planning and development, central quality control, and marketing. Furthermore, working conditions, namely, the rights and obligations of the workers, are anchored in agreements reached through collective bargaining and signed by trade unions and employers. These concerns are the main employers in the industry.[15]

The second type, mainly subcontractors, comprises those sewing plants that provide outsourced production for the large concerns and to wholesalers and retailers. The subcontractors are essentially production facilities that engage in sewing. They do not deal with linkages and logistics beyond the production.

The third type consists of small sewing workshops run by local entrepreneurs who act as subcontractors for Jewish companies and produce for the local market. These workshops, typically located in private homes, employ a small number of workers, usually members of the immediate or extended family. Technologically, they are simple, concentrating only on sewing operations.

These three types do not overlap, but one can identify certain interfaces, such as the outsourcing of work from the concern to subcontractors. Such relationships can be seen in Table 1, which summarizes the main characteristics of the three types of sewing enterprises.

Until recently, the sewing plants were the main industrial organizations in the Arab and Druse villages in Israel. Jewish and Arab companies, large and small, enjoyed the benefits of a cheap and reliable labor force. The year 1997, however, marked a new era for the sewing plants. Israel, like many emerging economies, is heavily influenced by globalization and its afflictions. The chairman of the textile division of the Israeli Industrialist Association claims that the main reasons for the collapse of the sector and the closing of plants are the the rising costs of labor, frozen currency rates, and an increase in exposure to imports because of the lowering of protective tariffs from 40 percent to 8 percent.[16] Taking ad-

TABLE I

Comparison of the three main types of industrial textile enterprises in the Arab sector in the Galilee

	Type of Plant		
	Concern	*Subcontractors*	*Workshops*
Organization of production	Vertical	Horizontal	Horizontal
	State-of-the-art technology	Adequate technology	Outdated technology
	Multiple assembly lines with production volumes of millions of products a month	A few assembly lines	One or two assembly lines
	Produce high-quality undergarment and athletic wear	A limited but diverse range of products with different degrees of quality	
	Professional management at all levels	Basic management on the shop floor	Owner is manager
	Workers are young women from the plant's location and its vicinity	Workers are young women mainly from the local community	Workers are women from the owner's immediate and extended family and the community
	Plants located also in Egypt and Jordan		
Number of workers in the plant	150–350	Up to 200	up to 30
Working conditions	Terms of employment set according to the Israeli labor laws and collective agreements, including minimum wage, pension, health insurance, welfare, and social amenities	Minimum wages and social amenities as required by law (social security and health insurance)	Wage negotiated with owner, with no social amenities

TABLE I, *continued*

Comparison of the three main types of industrial textile enterprises in the Arab sector in the Galilee

	Type of Plant		
	Concern	*Subcontractors*	*Workshops*
Working conditions, *continued*	High standard of physical working conditions with a modern infrastructure, air conditioning, space, light, and a cafeteria for lunch	Adequate physical conditions on the shop floor	Poor physical conditions, usually domestic spaces that were converted into workshops
	Workers' committees	Labor not organized	
	Social events	Almost no social activities	
Ownership	Public: Israeli (Jewish) and international companies	Joint ventures between Jewish and Arab entrepreneurs	Arab entrepreneurs
		Jewish or Arab ownership	Joint ventures between Arab and Jewish entrepreneurs, whereby the Jewish partner is responsible for marketing and the Arab partner is responsible for production
Clients	Local and export to leading fashion chains in the U.S. and Europe	Concerns	Local retailers in the Arab sector
		Jewish wholesalers and stores	Jewish wholesalers

vantage of the relative normalization with neighboring Arab countries, the industry began to drift to Egypt and Jordan, following the cheap labor trail. The immediate consequence was the firing of workers and the closing of plants in Israel. Industry sources claim that the salary differentiation between Arab Israeli workers and Egyptian or Jordanian workers is 10 to 1. Moreover, rising minimum wages hurt the textile industry more than other industries that were able to compensate through mechanization.

The portion of the labor force in the textile industry declined by approximately 11 percent from 1991 to 1996. Since 1996, with the massive closures of plants, another 24 percent have lost their jobs. In the first half of 1998, more than 1,500 seamstresses were fired. Overall, about 25 textile plants from the Galilee have relocated to Egypt and Jordan.[17] In the Galilee, numerous sewing plants, including four of the six plants I researched, have closed. The closing of the plants belonging to the main textile concerns created a chain reaction whereby many subcontractors and small workshops, which depended on the concerns for orders, also shut down. Nimer Hisam, the mayor of Shefaram, one of the biggest Arab cities in the Galilee (population about 40,000), estimates that in 1996–1997 about 50 million NIS were withdrawn from the Arab family income in his city and its vicinity.[18]

The following chapters present a comprehensive ethnographic account and interpretation of the interrelationships between management and workers on the shop floor. The book is presented as an ethnographic study in narrative form: it describes various events and happenings in the sewing plants, stories, conversations, and the differing interpretations given to them. The narrative also presents the thoughts and opinions of the participants on their work world. Chapter 2 contains a methodological discussion on the theoretical and practical significance of this approach.

Chapter 3 reviews theories and presents a framework regarding women in the global factory and the attributes of work culture. The chapter integrates the conceptual framework of patriarchy and the structural inequalities prevalent in the factory setting with analyses of the organization of production, shared meaning, and conflict.

Chapter 4 describes the setting of the ethnography. It portrays key organizational attributes and presents the context of everyday life—dilemmas in the ongoing organization of production, work values, and conflicts over interpersonal and working relationships in the plant.

Chapter 5 documents and analyzes the perspective of the seamstresses on various experiences at work. It focuses on the nature of the work, issues of discipline, behavior, and attitudes. It also addresses some of the seamstresses' personal and familial concerns. The chapter investigates the social and work relationships among the seamstresses and between them and the supervisors and managers.

Chapter 6 focuses on the supervisors, describing their everyday work processes. It looks into their role as mediators between managers and workers and between families and the plants. The chapter also demonstrates how the supervisors convey the point of view of management to the seamstresses and discuss the supervisor's perception of work and supervision. The personal relationship between the managers and the supervisors and its significance is also examined, with a focus on the dependency that develops between them.

Chapter 7 centers on the managers. It portrays their everyday management systems, techniques, strategies, and manipulations. A key issue is how management ideology adapts to a situation in which traditional values must be taken into account. Also examined is the relationship between managers and supervisors and seamstresses. The chapter also deals with the relationship between the managers and the community.

Chapter 8 presents the changes in the organization of production and work culture that have occurred during the past few years in the sewing plants, with the relocation of some of the plants to Egypt and Jordan.

Chapter 9 provides an integration of the main observations. It presents and analyzes the implications of the findings for the plants' organizational culture. The conclusion also presents a framework for understanding the evolution of work culture in a multicultural setting.

CHAPTER 2

Methods: Reflections on the Field

You will ask questions and remember what you are told.
Do not disdain to engage common men in conversation
who for a few coins will disclose everything. But let the
sum be small, and it must appear a gift, not a bribe, else
they will grow suspicious. You will never ask anything
directly, and after questioning someone one day, you will
ask the same questions on the morrow in different terms,
so that if the man at first lied, he will be led to contradict
himself: foolish men forget the tales they tell, and the
next day they invent an opposite story.

—UMBERTO ECO
The Island of the Day Before

MY ENTRANCE to the plants was initiated by the human resource
manager of the concern. She knew of my experience as an organizational anthropologist who has worked with "developing popula-
tions," referring to my extensive field research experience in developing countries such as the Caribbean, Central America, and
Africa. My career began when I was a graduate student in anthropology at the University of California at Los Angeles and continued through research projects in academia and in the service of the
World Bank and UNICEF (Carvajal and Drori 1987; Drori 1990;
Drori and Gayle 1990a, 1990b).

The concern sought my help with what the human resource
manager termed the different mentality and culture of the Arab
and Druse workers and the Jewish managers. She believed that a

professional anthropologist would be able to improve working relations in the plants and serve as a cultural intermediary. I was to "interpret for the managers the aspects of the Arab women's behavior and mentality that are relevant to everyday management and expose the workers to the values and appropriate behavior of a modern textile plant." The human resource manager thought that misunderstandings about these issues were responsible for the high rate of absenteeism and turnover that the plants had encountered for the past few years. She exhibited her knowledge about the requirements of research (she was a graduate student in social psychology) and assured me, "You can conduct appropriate academic research without compromising your personal integrity."

I must admit that I saw this as a unique opportunity for research.[1] Conducting an organizational ethnography in the Israeli textile industry, notorious for employing cheap Arab labor, seemed academically, socially, and politically important. I was enthusiastic because I knew that no Israeli, Palestinian, or other social researcher had ever studied Jews and Arabs under a single organizational roof, particularly in the context of Jewish involvement in the industrialization of the Arab communities in Israel.[2] As a Jewish male from academia in Tel Aviv, I realized that this was an unmatched opportunity to gain access to a pluralistic workplace. I appreciated the rarity of doing participant observation in textile plants located in Arab and Druse villages and the possibility of interviewing managers and working women on the shop floor.[3] In the anthropological literature, entrance into the field lays the foundation of the work and always presents a physical, emotional, and intellectual challenge to the outside researcher who attempts to immerse himself in fieldwork. I almost blew it.

Eli's Car

During the first period of my work at a sewing plant in one of the Druse villages, I used to arrive with Eli, then a graduate student who had recently gone into early retirement from an army career in organizational development. We would arrive at the plant in his small car, which had an army license plate.[4] At that time, the formative stage of my fieldwork at the plants included mainly interviews with the supervisors and seamstresses on issues related to the production process. The managers explained our presence to the seamstresses by indicating the importance of research to reveal their needs, improve the work process, and increase their work satisfaction. From the start, we received full cooperation, and the workers saw the personal interviews as a break from the sewing routine.

Late one morning, during an interview, the manager urgently calls me to the production floor. Havoc reigns—the seamstresses are excitedly talking with one another, the supervisors are helpless, and the manager tries to calm Shirin, one of the seamstresses. She cries and mutters, "I'm quitting, I'm quitting, I can't work here anymore. My fiancé won't allow me to work, I must quit."

We are surprised, not understanding why she had suddenly stopped working and why she is quitting.

Soha, her supervisor, says, "The best thing to do is go to her fiancé. He's home now, he'll explain." Shirin looks at her gratefully.

Amos, the manager, and Eli and I are sitting on couches with red cushions in Samir's square guest room. He is Shirin's fiancé. Expressionistic paintings of mountainous landscapes, galloping horses, and photographs of men in army uniforms hang on lightly blue painted walls. In a central spot is a big picture of the Sheikh Amin Tarif, the spiritual leader of the Druse faith. Nahala, Samir's sister, and Soha, Shirin's supervisor, serve us coffee and sweets. Samir, a young man in his late twenties, enters the room. He is tall and well built, with wide shoulders and a strong sharp face. He is wearing the army uniform of a paratrooper with the shiny ranks of a Captain.[5] We introduce ourselves and shake hands. For a moment there is an uncomfortable silence.

Suddenly, in a loud and determined voice, Samir says, "I'm an honest man, a good officer. I love the army. The army is my life, and if I do something wrong, I will give up my life." In front of our astonished eyes he crosses his arms, grips the ranks on his shoulders and tears them off. We are shocked; we do not understand what it is all about.

I realize that Samir's face is familiar. I ask him, "Did you by any chance study at the university in the Middle Eastern and African History department?"

He looks at me with surprise and says, "Yes, I studied there. I finished a year ago and returned to the army."

"You don't remember me?" I ask.

He tries but does not remember. I help him. "I taught the courses on African anthropology."

He recalls and asks, "Then what are you doing in the sewing plant?"

Amos explains, "He is doing research to help us understand the mentality of the workers so that we can be more attuned to their needs."

Samir breathes a sigh of relief and says, "Now I understand everything. It's all a misunderstanding. I was told that the army was making investigations about the married seamstresses, and so I told Shirin to quit right away."

He explains that the army recognizes the engagements of Druse soldiers as marriages. Married soldiers are entitled to receive higher salaries. If their fiancées or wives work, however, they must report it to the army for readjustments of their income tax deductions. Samir tells, "It is common not to report that your fiancée is working so that you pay less taxes. Today, Shirin's relative saw the army car outside the plant, and she suspected that the army was there to investigate those engaged seamstresses whose fiancés have not reported their employment. She spread the rumor in the village." Samir relaxes and apologizes. We finish our coffee. He then asks Soha to explain on his behalf to the workers that it was all a misunderstanding and a falsely based rumor.

By the time we returned to the plant, our label as "army investigators" had become a matter of fact. Amos assembled all the workers, and Soha, the supervisor, conveyed Samir's message. For many months, I carried the stigma of army investigator and encountered difficulties in interviewing workers, who were always suspicious when I asked personal questions.

The workers' reaction to the incident represents their suspicion that the research had an underlying purpose beyond its declared aim of improving their work life. Research done in the plant was seen as an intervention with ulterior motives that would not necessarily benefit the community and its people. It took me substantial time to dissolve the impact of the incident and gain the seamstresses' confidence and openness.

I conducted fieldwork from 1992 to 1997 in six sewing plants in the Galilee. Throughout these years of research, I constantly had to tackle suspicions regarding my work and to justify my presence. I had to provide reasons for my questions and explain to my informants why their answers were important to the research. The workers held me accountable for the information I received and emphasized that it was given to me exclusively because of trust and friendship.[6] Through this process of reification and relegitimization, I was deemed worthy of hearing the workers' and supervisors' secrets, ideas, stories, and complaints. It took a great deal of interpersonal sensitivity, an understanding of the informal setting and statuses, and an awareness of the social relations and the normative behavior and values of Arab and Druse people (see also Rabinow 1977) to earn their trust.

The interplay between managers, supervisors, and seamstresses—each with different roles and characteristics—influenced my understanding and interpretation of the work culture. It was relatively easy for me to link with the managers. They gave me access to the shop floors and allowed me to spend numerous hours with the workers during work hours. We were all Jewish males who had experienced active army service, we were about the same age, and we had more or less the same concerns of the Jewish middle class in Israel. My link to the supervisors and seamstresses was more complicated.

I tend to agree with those anthropologists who claim that the social role that the informant ascribes to the researcher is the key to understanding the interaction between researcher and informant (Berreman 1972; Kondo 1986; Tsuda 1998). I had to constantly reaffirm my identity in relation to all the actors in the plant. My identity encompassed several roles—researcher, consultant, male, and Jew. I had to "bear the cross" of all four identities, waiting in anticipation for my informants to assign me a role in order to design my response. Decoding the meaning of my various roles to my informants was a difficult analytical endeavor. I felt like Woody Allen's "Zelig," the human chameleon.

Nevertheless, in each role I took an active position and also constantly engaged in impression management. My relationships and interactions in each role were geared toward achieving access to more information. The following story illustrates this process within my role as a consultant.

Gina's Djinny

It is a hard winter with frequent thunder and lightening storms. Naturally, these storms are accompanied by electric blackouts that darken the entire shop floor, which is located in a large cellar with no windows. Whenever the electricity cuts out, the machines stop. In the split second before the pale emergency lights automatically activate, the seamstresses shout loudly. When they settle, only one voice continues its high pitched cries. All of us, supervisors, managers, and I, rush to Gina, who is sitting on her chair at the machine, waving her arms, and pulling her hair. We grab her and take her to the office, pour water on her face, give her a tranquilizer, and let small-figured Sarweh, her supervisor, embrace her large frame for a long hour. This winter Gina's outbreaks are a common occurrence. On rainy days, we all wait anxiously for the first electrical breakdown.

My identity as a consultant is established, not only with the managers but also with the supervisors. They use my intensive interviews and talks with the workers for practical advice regarding ad hoc managerial issues. Naturally, professional advice quickly crosses the line toward personal matters. I am close to Sarweh. I do errands for her in Tel Aviv, buying *chamsas* [good luck charms] for her collection. When the frequency of Gina's attacks becomes unbearable, as do the electrical blackouts, Sarweh approaches me with a blunt demand. "You are our advisor. We give you our secrets. You know us. You should help Gina."

I try to give Sarweh some popular psychology rationalizations to get her off my case, saying that Gina should seek professional help.

She says, "Gina has seen the best healers in the villages. It doesn't help, and nobody dares to speak with her father about psychologists." She adds sarcastically, "Believe me, they are all *majnun* [crazy] in her family."

She insists that I find a solution, disguising a threat by saying, "I know you will not disappoint me."

Sarweh, the manager, and I have a consultation, and my attempts to abort the mission of solving Gina's outbreaks are again in vain, because the manager joins Sarweh in cornering me. I ask Sarweh to convince Gina to accept my help and to glorify my abilities to solve her problems. I say, exasperated, "Tell her that I am the firstborn of seven generations of male firstborns. Tell her that I am a healer and can read palms; tell her anything to convince her that I can help her."

Sarweh doesn't laugh. She says, "Gina is suffering. You should help her. And don't forget to bring me a new *chamsa*."

The blackout, pale emergency lights, and Sarweh's *chamsa* ultimately inspire my intervention. A few days later, arriving early in the morning from Tel Aviv, I speak with Gina before work. She sits tensely in front of me, her eyes revealing fear and anxiety. I ask her to tell me her story, why she fears the dark so much.

She tells, "It's not the dark. It's the djinny that enters my heart when the dark suddenly comes."

I ask her, "What happens at night?"

She says she is not afraid at night, only in the cellar of the factory. She says that when the djinny enters her heart, she feels suffocated.

I give her a small golden *chamsa* and tell her that when there is a blackout in the plant she should hold it strongly to her chest and not let the djinny enter her heart.

She says, "What about the dark?"

I have a solution for this problem as well. I have brought from home a small emergency light to attach to her machine. I emphasize to her that she will be the only one in the plant who will have a personal light when there is a blackout.

That day and for the next two days, I sit near Gina's workstation in the middle of the shop floor. When the electricity fails, she gives one loud shout and firmly holds the *chamsa* to her heart. Then, when the luminescence of her personal light surfaces, she is quiet. All the seamstresses, managers, and supervisors look at us intently and burst into laughter. Gina laughs as well. Apparently she enjoys this attention very much.

Within days, Gina's story had spread to all the plants. For a period of time, I was very popular as an advisor for personal matters. I had to refuse many demands for help by the workers, instead attributing success to the *chamsa* and the emergency light while minimizing my role. During that year, many seamstresses and supervisors wore *chamsas* around their neck.

My identity was constructed by the managers as a consultant who could remedy problems in the organization. The workers reconstructed my role as a healer of souls. I was forced into the role of personal consultant and not given an avenue to withdraw. I felt that my intervention in Gina's case was cheap manipulation, too stereotypical and exploitative. The reconstruction as a personal consultant who directly intervened in Gina's private matters accentuated the differences between the informants and myself, in terms of gender, ethnicity, and power.

My closeness to the people in the plants was recognized by managers and workers, who both manipulated it for their own needs. I was both confidant and mediator, as required by the circumstances. I mediated between management and workers on issues that had potential to create a crisis, as the following story illustrates.

Mediating Between Oren and Waffa

Waffa lives near the old mosque in one of the mountainous communities in the Galilee. One must maneuver cautiously through the narrow winding roads, being careful not to hit the children playing soccer on the street. It is afternoon, and Oren, the manager of one of the plants, and I are paying a visit to Waffa, one of the department supervisors. Earlier that day, she had left the plant, slamming the door in anger. Before leaving she tells me,

"Believe me, Israel, I love my job. I do everything for the work, and everybody knows that. When Oren assigned me my department, I worked very hard to learn the new machines. I promised him 3000 undergarments per day, but I asked for time. There were problems with the new machines; they were breaking down, and the machinist was stressed out, not helping much. Oren did not believe that I could do it, so he forced me to work with Wahiba [a veteran supervisor]. I agreed because I thought we would work together as equals, but suddenly she became my boss. I've been a supervisor for five years now, and I will not let anybody damage my honor in the presence of my workers. So I'm leaving and going home."

While we drive, Oren complains about the pressure from the division manager to finish up an urgent order from Waffa's department. "This is a severe breach of discipline, and normally I would never try to get her to come back. But we need this order." Referring to the division manager, he says, "It's always like this. He always uses the same tactic." Oren mimics him, "You have to finish the order on time. Otherwise we lose the order. If we lose the order, we lose the client. We lose the client, we lose business. We lose business, we're all fired." Oren hates to be in this position of depending on Waffa. But he needs her to stop the work slowdown in Waffa's department. Her seamstresses are not cooperating with Wahiba, who is Waffa's replacement. He hates even more having to visit Waffa at home, so he asks me to go with him and mediate between them about her return.

I try to talk him out of it. I offer the argument that if he visits Waffa alone, this will exhibit generosity, largeness of spirit, and a willingness to admit his mistake. He looks at me with contempt and spits out, "You're crazy. If I visit her alone, they'll think that I'm weak. When you are with me, I am not visiting her—I am only accompanying you." I try again, telling him that a manager visiting his worker shows his respect and trust for her and her family, which she will reciprocate on the shop floor. He does not accept this argument either.

Waffa sees the car from the window and rushes to greet us. She is friendly as she leads us into the guest room. We barely sit down before Waffa and her little sister serve us sweets and drinks.

I begin to review Waffa's achievements in the plant, her commitment, her success, and the great responsibility she took upon herself in volunteering to be a pioneer in adopting the new seamless technology. This, I said, is a sign of confidence from the manager, who has a high appreciation of her technical and leadership skills. Oren nods in agreement. Waffa comments, saying that the issue of technology is not so important. She says, "The problem is controlling the department. The new machines are good for the women. They don't have to do anything; the computer does it all. You can operate this machine even if you are completely dumb. But for me there are a lot of problems, and I have to work harder because I have to set the machines all the time. I don't have time to supervise my workers and organize the work. There's been a lot of pressure lately. You know I worked so hard that blood ran out of my eyes instead of tears. Now at home I can't even watch television."

Oren says victoriously, "This is exactly why I asked Wahiba to help you."

Waffa, ignoring Oren, continues with her arguments. "I told Oren that I'm ready to work with Wahiba because it was an urgent situation. But I also told him that I know her, and she is too bossy. It is my department. I spat blood, not saliva, to build it, to make it the best department in the plant. This work has raised my blood pressure. I have committed myself to the plant; it is like my husband." Waffa has been working at the plant for fifteen years. She is unmarried.

Waffa, Oren, and I attempt to reach an agreement and move toward practical decisions. The tactic that eventually works involves acknowledging Waffa's ability to work under pressure, in particular recognizing her ability to finish the order with the required quality asked by Marks and Spencer and on time. Thus, her return to work and subsequent completion of the shipment prevents great shame to the plant, the managers, and the workers. With regard to Wahiba, Oren had already decided that she will be compensated by nominating her to be chief instructor of the plant.

Waffa agrees to return to work the next day. She says, "You are a witness and you are obliged to ensure that both the manager and I will keep our words." Ultimately, my presence guaranteed that each of them saved face.

I knew I was being manipulated by Oren and, to a lesser extent, by Waffa, but I also knew that this was the price for being allowed to conduct my research, and I did not feel too bad about it. It seems that at least both sides attempted to use me as a fair broker.

Extensive participant observation and endless talks and interviews eventually built trust and confidence through constant testing and reexamination. Gradually, I became a confidant and was exposed to intimate and sensitive information concerning the everyday lives of the workers in the sewing plants.

In one of the plants, there are seamstresses who live in southern Lebanon.[7] These seamstresses have developed social relationships with the local seamstresses beyond work. One of the main manifestations of these social relationships has been the establishment of an informal bazaar in the plant bathrooms, where products such as clothes and perfume, which are considerably cheaper in southern Lebanon than in Israel, are offered for sale. The southern Lebanese workers engage in this petty capitalism to complement their income. The bazaar is strictly prohibited by the managers because of a security directive that sees any illegal transference of goods across the border as proof of its permeability (this issue is considered important in light of potential terrorist attacks). If the southern Lebanese workers are caught at the border smuggling goods, security officials hold the managers responsible for breaching the central condition of the employment contract between the plant and the authorities. The managers are obligated to report to the authorities any irregular activities in the plant with regard to the southern Lebanese workers. The penalty for not doing so can be a temporary denial of workers. Additionally, managers strictly object to any commercial activity that might distract the work process. In instances where the managers surprised workers in the midst of this kind of commercial activity, both the buyers and the sellers were fired on the spot.

I was witness to this market after two years of research in one of the major plants. As Amne, one of the seamstresses, said, "We know you by now and we know you won't tell the manager."

My ability to collect relevant and reliable data stemmed from a relationship of trust and candor that developed during my years of work. I gradually underwent a transformation from participant observer to active participant, operating along the continuum of outsider and insider, stranger and friend. Eventually, the distinction between the self and the other was blurred.[8] I experienced the various roles of the researcher and ultimately became part of the experience of the seamstresses and the managers, a part of the plant narrative.[9]

As a confidant, I was exposed to intimate and in-depth personal information about the private lives of workers. These confessions were painful reminders of the extremely precarious position of a Jewish man researching Arab women. One of the most notable examples, which could have been messy and risky, involved a worker asking me in utter secrecy to arrange for a private medical operation to renew her hymen in anticipation of her wedding. Incidents such as these strongly exposed me to the essence of patriarchal relationships and, consequently, to the paternalism that the managers exhibit toward the women in the plants. It is a most effective strategy for domination, control, and manipulation of men over women, as will be seen in the pages of this book.

From their actions and words, I ascertained that the seamstresses and supervisors assigned me the role of their consultant and confidant. My ongoing questioning was met with openness and was perceived as a means of providing me with the necessary information for our ongoing interaction and not as a means to an end.

In accordance with the reflexive and postmodern traditions (Marcus and Fisher 1986) regarding my roles in the plant and as a researcher, I am acutely aware of my subjectivity in narrating the field experience and my sensitivity to the formal and informal positions of the participants on the shop floor, which led to empathy for the seamstresses and sympathy for the "underdogs." I hope that this attitude did not make me prone to arrogance.

Being a Jewish male in Arab society automatically engenders a certain response toward me, mainly simultaneous respect and suspicion. With time, my role changed from the stranger to the familiar, and the seamstresses began to refer to me as their brother, which implies closeness, confidence, unconditional help, and reciprocity, as in their own families (Joseph 1994). It structured a relationship of trust and openness and gave me greater role flexibility in the context of the patriarchal relationships on the shop floor.

During my entrance into the field and my many years of research, my Jewishness was never categorized in explicitly political terms. Even during politically charged times, politics were downplayed. However, many interactions demonstrated the workers' sensitivity to the political and economic circumstances of Israeli life. My Jewishness was manifested, for example, through the women's response to my female research assistants from the university, who occasionally accompanied me. The workers continually compared their way of life with the assistants, who were also young and single and thus served as a comparison.

Reflecting back on the field, one of my assistants said, "When I used to come and speak with the women, they always asked me questions that tried to investigate our differences. They always compared and tried to get me to tell about my way of life, how it is to be a single woman, living alone in an apartment in Tel Aviv, with my own car. They would feel my hair and ask about my clothes. They said I looked like and dressed like the women in soap operas."

Although the workers constructed Jewish-Arab relationships in terms of differences in culture and degree of modernity, the inequalities and limited opportunities remained an undercurrent. I sometimes initiated conversations relating to the Israeli-Arab situation and Arab minority position, but the topic was considered too political and was never pursued. Being a Jewish researcher among Arab working women sharpened my consciousness regarding issues of exploitation, periphery, gender, ethnic differences, and marginalization. I hope that this consciousness is manifested in my conceptualization and writing.

My years of intense work in the plants produced exotic and unique data. Without these data, there would be no base for my theoretical understanding, which allowed me to glean the meaning within the everyday stories. I chose to focus my work on power relations, male-female inequalities, and conflict. Although this ethnography is a realistic text, my reconstruction of the reality is juxtaposed upon my interpretation of the plants and their environment. In particular, I was influenced by the crisis in 1997 and 1998, when four plants closed and were relocated to Egypt and Jordan. These closures raised my sensitivity to globalization and peripheralization issues and their linkage to women's employment. This sobering experience shook any idealism left in me regarding the true nature of harmony in the workplace as I discovered the ugly face of domination and the manipulative aspects of patriarchy.

The sewing plant is an unequal social arena. A pluralistic setting in which the managers are Jewish men and the workers and supervisors are Arab and Druse women, it is organized according to a strict hierarchy. Although they work under the same organizational roof, each of these different groups has its own perception and interpretation of the working life of the plant, derived from its organizational role, its cultural heritage, and its social identity. For me to understand this diversity required a strategy of thorough and active participation and closeness to the events. I tried to simultaneously take into account the experience and the interpretive framework of each group. I had to engage in an enterprise of interpreting and organizing apparently separate thick descriptions of each group into a unified analytical framework. I embarked on this task using Van Maanen's (1979) principles for organizational ethnography. He states that an organizational ethnography should

> uncover and explicate the ways in which people in particular work settings come to understand, account for, take action, and otherwise manage their day-to-day situation. (p. 540)

Presenting various voices of interpretation calls for an integration of the emic and the etic (Headland, Pike, and Harris 1990). The ethnographic description in this text presents narratives that include a description of the event and interpretation as seen by the informant. Also included are narratives in which I played an active part. Both types of narratives contribute to my conceptual framework, both have validity and reliability for capturing the human experiences in the plant, and both serve as building blocks in understanding the work culture. Thus, the research advocates a multivocal viewpoint rather than monophonic voices (Clifford and Marcus 1986).

The ethnography was conducted in sewing plants located in various communities in the Galilee. This is not a single-site ethnography. It is characterized by its multilocality (Marcus 1986; Marcus and Fisher 1986). The narrative, however, presents the sewing plants as a single organizational and cultural composite. Components of social behavior in specific plants also represent the common behavior in others. My assertion is that values, norms, and perceptions related to work and interrelationships among managers, supervisors, and seamstresses have shared meaning.[10]

CHAPTER 3

On Factory Daughters and the Culture of the Workplace

Sana is seventeen. It is seven o'clock in the morning, and it is her first day at work. She is a little frightened and embarrassed. It is the first time she has set foot in an industrial factory.

"This is the first time that I do something for somebody, but also for myself."

I ask, "What would you like to do?"

"Lots of things. Buy clothes that I like, buy a television for my room, buy CDs." She thinks a bit and adds, "Maybe to help my mother, maybe save a little. Maybe I'll travel to Egypt, buy a car, or get things for my wedding, which will eventually come."

WOMEN constitute the majority of production workers in textile manufacturing—more than three-quarters of its workers throughout the world.[1] Textile factory work is seen as women's work, with the implications of a sexual division of labor, semiskilled or unskilled jobs, low wages, and routine, repetitive, and monotonous manual work. The feminization of sewing work is linked to an essentialist view that considers feminine traits of dexterity, patience, obedience, endurance, and order as fit for sewing work. The textile plants are hierarchically organized and reflect a system of control, power, and domination in which the position of men as managers is seen as resulting from a natural and objective differentiation in personal traits, skills, and social role (Elson and Pearson 1981). The differentiation between men and women in the textile industry also bears on employment conditions. The industry is notorious for its extremely low wages and very long hours, particularly in developing countries (Dicken 1986; Elson 1994). Thus, women's incorporation into the labor force is described by numerous researchers as a system of exploitation based on the capitalist mode of production and the continuous construction of women's identities as housewives, which makes it possible to gain political and ideological control over them as well as cheapen their labor (Elson and Pearson 1981; Mies 1994).

Traditionally, garment production was considered the craft of a tailor, but with the evolution of the industry and the development of technological innovations, the craft has been subdivided into multiple processes that are geared toward mass production (Webster 1996). The organization of mass production is delineated in dichotomous terms: women perform unskilled, routine, tedious, low-status, and low-income work, mainly operating sewing machines on the shop floor, and men occupy managerial and planning roles as well as the physically strenuous jobs associated with fabric production (Cockburn 1985). Occupations in the textile industry fully encompass gender constructs in terms of what Sundin (1995) calls gender systems. These systems carry gender labels that distinguish between men's jobs and women's jobs and, subsequently, division of labor, roles, employment conditions, and remuneration. Additionally, they refer to women in their double role at work and at home and the inseparability between the domains of home and work.

Much research on women in the textile industry focuses on the interrelationship between deskilling and the gender construct (Phillips 1998). Deskilling is associated with developments toward automation of the shop floor; it reflects on the position of women in a vulnerable, usually temporary, workforce, characterized by low pay and limited mobility. Deskilling breeds a patriarchal management system that delineates male gender roles as leaders, holders of power, resources, and authority, and female gender roles as weak, subordinate, and dependent on men for protection and subsistence. Patriarchal management is instrumental in reconstructing the male-female relationship at the workplace, deriving its principles and content from the familial and social sphere (Cockburn 1985; Webster 1996; Westwood 1984).

The prevalence of global factories has spawned diverse systems of production, ranging from huge mills employing thousands of workers, to medium-sized family-run firms, to tiny sweatshops and subcontractors (Elson 1994). Accordingly, the large textile concerns of the Galilee generate various complementary textile activities and enterprises that can provide opportunities for women entrepreneurs.[2] However, calling these opportunities valid entrepreneurial enterprises for women is overly optimistic. In the Benetton model (Belussi 1992; Clegg 1990), which is based on a company policy of hiring numerous subcontractors, women subcontractors still perform sewing work and have the lowest added value in the production chain in terms of remuneration and opportunities. Although wage employment can improve the condition of women and allow them to exercise more personal freedom, decision making, and autonomy, these changes occur within a system of patriarchal relationships of gender inequality (Dicken 1986; Elson 1994). Tiano (1994), in her study on women's work in the maquiladora industry in northern Mexico, reported that entering wage labor has given women more options to get out of the house and more leeway to structure their careers, but it has not significantly raised their consciousness of the male domination and exploitation in the industry.

Women and Global Industrialization

Theories that explain the global factory and women's employment on the assembly line assert that women are the ones who suffer the consequences of industrialization and the international division of labor (Boserup 1970; Robert 1983). As companies relocate production into Third World countries, women are hired for unskilled assembly line jobs, thus perpetuating the gendered construction of factory work (Safa 1983).

Many feminist scholarly studies of labor processes and women in industrial work attempt to understand how work became sex typed. Many sociological feminists believe that a combination of structural, social, and ideological forces explains both vertical occupational segregation (whereby women are lower than men in the organizational hierarchy) and horizontal sex segregation (whereby women work in particular industries and occupations, usually at unskilled or semiskilled and low-paying jobs). These forces include the government and its policies, educational system, availability of child-care, employment practices of companies, exclusionary practices of trade unions, sex typing of occupations, responses of women to these structural conditions, and the social relations in the workplace (Eisenstein 1979; Webster 1996).

Thus, industries consider women suitable for assembly line work not only because of their low wages but also within the context of the patriarchal paradigm that defines them as dominated by men and consequently obedient, patient, dexterous, and capable of performing routine work. Furthermore, women are considered secondary to economic processes; their primary obligation is their role as mother and wife. As Fernandez-Kelly (1983b) writes:

> At certain stages of its development, the domestic unit tends to produce and put into circulation young factory workers, that is, *daughters*, who after a few years of work in one or several factories tend to be reabsorbed by newly formed homes as wives, while a new wave of younger women take their place along the assembly lines. (p. 220)

The textile industry enjoys a steady supply of fresh assembly line workers who have no expectations from the work, no awareness of their rights, and no intention to stay after assuming a domestic role as wife or mother.[3]

The incorporation of women into industrial employment is shaped by characteristics such as technology; economic, social, and political settings; cultural attributes; geography; and structure of the labor market (Pearson 1992). Complementary views of women in global assembly lines have been reported in the literature. Integration theory sees the participation by women in the labor force as a springboard for autonomy and emancipation, whereas marginalization and exploitation theories emphasize discrimination, sex segregation, and channeling of women into undesirable and unrewarding jobs (Tiano 1987). Although wage earning and personal independence may expand their consumption levels and give them greater social freedom, this interrelationship does not necessarily result in real economic independence or decision-making power (Fernandez-Kelly 1983a, 1983b; Kung 1981; Salaff 1981; Stichter and Parpart 1990).

Most of the research reported in the literature on women and industrialization has been carried out in Southeast Asia and Latin America. As Moghadam (1993) states, work on the Middle East is scarce "partly because of the difficulty of obtaining data, and partly because of a common view that in the Arab world cultural and religious factors influence women's lives more than do economic factors" (p. 8). Taking into account the research on women in industry, particularly Arab women in the Israeli textile industry, this book is based upon two basic propositions: (1) the employment pattern of women is shaped by the pattern of patriarchy that encompasses their families and communities and the capitalist development of the global textile industry; and (2) the culture of the workplace is a dynamic interaction between managers and workers for the creation of shared meanings within the context of the global textile industry.

Although working relations can be characterized as predominantly patriarchal, women are not passive recipients of male domination. Women do play a role in shaping their labor market position and their individual experience at work. Within the context of the shop floor, some researchers refer to the active participation that women have in shaping their working lives as *resistance* (Benson 1986; Lamphere and Zavella 1997). This resistance can take the form of tactics and strategies on the shop floor, changing labor processes, forming workers' organizations, and curtailing managerial control, as in the case of Hispanic and Anglo Sun Belt workers (Lamphere and Zavella 1997, p. 340–341). Furthermore, resistance also includes using spiritual manifestations in fighting discrimination and oppression, as described by Ong in a Malay factory under Japanese ownership (Ong 1997). Resistance expresses an understanding of power and leverage on the shop floor relative to management. This book presents the context of resistance strategies and tactics on the shop floor as a process of constant negotiation and conflict. The Arab seamstresses not only confront their managers and their tactics of normative control but also advocate and shape their own version of working relations, power relations, and prevalent norms and values at the workplace. They participate in constant delineation of the boundaries, both of their personal autonomy and their role on the shop floor.

Patriarchy and Paternalism

Patriarchy and paternalism constitute the essence of the interrelationship between the Jewish managers and Arab supervisors and workers. The dynamics of mutual sense making in the context of workplace inequalities are best exemplified through an analysis of the meanings of patriarchy and paternalism. Although the two concepts are distinct in definition, content, interpretation, and representation, they can be analyzed as complementary. Patriarchy represents the ideological and structural aspect of the interrelations between the managers and the workers, and paternalism is its concrete pattern and behavioral manifestation in the plants.

Patriarchy can be defined as "a system of social structures and practices in which men dominate, oppress, and exploit women" (Walby 1990, p. 20). It includes a set of assumptions about the natural differences and roles of the sexes. As Pateman writes, "Men's patriarchal right over women is presented as reflecting the proper order of nature" (1997, p. 321). Walby conceptualizes patriarchy as a system of social relationships and applies the principles of operationalism to it within the context of various structures, such as patriarchal relations within paid labor in which women are segregated into undesirable, unskilled, and low-paying jobs. The operationalization of these structures is disputed by Pollert (1996), who sees the concept of patriarchy as static, tautological, and unsuccessful as an explanatory tool of gender inequality. Patriarchy at best is seen as a general description of male domination over women within particular social and historical contexts. Gottfried (1998) also rejects patriarchy as an explicit explanatory concept of gender in the world of work. She broadens Burawoy's (1979) metaphor of *making out* (which describes the role of the workers' shop floor subculture in perpetuating the capitalist mode of production) to include other power plays through what she terms excavating practices. These excavations reveal the gender processes within the context of interaction between men and women, management and workers.

I believe the operational concepts of patriarchy in this book are valid and will be seen when the male-female relationships on the shop floor are excavated, uncovering the layers of meaning that shape the work culture in a setting of situated inequality. The social and historical context goes beyond the shop floor itself. The social arena within which the sewing plants operate presents inherent inequalities between managers and workers along gender, ethnic, and religious lines. Furthermore, the process of globalization that the textile concern is currently undergoing brought about plant closures in Arab villages. In this regard, the patriarchal relationships represent inequalities inherent in a capitalist organization operating in peripheral areas that are structurally and institutionally discriminated against.

Patriarchal relationships in the plant are also concomitant with Arab society, reflecting the supremacy of men and their control and subordination of women. This gender-based structure of domination in the broadest sense is embedded in the structural setting. As Ecevit writes:

> Men [at work] behaved towards women as if they were their fathers or husbands. What is more, this behaviour was exhibited not only by the male foreman and supervisors, but also by the other male employees. . . . What is more interesting, the women did not oppose this. They conformed, without question, to the traditional stereotypes of feminine behaviour. Existing forms of gender subordination are reproduced in the factory. The argument that women's subordinate positions stem from a lack of job opportunities and can be ended by the provision of sufficient jobs does not hold true as long as women cannot free themselves from this subordination. (1991, p. 71)

The workplace simulates patriarchal relationships, whereby women construct the role of men at work according to the role of father or brother. In her study on satellite factories in Taiwan, Hsiung (1996) describes a different version of women constructing their roles at work and their relations to men by emphasizing their dependency on their kinship relationships with men. These kinship-oriented features make patriarchal order an important aspect of fostering capitalistic production. Hsiung describes two underlying patriarchal forms—Chinese familial patriarchy, which defines women according to their kinship relations and reproductive role, and capitalism, which sees women as available cheap labor. Thus, patriarchal relations at work simulate the Chinese family, whereby the worker is "molded into mother, wife, and daughter-in-law for her reproductive responsibilities, and into waged and/or unwaged worker for her productive responsibilities" (p. 107).

As this book demonstrates, workers and managers reconstruct their roles and subsequent behavior, attitudes, and values within a context of patriarchal relationships. These patriarchal relationships generate from the control Arab men have over women in the domestic sphere, which translates into paternalistic behavior at work. Patriarchy at work has a twofold manifestation. First, the ideology of discrimination against women and male domination is reflected in the ubiquitous institutional patterns. Second, patriarchy is manifested within the patterns, structures, and specific actors that dominate women in public and private spheres. In this regard, patriarchy can be translated into an operational content—analyzed and defined as an attribute of work culture. Patriarchy is an integral part of the values and norms of the workplace in those industries that take advantage of tensions between local culture and capitalist development. Patriarchy can be interpreted by families, workers, and managers to promote their individual agendas and reconcile their differences. In her work on female workers in the Moroccan garment industry, Cairoli (1998) writes:

> Inside the factory, the garment workers struggle to retain a notion of themselves as family members, specifically as daughters (or sometimes as wives) in patriarchal households. They have accepted a notion of themselves as subservient and dutiful long before they enter the garment factory. They model their position in the factory hierarchy on their role in the household and so are able not only to accept the domination of the factory, but to find in that domination their own sources of personal self-worth and power. Thus, workers transform colleagues into loyal sisters and factory owners into concerned fathers. They are able to accept the constraints that the factory imposes by assimilating the owners' dominance into other, more acceptable forms of relationships.

This re-molding of relationships formed inside the factory to fit the prototypes of ties formed outside ultimately makes the workers available for increased exploitation. Persons with authority in the factory capitalize on workers' interpretations of their roles to maximize production and ultimately increase profit. (p. 182)

Within the context of globalization, the textile sector is based on an industry of women, a relatively weak social group in many countries, which gives special meaning to social relations at the production level and paternalism as a system of normative control.[4] Numerous studies document a paternalistic framework in all aspects of the work cycle—from recruitment, to management style on the production floor, to contacts beyond the workplace[5] (Dick and Morgan 1987; Newby 1977; Newman 1980). The paternalistic approach in the workplace thus elicits commitment and loyalty from the workers. In her work on Amoskeag, a New England industrial community, Hareven (1982) describes the paternal authority of the bosses as conforming to the family and religious tradition: "The bosses symbolized paternal authority to many younger workers, who treated them with awe and often turned to them for help" (p. 134). Paternalistic social relationships in the textile industry enable the managers to design managerial tools and determine behavioral standards geared toward maximizing production. Furthermore, paternalism softens the impact of formal coercive and control measures. It is meant to be a personal, reciprocal, emotionally committed, and informal style of management.

In sum, paternalism is a Janus-faced system of managerial exploitation grounded in personal sentiment ultimately aimed to soften potential conflict and raise loyalty through personal attachment (Padavic and Ernest 1994). Paternalistic behavior is a weapon in the managerial arsenal, an ad hoc strategy for perpetuating managerial control over labor.

Work Culture on the Shop Floor

The work culture in the plants is the result of an organizational process of creating shared meaning, fostering a common interpretation of the organizational experience, and deriving behavioral guidelines, whether conscious or automatic (Hofstede 1991). Shared meaning is seen as common feelings, experiences, communication, and interpretation of activities (Schein 1985). Shared meaning tends to preserve itself by channeling the perception, interpretation, and behavior of organizational members toward a common worldview. Thus, shared meaning is an organizational attribute, a complex of multifaceted processes embedded in the daily interactions and worldview of the organization (Daft and Weick 1984). This study shows how shared meaning has multiple origins. It depends on both the organizational setting and the local environment for making sense of behavior at work. Family involvement is an essential component of the work at the plants and, as this book shows, the work culture simulates the family's main tenets through dictating values, attitudes, and practices on the shop floor.

The members of the organization participate in determining the logic of their social and organizational world, complying with its norms and rules and modifying their behavior accordingly. The shared meaning is not static or inert. Ongoing conflicts and negotiations create a process of redefining meaning, identities, and objectives in the organization. As this book shows, the managers and leaders of the organization are not the only ones who shape this process. Meaning is transferred and molded through the interaction of all the actors on the shop floor. Although they all structure the ideology, values, and practices of the sewing plants, not all players are equal in creating shared meaning. In the sewing plants, the process depends on the division of labor, formal and informal roles, local events, demographic composition of the plant, and characteristics of the managers and supervisors.

In this study, the work culture on the shop floor is a *shatnez*, which in Aramaic denotes the commingling of dissimilar elements, the merging together of components appearing to be different in form and content. The content of this familial culture and its shared meanings rests on production agendas, characteristics, and social identities[6] of the organizational members.

Many researchers portray managers as creators and manipulators of organizational culture (Deal and Kennedy 1982; Peters and Waterman 1982). The principal aim of these strong organizational cultures is to produce normative control and organizational structures that enable the management to achieve its goals.[7] As Kunda (1992) mentions:

> The evolution of organization forms based on a managerial ideology of normative control leads to heavy claims against the self— the thoughts, feelings, and experiences of members of work organizations. More than ever, domains of the self once considered private come under corporate scrutiny and regulation. What one does, thinks, or feels—indeed who one is—is not just a matter of private concern but the legitimate domain of bureaucratic control structures armed with increasingly sophisticated techniques of influence. The significance of this development goes beyond the boundaries of organizational life. The power of organizations to shape individuals raises the more general problem of the relationship of self and society. (p. 13)

Unlike the popular managerial literature on strong culture and leadership, many writers on women workers portray the active role of working women in constructing a workplace culture (Kondo 1990; Ong 1987). One cannot understand diversity in the workplace in terms of gender and ethnic composition without investigating the perceptions, actions, and interpretations of all the participants in the working life. Within the framework of the importance of gender in inserting meanings to the work culture, I relate to those attributes that best explain the dynamics of the organizational culture of the textile industry in the Galilee: organization of production, values and norms, and conflict.

ORGANIZATION OF PRODUCTION

In Blauner's seminal work *Alienation and Freedom* (1964), the textile industry is described as constraining the workers' control over their work processes. The technology and division of labor on the textile shop floor confine the workers to the machine and require them to work at an accelerated pace, using a limited number of procedures. The textile industry resembles the classical Fordist model of mass production—product standardization, assembly lines, mechanization, and deskilling (Edwards 1978). Fordism entails the logic of Taylorism—reducing the independence of workers, accelerating the speed of work, limiting workers to the production floor, relieving them of authority and responsibility over the work, and maintaining a strict managerial hierarchy for anchoring managerial positions in the firm (Amin 1994). Thus, Fordism is a combination of two complementary principles:

> The semi-automatic assembly line, organizing work into a straightforward linear flow of transformations applied to raw materials . . . [and] the fixing of workers . . . In such a system individual workers lost control over their own work rhythm, and became fully adjuncts to the machine, repeating those few elementary movements designed by engineering departments as the rationalized sum of their formal organizational existence." (Clegg 1990, pp. 177–8)[8]

The major work value of the shop floor is the recognition that optimal production is a consequence of specialization in specific procedures. Optimization of shop floor production also requires an appropriate physical environment, optimizing concerns of space, air-conditioning, lighting, and so on (Kapferer 1972).[9]

The predicament of assembly line work is routinization. The more monotonous the work procedure, the higher the degree of specialization and production level. Routine work dictates an organization of production that emphasizes that line supervisors have optimal control of the worker (Edwards 1979). The work itself requires few skills, and training occurs on the job. The machines, not the workers, determine many aspects of production (Berger and Piore 1980; Hall et al. 1987; Sabel 1982). Furthermore, some argue that technological advances, especially electronic and computerized advances, accentuate the deskilling of the workforce (Leman 1992).

Assembly line procedures prevent the worker from grasping the overall production process. The worker usually concentrates on a particular part of the garment and is not responsible for the production of the entire product. Production planning is not an integral part of shop floor activities and is not the concern of the workers. The common practice is to restrict the worker to his or her own workstation. This specialization and distance from the overall work process reduces worker commitment and identification with the work and the organization.

Research of the contemporary textile industry (Rainnie 1984; Spybey 1984) finds that management still preserves the hierarchies, norms, and symbols that were accepted in the nineteenth-century British textile industry. Managers still practice surveillance, strict discipline, direct supervision, and rigid control. The organizational structure of the shop floor consists of a clear and defined hierarchy that includes two management levels: general managers and supervisors, who directly control the workers and the line (Westwood 1984; Woodward 1965).

In the plants under research, supervisors are important players on the production floor (see also Kapferer 1972; Kung 1983). The role of these supervisors centers on close oversight of the worker's performance and ensuring the smooth flow of quantity and quality. The supervisors are expected to be authoritative because their main task is to enforce tough production demands. The production level depends on the workers' ability to optimally operate the machine and establish the flow of work.[10] Consequently, the supervisor must ensure a strict rhythm of production during the working day. Furthermore, the supervisors mediate between the female workers and male managers. In this regard, the supervisors are cultural brokers and translators of the work procedures and the organizational objectives. On one hand, they must adhere to the plant's strict regime of maximizing the use of workers' skill and dexterity through tight control. On the other hand, they must cater to and advocate in the interest of the workers. An important theme in this study is the supervisors' role as social and cultural mediator. They attempt to bridge the gaps between home and work and between the managers and the workers.

The supervisors' role as management's right hand in perpetuating the "evils" of the shop floor (unwitting victims of capitalist hegemony who do not benefit from it) was challenged by the modernization and computerization of the shop floor (Nichols and Beynon 1977; Rose, Marshall, and Vogler 1987). New developments, such as total quality management and teamwork, supposedly replace the role of supervisors with bureaucratic, technical, and cultural control. Furthermore, the new organization of production and information technology purportedly encourages normative control whereby the workers themselves internalize the values and practices that were traditionally embodied by the supervisors (Edwards 1979; Sewell and Wilkinson 1992).

The views that supervisors will no longer be needed or are derivative of the organizational structure and its technology are rather simplistic (Perrow 1970; Woodward 1965). They fail to capture the essence of the supervisors' complex role on the shop floor, particularly the complex social relations involved in bridging the gap between managers and workers and in negotiating and reconstructing their role (see also Delbridge and Lowe 1997, p. 411). This book attempts to develop a conceptual framework regarding the social relations of supervisors on the production floor. The textile plants exemplify a reality that is far from the "death of supervisors." As this book shows, it is their role as mediator and intermediary between workers and managers that bestows them with increasing managerial and social content and ultimately aligns them with management.

WORK VALUES

Familial relationships, such as vacation, working hours, work arrangements, social events, and social services, have been prominent work values in factories since the nineteenth century (Joyce 1980). Employers know that by strengthening ties that simulate familial relationships at work, they can prevent some of the difficult consequences of liberal individualism and conflicts of interest between the worker and the work (Gutman 1977; Hareven 1982; Montgomery 1979).[11] Thus, industrialization is not necessarily a catalyst encouraging change but can actually reinforce the mores of the family (Hareven 1982; Tentler 1975; Tilly and Scott 1978).

The nature of the work organization of the sewing plants, particularly their situation in the midst of the Arab communities, may be seen as a culmination of a pronounced influence of local norms and values on management from the workers and the community. The values of the sewing plants represent characteristics of solidarity, cohesion, self-absorption, loyalty to the organization, and a blurred distinction between the organization and the individual and his or her family (Cairoli 1998; Seiter 1995). Consequently, the work culture in the sewing plants corresponds with what is characterized as a clan (Cameron and Freeman 1991; Quinn 1988). The clan form represents a family-like organization and supports a high level of commitment from its members. The clan form is perceived as an organizational culture that mobilizes workers by mimicking kinship relations, thus enabling the organization to become an integral component of the family and the community.

Although the clan form of organizational culture is considered stable, its reconstruction in the textile plants must be viewed against the backdrop of instability. Conflict and resistance are part of the daily life in the plants; each participant has an active role in creating the work culture. Understanding the work culture in the sewing plants in the Galilee requires consideration of the inherent conflict and the threat of imminent crisis that prevails in the daily work life.

INHERENT POTENTIAL FOR CONFLICT

The pluralistic environment of the plants makes it necessary to give primacy to the nature of the various members. The significant differences between the workers and the managers—in world outlooks, values and norms, behavior patterns, interests, and goals —generate a situation in which conflict is inherent.

Theories of conflict consider organizations as battlefields, not because of anyone's individual characteristics but because of intramural structural traits (Collins 1975). According to this approach, organizational conflicts can be solved by the intervention of managers who establish the parameters and mechanisms of organizational design and content (Galbraith 1977). A conflict may be resolved through structural factors and laws (Lawrence and Lorch 1967), by an appeal to norms and cultural values (Kunda and Barley 1988; Schein 1985), or by rituals and gestures (Trice and Beyer 1984; Trice 1984). Investigators such as Black (1990) and Nader and Todd (1978) focus on conflictive behavior, examining how specific social context influences how people deal with their disagreements.[12] As this research attempts to reveal, however, conflict is negotiated incrementally through an exchange process, with each party appropriating the symbols, values, rationale, and interests of the opposing side.

The sewing plants contain several sources of conflict:

conflicts related to the organization of work, such as rights and duties, manner of implementing work, remuneration, and discipline;

conflicts related to views on family values and norms of behavior as against management norms; and

conflicts brought into the sewing plant from outside society, such as the community social and political issues and the status of the Arab minority in Israel. (Drori 1996)

In the sewing plants, a dialogue is set in motion whereby managers and workers advance their specific interests within the constraints of production goals. The sides of this dialogue are unequal, and this power inequality determines the processes through which each group influences the other in the domains of action, values, and norms (Etzioni 1961). Each group assesses the words and actions of the other through its particular cultural standards. The implication of cultural difference on this process is that workers and managers have divergent perspectives and sometimes receive conflicting messages. Thus, conflict commonly arises out of mutually mistaken interpretations.

Following previous research on conflict, this book assumes that each group in the organization has its own resources and interests, and it is through these that the conflict is developed and resolved (Kolb and Putnam 1992). Conflict is regarded as a calculated means and predesigned strategy for achieving one's goals, marking boundaries, seeking recognition, and confronting the differences in the social relations of production. These reasons surface as each side reifies its position, status, and role in an attempt to establish ownership of work values, behavior, justifications, way of doing things, and worldview. Through conflict, each side becomes aware of the other's positions, trade-offs, and concessions.

Conclusion

Two complementary theoretical perspectives guide my propositions in analyzing the work culture in the sewing plants. The first is linked to the literature describing the dynamics of women's employment in global factories and the variables and attributes that influence the content and pattern of women's roles and status at work and at home. This literature asserts that entrance into wage employment in assembly line industry accentuates inequalities and reasserts patriarchy at local and global levels. It also portrays the workplace as a mechanism for increased autonomy and social and economic power for women. It presents a dynamic interplay between the various actors that influence women's entrance into wage employment, such as the political state, the employer, the family, and the community.

The second perspective analyzes those attributes and factors that play a role in the creation of shared meaning. It emphasizes the interrelationship between the organization of production as a mechanism for arranging and managing work; the clan organizational culture, which emphasizes familial values and norms; and the conflict and negotiation that accompany the culture creation process.

The integration of these two perspectives, one relating to women in industrialization and the other relating to organizational culture, calls for the incorporation of everyday realities and social interactions in a context of the structural inequalities inherent in sewing plants.

CHAPTER 4

The Sewing Plants: Scenes
from the Social Arena

To see an individual in many contexts is to see what he
is. "Men reveal themselves in journeys," says the
proverb, not only because of the intimacy of constant
companionship but because changing circumstances
reveal situated characteristics. To go to another place is
to put oneself into a new context with all that implies for
those traits and tics that cumulate in the individual as a
matter of his surround. It is not time that shows us what
others are, but their placement in the social worlds
through which they move. It is not their intrinsic
qualities, their unrevealed selves, that make individuals
what they are but the words and actions they create and
display in the situations through which they move.

—LAWRENCE ROSEN
Bargaining for Reality: The Construction of
Social Relations in a Muslim Community

THE ARCHITECTURAL features of the Arab and Druse villages in
the Galilee merge with the sloping landscape. Narrow streets and
alleys, simple square stone dwellings with arched windows, tile
roofs, and balconies are cluttered around the mosque towers.
Some houses are local variations of the ostentatious style common to the villas on the outskirts of the Israeli cities. In all, the
architecture is a conglomeration of mixed building styles. The

streets of the villages do not have sidewalks, and people and vehicles wend their way haphazardly through them. The village centers are crowded with small buildings, containing apartments upstairs and businesses at street level.

From the second-floor balcony off the production room of the sewing plant in Beit Jann, one can see the mountainous landscape of the village, where houses built on long narrow supports cling to the slopes.

The entrance to the sewing plant in Julis resembles the security fence on the northern border between Israel and Lebanon. The plant is enclosed by a high, densely webbed fence, next to some private dwellings or, to be more exact, to their laundry lines.

An ancient olive tree shades the rectangular building of the Hurfeish sewing plant. In the yard is a small grove of pomegranate and fig trees. The building blends into its surrounding, and no one can tell it apart from the residential houses.

The sewing plant in Nazareth is located in an industrial zone. The access road to the plant ends at a busy quarry, and the trucks raise clouds of dust that blanket the heavy door of the plant in a thick layer of white sand. It is as though a heavy curtain separates the world of work inside from the rest of the world outside.

Looking from the north side of the street that leads to the sewing plant in Maghar, one can see the plant's barred windows along the long stone building. Directly across from the glass entrance door to the plant is a sign that reads "Galilee Roasting Factory." A heavy aroma of roasted coffee beans, cardamom, and sunflower seeds hangs in the air.

The sewing plant at Kfar Tavor is located in the heart of the industrial zone. It is a square, two-storied stone building without a single window. Large metal doors lead into a concrete passageway that extends the entire length of the building. From the plant, one can see glorious Mount Tavor and, seemingly suspended off the far end of the mountain, the square Franciscan monastery with the sloping roof.

These plants are the setting of this book. As can be seen in Figure 1, the plants are distributed within the Arab regional settlement system, characterized by its territorial continuity and predominantly Arab population (Schnell, Sofer, and Drori 1995). The

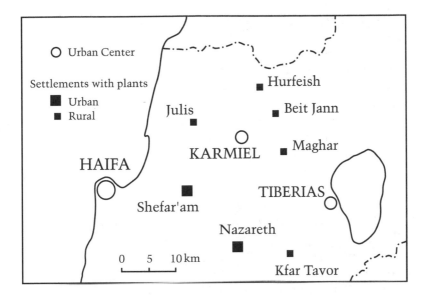

FIGURE I. Plants within Arab settlement region

plants are not of a uniform size. The one in Nazareth is the largest, employing about 300 women workers and staff. The one at Kfar Tavor has about 230 employees, and those at Julis, Beit Jann, Maghar, and Hurfeish employ between 160 to 200 workers.

The chapter attempts to illustrate through ethnographic examples how the managers, workers, and supervisors attempt to generate shared meaning on the shop floor. It reviews the organization of production, the shaping of work values, and the dynamics of conflict resolution. The dynamic pattern of action, interaction, and interrelationships constitutes a set of guidelines for the basic assumptions, values, and behavior that shape the work culture in the plant (Schein 1985).

Organization of Production

The production areas of the plants are all alike—large spaces, lit by long neon tubes casting diagonal rays of light from the ceiling and illuminating the clouds of lint covering the seamstresses. The women sit one behind the other, and at first glance it is difficult to discern exactly where one stops and the other begins. Row after row they sit at their machines, in white smocks, and a hodgepodge of movement merges into a single current. Their nimble fingers are never at rest. The seamstresses work according to the "bundle" system, whereby the supervisors provide them with predesigned components packed in bundles of up to fifty. The seamstresses collect the segments from the bundles next to the machines and sew them together, their heads bent forward first and then backwards, to take the next two segments. The segments are placed in the exact position on the track of the machine as the needles go up and down. The women's bodies sway back and forth like men at prayer. The synchronizing wheel at the back of the machine turns and stops. The joined segments are pulled onto the woman's lap and the next two pieces are taken from the tray. After sewing, the bundle is retied and the supervisor marks its completion on a form attached to the sewing machine. She gives the seamstress a new bundle and updates her on her work progress in relation to her daily quota.

Zohar, in a white shirt and black pants, stands at the far end of the production area of the Beit Jann plant, his arms crossed on his chest.

Rima says, "He is a handsome man, our manager, a real beauty. He's also a good man."

She lifts up her head from the machine while her hands continue sewing—automatically without cease. Zohar's keen eyes dart around the room all the time, not missing a single fly on the wall. With a slight movement of his head he signals to one of the supervisors. The supervisor wears a red smock. She understands his intention from his body language, and her response is immediate. She transfers piles of material from one place to another, throws a warning glance at one of the women chatting with her neighbor, and checks the way the quality controller in the brown smock is working.

"It's enough if I listen," says Zohar. "If the sound is uniform, the work is being done right. Listen to the tempo."

The grating noise of the sewing machines, the monotonous hum of the electric motors, and the high-pitched tones of the famous Arab Israeli singer Zoher Francis coming from a loudspeaker combine to produce what sounds like an avant garde symphony. I am standing next to Zohar surveying the production area. The women are making undergarments. The entire scene looks like a modern art display: there are women in smocks of white, brown, and red; black sewing machines; and colorful pieces of material of different sizes and shapes. One gets the feeling of a dynamic flow, of movement and the meshing of gears.

The women arrive at work at 6:30 in the morning, usually by bus or van.[1] Each one has her own assigned place in the plant, but the supervisors may make changes when workers are absent and empty machines need to be filled. The departments are built on the principle of specialization, each one complementing the work of the other. Each product has its own sewing file describing the procedures and quality requirements and the standard production time of each component. Each of these products has a distinct production process and requires specific sewing machines for various stitches. If one line stops working, a production bottleneck is created. For this reason, balance must be maintained. The balance within each department is the supervisor's responsibility; between the departments, balance of the production lines is maintained through consultation with the production manager. The guiding principle is to ensure that every sewing function is adequately staffed, and a situation is maintained in which the output of each production line is synchronous with those of the others.

The organization of the work is structured such that the flow of work is the dominant process. This flow allows for a continuous, uninterrupted process of production, from the beginning of the sewing to the finished product. Productivity depends on the flow, which in turn depends on the proper balance between the seamstresses in their different functions. Each line has a predetermined quota that must be attained. The supervisors organize the daily operations according to the availability and abilities (in production terms) of seamstresses in each workstation. Absenteeism hurts planning and the reaching of production quotas. In such cases, there is a need to reshuffle the department, moving seamstresses from one workstation to another and balancing the department in an attempt to minimize the effect on production level.

ORGANIZATIONAL STRUCTURE AND SPAN OF CONTROL

The structure of the sewing plant is usually based on three departments. Each department is responsible for its line of men's underwear designated to a specific client. After completion, the finished product is brought to the packing room, and from there it goes to the warehouse. Clearly, the division of labor is simple and mechanical. Each worker concentrates on her small world—one or two operations, with emphasis placed on speed and quality.[2] This limited realm narrows her work to a mindless, technical, and automatic set of movements.

Accordingly, the organization of the sewing plant is relatively simple and schematic, reflecting the structure of authority and formal responsibility. It represents an ongoing production process typical of assembly line plants. There is a strict linear hierarchy of managers, supervisors, and seamstresses (Fig. 2).

The Jewish managers divide responsibilities among themselves. Usually, the general manager is responsible for dealing with all outside contacts. He has overall responsibility for the plant. He represents the plant, the workers, and their families to the divisional headquarters and he represents the concern to the community. The production manager is responsible for everything that happens on the floor. He determines priorities in the work and supervises quality control, order, and discipline. Cooperation between the general manager and the production manager is total, with one complementing the other. Sabi, the manager of the plant in Nazareth, sums up the subject:

"We work together. As a matter of fact, all of our work is done together. Cooperation between the production manager and me is of pri-

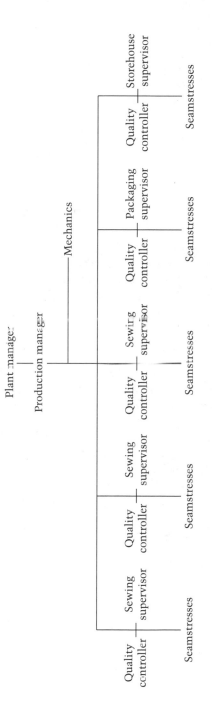

FIGURE 2. Organizational structure of the sewing plant

mary importance. In fact, he has to know what is going on in the plant even more than I do. I have to know in general terms; he has to be familiar with the fine details. Apart from that, it is important that someone be able to replace me when I do [military] reserve duty or go on vacation. If the general manager and the production manager don't get along, the production manager has to go."

The supervisors run the departments, and their main job is to mediate and translate the work plan of the production manager into the smooth operation of the departments. The supervisors are directly accountable to the production manager. They act as his right hands and have a wide scope of responsibility on the shop floor. As Ofer, the production manager of the plant in Nazareth, notes:

"The supervisor reports to me. But what concerns her is the department. She has to perform her duties in order to assure that work as a whole proceeds in a balanced and synchronized manner. The supervisor has to cooperate with the other supervisors and with the production manager so that in the final analysis the finished product will be of the quality and the quantity required. In order to fulfill the production schedule, I sit with each of the supervisors and check her needs: manpower, machines, and raw materials. That's how I make plans. Together we can estimate how the month will go. When there is cooperation among the supervisors, they can help each other with all kinds of problems, from getting new women to transferring workers from one department to another when there is a bottleneck. The main task of the supervisor is to watch the flow of work. If she is organized in her work program and balances the department, everything runs smoothly."

The grating noise of the machines and the hum of the motors dominate the entire shop floor, accompanied by the trill of the music. It is a rhythmical monotony. An experienced ear can judge from the noise the tempo of production. Monotony and uniformity are an indication that the tempo is rapid, that the machines are working smoothly.

Fatma, a supervisor, finishes her morning rounds, balancing work between the various production lines, distributing raw material, and registering quotas. She contentedly observes the department at work.

"I've got a good department," she says. "I taught all the women how to work, but I also taught them that they have to cooperate with the supervisor. Without cooperation I won't treat them nicely, and if I don't treat them right there's no cooperation. I keep telling them that if we don't all hang together we'll all hang separately."

Within the formal division of labor and authority, the supervisor operates only within the boundaries of the department. Her enclosure within the department generates intimacy with her workers and the development of informal relationships.

In the production line, next to one of the seamstresses, Aysha sits on a crate used for storing segments. Aysha is a quality controller, and as such her job is to make sure that the pieces sewn together meet the strict standards of the clients. She selects a "victim"—"That's what I call the woman whose work I decide to check." She checks the underwear—a seemingly slow process, with rapid, rhythmic hand motions, moving in a set track and seeming to draw a fanciful picture of a clothes hanger. Her fingers are long and bedecked with gold rings. One of them has a red stone embedded in it in the shape of a heart. Another glistens with diamond flakes. A third is simple and of white gold and yet another has silver threads woven into the gold. She sees that I am observing her hands, and she herself looks at them with their bright red nail polish with obvious pleasure: "Soon my hands will have the shape of underpants."

Quality controllers have a neutral position in the hierarchy of the plant. Their perception is that they are independent professionals and as such do not deal with the workers and managerial problems but are affiliated with the products. The manager and supervisors challenge this view, however, and are inclined to assign them the tasks of helping supervisors with allocating raw materials to the workers and teaching quality standards practices to the workers. Quality controllers do not tend to see themselves as accountable to the overall quality performance of the department. This view is another source of dispute with the managers, who attempt to link responsibility for the quality of the department to the work of the quality controller. The painting of boundaries of accountability are a constant source of tension between quality controllers, managers, and supervisors, whereby the former attempt to narrow their terms of reference to the product itself and remain detached from the department, and the latter attempt to integrate them into the department. The managers and supervisors attempt to delineate their position within the hierarchical setting of the plant as under the responsibility of the supervisors.

PRODUCTION CONSTRAINTS

Work in the sewing plant is demanding. Insistence on high quality and output stems from the fact that the products are for export. The plants are under heavy pressure to meet quality standards and production schedules because the concern operates within the competitive and lucrative market of leading garment labels. In some cases, logistics problems not directly connected to the plant itself, such as shortages of raw materials—elastic, labels, ribbon—cause delays. A good part of the time and energy of management is invested in coordinating production lines with changing demands.

"You see," says Even, the plant manager in Maghar, "it's always like that—zero landing time. They [the division] want immediate responses." He asks the secretary to call the supervisors into the office. The supervisors are soon there. Even stands behind the desk, the supervisors in front of him.

"This is not a meeting. We'll have one tomorrow," he says. "Too many women are out this morning. I don't agree that just because it's raining they decide not to come to work. Believe me, I would also like to stay in bed." The supervisors laugh. "Pick up the phone or go to their homes and get them out of bed."

Nadia asks, "What if they're sick?"

Even interrupts her impatiently. "We need them all here. There's an urgent order. Besides, they're not sick; they're just playing sick."

Later Nadia tells me that "it's always like that in the winter. Lots of women are missing in the morning. They just don't feel like coming to work. You think I like going over to their houses and arguing with them and with their mothers? When I came to Rashida this morning, her mother said to me that I would have to take responsibility for her health. That's a big problem. The parents are always anxious about their daughters' health. There are some who complain that the work causes the women backaches and breathing problems and they don't want to let them come to work at all. They'd rather have them sit at home until they get married. They want them to be healthy when they marry."[3]

Although the managers attempt to achieve maximum control over work through a formal structure and bureaucratization of procedures, in reality, the workers' own behavior and values collide with the plants' desired organization of production. This tension is absorbed and embodied by the supervisor who takes on the complex role of mediator. She must simultaneously represent both the managers and the workers and solve the contradictions that emerge from these two apparently mutually exclusive systems of expectations.

The conversation with the supervisors ends. Even sits down in his chair. "We're caught between the devil and the deep blue sea—the production on the one hand and the women's priorities on the other."

He looks worried. He attributes the difficulties in the plant to the unreasonable demands of the executive division management and complains about the inconsiderateness of the division manager.

"They refuse to understand our problems. We're dealing here with a peculiar kind of workforce, and we have to measure every step carefully. We can't force the women to work overtime and on Fridays for too long a period. It's too problematic."

Friday is the Muslim Sabbath. The seamstresses are outspoken about their dissatisfaction with working Fridays, and some of them just walk out. On Fridays, absenteeism is worst. The managers don't want to apply severe sanctions against the seamstresses for fear of losing them entirely and arousing the antipathy of the village.[4]

"Sometimes things become absurd," says Even. He is speaking in a low and monotonous voice. "You remember that we didn't work on *Iyd el-Adha* [a Muslim holiday following the Ramadan fast], and afterward we tried to make up for lost time? The pressure to step up production resulted in a decline in quality, and this produced a kind of snowball effect. Because of bad quality, more of the merchandise failed to pass quality control and had to be returned for fixing up. At the same time we had to continue production."

The nature of assembly line work is its potential for "causal collapse," whereby a break in one link in the chain leads to an escalating series of problems. The organization of production is designed to ensure continuous monitoring and control of processes and workers in order to reduce stoppages in the production flow (Edwards 1979).

"The sewing plants pay a price. Because of a drop in quality and the pressure of production quotas, I have to keep the women working overtime. This results in absenteeism and in women leaving. It's a vicious circle. I pressure the women who are still working, and because they can't take the pressure they don't come to work the next day. So there are more production problems, and I continue to apply pressure and then the quality drops, and this goes on endlessly.

"I told the women that we were in an emergency situation and that we were all in it together—like a family. I begged them to work longer hours and produce more. Not just for me, but for us, working as a united family toward a common goal."

Because of the oscillations in production, the managers continuously need to mobilize workers to invest additional time and effort in the plant. The managers realize that they cannot rely only on their formal authority and the organization of production to coerce their workers. They must comply with the pressure coming from the workers and their families on issues such as overtime, as the next story illustrates.

There was a lot of unrest at the plant. Some of the women were not prepared to stay on and work overtime, and they went home. They weren't even deterred by the fact that the manager confiscated their timecards and they were unable to clock out. This meant, in fact, that they were losing a whole day's wages. The situation developed into a major crisis, and the women's parents came to the plant demanding an explanation. A meeting was arranged between the management and the parents, but only on condition that the women return to work.

"The parents' meeting was a total farce," says Even, playing around with a pen. "It was a dialogue between deaf people. The parents spoke about low wages and overtime, and we spoke about production needs and the significance of losses which would result in closing the plant. Their response is always the same: 'We're not the slaves of the company.'"[5]

These clashes are the daily routine of the plant. They are either spontaneous or initiated by managers, workers, or family members. Sometimes a clash is a "dialogue between deaf people," and sometimes it is a negotiation process. The games have rules that are meant to diffuse conflicts and to save face. Although pressures on the shop floor tend to resemble the pattern of tension, conflict, and negotiation, these pressures still occur on the backdrop of managerial dominance. This dominance is rooted in the structural reality of the Arab sector and its position within the overall pattern of the Israeli labor market, whereby labor-intensive industries exploit the lack of employment opportunities and the availability of cheap labor (Schnell, Sofer, and Drori 1995). The workers and their families seek to identify the weaknesses and vulnerabilities of the system and manipulate it to demand better terms of employment. Thus, the work culture of the plant is not based exclusively on the terms of the plants, which are part of capitalist industrial development of the Arab communities, but also draws from and is shaped by local norms, values, and social relations (see Calagione and Nugent 1992).

THE RECRUITING SYSTEM

We sit in the manager's office in the Kfar Tavor sewing plant. It's a small room with a few chairs and a desk with piles of assorted merchandise. The office is separated from the production room by glass windows, permitting a view of what is going on there. Monta, a woman of about 30, is sitting across from Ronnie, the manager. She is wearing a long pink dress, and her head is covered with a white kerchief. She has come to discuss the possibility of working in the plant. She has fifteen years' experience, among them eight years as a supervisor in a sewing plant. She worked in a large plant belonging to a rival firm, but after a falling out with the manager, she decided to see if she could find work here. Experienced supervisors are in demand and Ronnie is making an effort to convince her to join the staff.

He says, "I came to work here even though I was offered three times as much money in another place. Today I am sure that I was right. When I came, the conditions were not what they should have been, and I even had physical difficulties. But I believe in the company. My salary is always paid on time. And I always get the vacation coming to me. When I needed a loan, I got one. It's a good company."

Monta is listening patiently, nodding her head in agreement. He continues, "You know that there are companies that pay better, but here you have the possibility of learning and getting ahead. Anyone who wants to study can do it at the company's expense. This place is not a short-term venture. If you want to succeed and enjoy all the advantages that a large company has to offer, you have to look at it from a long-range point of view."

Monta says: "Not everything in life is money."

Ronnie understands which way the wind is blowing and confirms Monta's feelings. "No matter how many places you've worked in, you still haven't seen a place like this. Ours is one of the nicest and best organized sewing plants—and not only in Israel. Our plants are the leading plants in Israel. We're in the fashion trade—and that's not what it used to be. I mean real fashion and not just ready-made clothing. Therefore, what's important to us is professional skill and the ability to teach the women. We have to get across to them the idea that sewing is a real profession and not just temporary work until they marry."

Monta continues to listen patiently and when Ronnie finishes, she asks, "And how much will I make?"

"I'll give 2,000 shekels a month. There are supervisors who make less, so promise me not to tell them how much you're making; otherwise I'll be in trouble."

Monta says, "I'm familiar with things like that. But it's nobody's business how much I earn except my husband's."

Ronnie continues, "I'm giving you more than a starting supervisor because you are experienced. But here it's not quite the same as in the other places you've worked. We have a different set-up and it takes time to learn. It's important that the supervisor deals with professional matters but also that she maintains good human relations with the women and cooperates with the rest of the staff."

Monta says, "You're 100 percent right."

Ronnie continues, "Don't decide right now. Take a day, talk it over, think about it, and then come back. Just remember that if you can prove yourself, if you can find your place here and get results, your salary will reflect that. I want you to remember this. As general manager I am telling you the truth, and I want it to be absolutely clear. You have to decide. It's your decision and not your husband's."

Monta is offended by Ronnie's last remarks. "My husband never decides for me. I decide. But I talk it over with him."

Unlike seamstresses, who have a high turnover rate and consider work as temporary, supervisors are expected to see the sewing plant as secure and permanent employment. Usually, good supervisors are in great demand. There are two avenues for recruiting supervisors. The first is by "raising" a promising seamstress from the production line, usually one who is good at the work, intelligent, and a natural leader. The second is by recruiting experienced supervisors, either from other sewing plants or ones who left work because of marriage and decided to return because of economic necessity. As this conversation illustrates, the managers market the plant as a modern and progressive workplace, emphasizing its international stature, its economic strength, and especially its ability to provide long-term job security and satisfaction. The plant managers present the work and negotiate with Monta in terms of recruiting a professional with a career path, and not in terms of the work itself and remuneration, as done when recruiting seamstresses. Another important point with regard to recruiting supervisors is that the manager sees the candidate as an independent individual, capable of making decisions according to her own interests and not as bound to external agents such as her father or brother who have the final say regarding her employment. This view emerges from the fact that most of the supervisors are unmarried women who have been working for many years and who may be sole breadwinners.

I ask Ronnie, "How do you recruit your nonprofessional workers?"

Ronnie answers, "You've touched on a very interesting point. Our system, actually the system in all the sewing plants, is that the women themselves and the supervisors bring in new workers. Usually they bring in friends or relatives, and in that way they more or less guarantee that the women they bring will work well. The system is such that one worker brings another. Everyone who brings in a new worker is responsible for her. The supervisor alone is responsible for her absorption into the work. You absorb her into the work, you train her, you teach her, you make sure that she's OK as far as production quotas and discipline. If she's good, it's your gain. If she's no good, it's your problem."

The system of "friend brings friend" and mainly "family members bring family members" and "sister brings sister" is the preferred recruiting channel in the sewing plants. It is an intricate system of obligations. The manager exhibits confidence in the judgment and discretion of the recruiter, thus demonstrating that she has been bestowed a right to represent the plant in the community. The recruiter, in turn, is committed to meeting the manager's expectations and recruiting a woman whom she knows intimately and is sure will become a good worker. She also has an obligation to the worker, whom she has convinced to join, and to the worker's family, thus supporting and mentoring her during her first period at work. From the perspective of the new recruit, she is obliged to the managers because of their capacity as managers and her desire to prove herself. The obligation of the new recruit is very prominent because a failure to meet the expectation of the manager with regard to her progress at work means insulting her recruiter and mentor—disputing her judgment and hurting the manager's trust in her. The recruitment system is a manifestation of what can be termed composite manipulation, whereby each actor attempts to promote his or her own interest through creating overt and covert obligations from the other side. Thus, the manager relinquishes his right to recruit and in return receives a loyal and effective workforce. The supervisor, in turn, is able to shape and control her own department and ensure loyalty from her workers and thus increase her relative power in the plant. The worker has a mentor and advocate, and the family has an address and a channel to the plant through both their daughter and the recruiter. The composite manipulation creates a comprehensive system of accountability that ultimately ensures, from the management's perspective, an obedient and obliged labor force.

Another avenue for recruitment is through the drivers who bring the seamstresses to the plants from their village. The seamstresses who come from other villages are driven at the plant's expense. The drivers are usually private subcontractors. Their role, however, is much beyond that of a driver. The driver is a trustee of the family and often a relative—families entrust their daughters in his care and rely on his discernment. He is a liaison between the family and the workplace. The driver also serves as an employment agent and provides workers for many of the plants, usually via his wife, who inquires in the village about women who are interested in work. The driver is a reincarnation of a well-known institution in the Arab villages, the *rais*, which represents a basic form of mediation for work and a mechanism of control of men over women (Haidar 1993). The family entrusts their daughters to the *rais*, who provides them with work while ensuring that the social codes and mores toward women are not adversely affected by leaving the protective domain of home.

Although the driver claims ownership over the seamstresses, in practice he is not a *rais*; the seamstresses consider him to be only a driver. In this regard, the work in the sewing plant reduced the role of the *rais* to that of a recruiter and a driver and eliminated his role as a guardian. This role was appropriated by the plant managers. For the managers, the drivers are accountable for the arrival of all the seamstresses at work. They pay him according to the number of women he brings, and it is in his best interest for them all to arrive. In times of need, in particular when there is a shortage of workers, the managers prefer to contact drivers who can promise a full load of seamstresses. Friction does exist, however. The drivers will attempt to have workers transferred to other plants if these plants offer higher transportation fees. Or, drivers will demand higher fees and refuse to deliver workers if their fee is not paid. These demands are frustrating to seamstresses and managers alike.

The seamstresses are divided into three main age groups—youth[6] (ages 15 to 18), before marriage (ages 18 to 25), and a small group of married and unmarried women 25 years and older. The youth are a distinctive group in the sewing plant. They are considered undisciplined, unripe for physical labor, and lacking a serious attitude toward work. The managers are uncomfortable with young seamstresses because they cannot expect the same quantity and quality of work as with the adult seamstresses and do not allow themselves to apply strict managerial sanctions against them. Furthermore, legally, youth work one less hour than adults and must be provided with a ride home at a different time. The managers recruit youth only in times of labor shortages or as a special favor to a family or a person close to the plant, as the next story illustrates.

Salah has been driving a group of ten seamstresses from his village to the sewing plant for many years. He owns a minibus and has always brought ten women. If one left, he would find a replacement. Unfortunately, in one instance, when one of the seamstresses in his group married and left, he had difficulties finding a substitute. Salah was the head of his family because his father was dead, and he took care of his mother and two unmarried sisters. He decided to recruit his youngest sister, who was twelve years old but looked considerably older. Knowing the limitations of the child labor law, he provided her with her sister's identity card, who was at that time sixteen and in school. For four years Bushra worked in the plant under the identity of her sister

Hamuda. When Hamuda got engaged and needed money to buy appliances for her new house, she wanted to work at the sewing plant. Salah went to the manager and revealed the fraud, suggesting a solution to the problem:

"The real Hamuda will replace Bushra at work and Bushra will be rehired as Bushra. This way both of them will work."

The manager was under a lot of pressure. On one hand he needed Salah and did not want to hurt many years of cooperation. On the other hand, he was not so happy to be a conscious accomplice to fraud. The final arrangement was that for a short period both Hamuda and Bushra work together at the plant as Hamuda "entered Bushra's shoes" in terms of her identity. Bushra's years of work were then granted to Hamuda, and Bushra was stripped of her years at work and was hired as a novice. After a few months, Hamuda resigned and received Bushra's compensation, an amount sufficient to buy a refrigerator, stove, washing machine, and television. Bushra stayed on in the plant, this time under her real name and legal to work by law.

When I ask her why she agreed to give all her years of compensation pay to her sister, she replies, "This whole trick was my brother's decision. This way I helped my sister, and now I can be me, Bushra. When I get married, my brother will take care of me too."

The cooperation between the managers and the fathers and brothers of the workers exemplifies the system of patriarchy pervasive in the sewing plant. The local practices, interests, and values of the family and the community are sometimes linked with the manager's use of patriarchal control in the plant. Through consent and cooperation from the brothers and fathers, the managers strengthen their internal control and create alliances with male members of the community.

Work Values

SHARED MEANINGS

All the plants have organized forums for managerial presentations of various issues regarding the daily and future operations.

The workers, the supervisors, and the managers all take part. Subjects of importance to the operation of the plant are raised, and a dialogue is conducted among all the parties. It is, in fact, a form of negotiation between the workers and the managers in which each side has the opportunity to present its point of view and argue on its behalf.

The women are all gathering in the cafeteria for a talk with the manager, as is the custom from time to time. Here they receive news concerning major events affecting the plant, such as changes in work plans and personnel, new products, forthcoming visits, or a serious decline in production or quality. These meetings provide a stage for the managers to articulate their philosophy of management and to demand discipline, production, and work norms from the workers. It is here that the negotiation for a mutual agenda of the plant takes place.

Zohar, the Beit Jann manager, begs for quiet and begins talking. Sami, the production manager, is standing next to him. The supervisors are sitting separately in one corner of the cafeteria.

"We are known for the quality of our work. We are working for a number of prestigious fashion chains in the United States and Great Britain. It is important, therefore, that we maintain higher standards than those of our competitors. We have to be the best at all times. Two years ago, we had a lower standard of quality than we have today, and in another two years our standard will have to improve if we are to remain in the market."

The workers seem to listen attentively to the manager, who speaks slowly and clearly, but one can only guess if they fully comprehend what he is talking about.

"Every worker in Israel costs the company $900 a month. In Egypt the same worker costs only $40 a month.[7] In Egypt the sewing is cheap, but an Egyptian seamstress is not capable of doing what you do. The standard is different—like the fact that a kid of twelve cannot sew as well as a grown man. You are what makes the difference. Your standard of sewing is one of the highest in the world. We export and sell the best and most beautiful merchandise in the undergarment industry."

In conversations with the women after the meeting, it is apparent that they do not attribute much significance to the comparison with Egypt. The veiled threat that production might be transferred to Egypt if the plant does not prove profitable seems to contradict their perception of the essence of relations of the workplace. The managers, who are under pressure to profitably operate the plant, attempt to internalize it to the seamstresses. By emphasizing values of cohesion and solidarity, the managers harness the workers for their own objective of achieving operational profit.

The manager continues. "Every worker is responsible for the quality of the merchandise she produces. Personally responsible to me." He turns to the supervisors who have stopped chatting and are listening attentively. "Every supervisor is responsible to me for the quality in the department as a whole, and I am responsible for the quality before the head of the division." He stops and surveys the audience. "Are there any questions?"

The women look at one another, then at their nails, then at the manager, until one of them, Alya, says, "I want high quality and a high rate of production, but they don't go together." Sounds of protest come from the supervisors and the production manager, and they begin to argue with the workers. The argument revolves around the question of whether output and quality are connected—whether a high rate of production adversely affects quality because of the fact that when one works fast, one concentrates less and therefore is less careful.

The manager lets the argument take its course without interfering. When the heat dies down, he says, "Our company has shown beyond a doubt that high quality and a high rate of production go hand in hand. A skilled professional seamstress with a high rate of production produces top quality goods."

He turns to a seamstress sitting in the third row. "Sana, how many pairs of underwear do you make a day?" The woman sitting next to Sana, a clumsy looking woman wearing overalls and a kerchief on her head, giggles. Sana appears uncomfortable. The manager persists. "Tell them all, Sana, how many pairs do you make?" Sana shoots out two words: "Twelve bundles." The manager reiterates, "Twelve bundles of excellent quality, and she has been working in the plant only three months. Twelve bundles means 120 percent, 20 percent above the quota. If Sana can do it after only three months, the rest of you can too.

"I am not asking you for something unrealistic, but anyone who can't keep up won't be able to stay at the plant. She can go and work at one of the smaller sewing workshops, located in people's bedrooms." He is referring to the spate of small sewing workshops that have sprung up in the villages. They attract workers from the larger plants by offering them slightly higher wages.

Zohar, the manager, is in a decisive mood. "All of you know exactly how much you produce each day. It's not a secret. Your daily output is listed on the bulletin board. Every one of you knows exactly how much she earned today and that if she produces more she will earn more. And I don't have to tell you what you can do with your money. All of us work for money. It's true that it's great working together and the plant is like a second home to all of us. But in the final analysis I don't want you working for me or for the supervisors. You work for yourselves. Whoever wants to stay here has to work well. I'm not asking anyone who hasn't yet reached 100 percent of the quota to produce 120 percent tomorrow. But you have to make progress, slowly but surely, another 10 or even another 7 percent more. Once you've reached that point, you don't go down."

The manager's last sentence is of great significance. One of the common truths in the plants is retention of the production level. Experience shows that any seamstress who reaches a high level of production maintains it. The ability to sew rapidly represents greater technical skill. The seamstresses are usually stable with regard to their sewing capabilities. In each department, there is a core of seamstresses who reach a high level of production and maintain it over a long period. A supervisor aims to expand this core to increase the efficiency of the department. Stability in a department enables the manager to plan his production schedules and to meet production goals. A stable department with a high rate of production permits a certain amount of flexibility in the work. The department can rapidly adjust to new products that require complex, new skills.

Zohar is reaching the end of his speech. "We are all full partners because this is where we all work. Anyone who does not respect his workplace has a problem. I respect the place I work in, and I want to do my job better. And I want the people who work with me to be the best there are. Remember, we are the plant, not the machines but us, the people. A person's respect for his work is reflected in what he produces. We sell quality along with our merchandise. Anyone who buys our product for $20 deserves the best." For a fraction of a second there is absolute silence. The production manager breaks it with evident impatience: "OK, women, back to work."

The manager used the argument about quantity and quality to manipulate the discussion into one about work values. Although the main messages of the managers relate to production quality and quantity, these messages are presented in terms of work values as well as in terms of quotas and remuneration. The workers recognize that they are being manipulated, and the regular ritual of the manager's motivation speech usually bears no immediate results on the seamstresses' production level.

TRANSFORMING MEANINGS

A common practice in the plant is to capitalize on local traditions. During the month of Ramadan,[8] the values and behavioral norms of the holiday are adhered to at work.

During Ramadan, work at those plants where most of the workers are Muslim stops at 2 p.m. instead of 4 p.m. The month of Ramadan marks changes in the atmosphere of the plant. Ronnie, the manager of the plant at Kfar Tavor, says:

"During Ramadan the workday is shorter but the production level is not affected. It's a holy month, and the attitude of the women toward their work is serious."

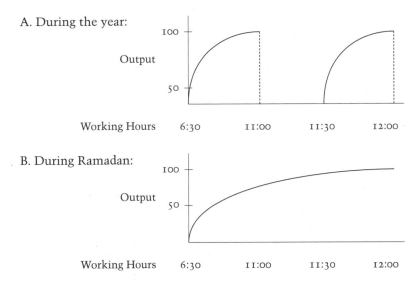

A. During the year:

Output

100

50

Working Hours   6:30   11:00   11:30   12:00

B. During Ramadan:

Output

100

50

Working Hours   6:30   11:00   11:30   12:00

FIGURE 3. Work flow during the month of Ramadan

He takes the pad on which I am making notes and draws two diagrams (Fig. 3).

Ronnie explains, "During the year, the workers take half an hour for lunch. It takes them at least a half an hour to get back to their previous tempo. A lot of time is also wasted in gossiping on the line, going to the bathroom, or getting up to drink water. According to my figures, about an hour and a half is wasted every day. Multiply that by 200 workers and that gives you 350 wasted hours. During Ramadan they don't take a lunch break, they don't get up to drink water, and so they don't go to the bathroom. During Ramadan, they are much more serious and don't gossip during work. Each one is absorbed in herself and in her work. What happens is that the tempo of work and the quality improve. I wish it could be that way all year round."

Ivtesam, the supervisor, talks to the seamstresses in her department about Ramadan. She is a religious woman, and during the talk she reminds her workers to keep up the production level despite the reduced daily hours of work during the Ramadan. She tells me, "This month is holy not only because of the fast. You have to be good all the time, including when you are at work. Because they're working without a break, it goes fine. Usually after eating, the women are a little lazy, eating makes them tired. They all want to sleep after lunch. They want to drink coffee. During Ramadan, there is competition between the women in my department. They all want to do better. They say to me that they wish it were like this all year round. During Ramadan, the women don't talk, and they don't get up from their machines. It's hard for them to talk. Just listen—the women don't make noise, only the machines."

In spite of the Ramadan, there is still pressure to maintain a high level of production, both from the management and from the seamstresses who see Ramadan as a time to express excellence.

"During Ramadan, the women want to prove that they're the best. On the first day of Ramadan, one of the workers, whose quota is 900, produced 1200 pieces. I praised her in front of the other workers. I said, 'You've done a great job.' The next day they all did 1200. There was one woman who missed a half day's work. I asked the other women to make up her quota. They all worked a little harder and made up another 50 pieces."

We are walking around the production line. The women are concentrating on their work, their heads bent over the machines. I stop near Yusra. A white kerchief covers her long hair. I ask her if there is a difference in the work between Ramadan and the rest of the year.

Yusra answers without stopping her work. "During Ramadan we concentrate on the work and don't gossip about this one or the other. During Ramadan we concentrate on the work all the time because that's part of being good, not lying, not talking nonsense, and not bad-mouthing anybody. During Ramadan we don't look at the clock. All of a sudden it's two o'clock and we go home. At home we have to help because in the evening we eat a large meal and we have to help with the cooking. Because the plant shows consideration for us and lets us off at two, I want to produce as much as the supervisor wants me to, even more."

The Ramadan represents the clan work culture and its main attribute of being one family. These familial relations are evaluated through behavior based on fairness and reciprocity. The management's consideration during Ramadan manifests itself in the shortening of the workday and is reciprocated by the seamstresses, who maintain a high level of production. Thus, Ramadan is another example in which a local value is appropriated by the organization and becomes a means of normative control. Ramadan, one of the most precious Muslim religious holidays, is brought into the domain of work and is integrated into the working process. Transforming the behavioral content represented by Ramadan is also the workers' normative interpretation and their contribution to the creation of shared values at the workplace.

MANAGERS AS FATHERS AND BROTHERS, WORKERS AS DAUGHTERS AND SISTERS

Chagai is a young production manager at the Julis plant. He is a member of a kibbutz, a cooperative settlement, but works in the plant because he could not find a job in industrial management at the kibbutz. Chagai's managerial worldview is participatory, and he claims that he still believes in the kibbutz ideology of togetherness and egalitarianism within the workplace. He says, "I look the worker eye to eye. I try to manage through consensus." On the shop floor, he is known for being gentle and mellow, not raising his voice, and for superimposing his authority through quiet leadership. In contrast to the manager of the plant, who is authoritarian and tough, Chagai has a soft image. In day-to-day management, the two have complementary styles and often play the good guy–bad guy roles. Their different styles reflect on the way they are perceived by the workers and define the boundaries of managerial practices and authorities beyond the formal division of labor between them.

Uda says, "Chagai is like my brother, and the manager is like my father."

I ask her, "What is the difference?"

She answers patiently, "With Chagai, I can laugh and joke around. I can come to him whenever I want, and I even tell him my personal secrets. He listens to me, not like the manager, who is very strict and does not tolerate argument. The manager always says that we are supposed to do what we are told to do with no arguing. He is like my father; we all have to do what he wants. Even my big brothers, who are married, have to do what my father says without arguing."

I ask if she argues with Chagai.

"A lot. I always argue with him about my quotas and absenteeism and everything else. But it's for fun; eventually I do what he wants, since he is the manager. But I like him. He is like a brother to me. I know that he likes me and takes care of me."

Patriarchal relationships between managers and workers are delineated according to a differentiation between managerial styles. The seamstresses construct managerial roles in terms of either brothers or fathers depending on the managers' characters, practices, and behavior. The construction of the manager's identity as brother or father also defines the worker's identity in this patriarchal dyad, whereby manager-father implies worker-daughter relationship and manager-brother implies worker-sister relationship. Thus, in the context of patriarchal relationships, both sides are assigned supplementary roles that determine the essence of their relationships on the shop floor, as exemplified in Table 2, which presents the ideal types of these relationships.

In reality, these dyadic patriarchal relationships between managers and workers show a degree of connectivity whereby, for example, the brother-sister type presents characteristics of both affection and closeness, power and control. In her study on brother-sister relationships in Lebanon as reproducing patriarchy, Joseph (1994) noted that this relationship manifests both love and nurturance, power and violence. Thus, in the plants, a patriarchal view of brother-sister relationships expresses an unmediated closeness within relationships of unequal power.

TABLE 2
Types of patriarchal views on manager-worker relationships

Managerial issue	Father/daughter	Brother/sister
Authority and control	Emphasizes uncompromised obedience	Emphasizes obedience through internalized obligation
Style	Patronizing, distant, reserved	Patronizing, close, warm
Practices	Formal, rule-following, inflexible, intolerant	Informal, flexible, tolerant

SOCIAL COGNITION

At the sound of the bell, the production area empties and the women hurry in groups to the cafeteria. It's an opportunity for them to be together, to chat, to gossip, or to show off something new in their wardrobe. At one of the tables the women are cooing at pictures of Amal's brother's baby boy. She proudly shows me the pictures.

"What about you?" I ask laughingly.

Amal looks at me, frowning. "The subject of marriage and raising a family is not something to make fun of," she says.

The women standing around us giggle. This is the subject that occupies them most of the time. The sewing plant has, since its inception, served as a matchmaking bureau. From among the brothers, cousins, and other relatives of the 200 women working here, there are plenty of potential grooms. Here, the women conduct their matrimonial "war councils," planning in detail stratagems and maneuvers, discussing how to decide whom to marry and what is really important in a groom.[9]

Rima says jokingly, "Amal has her eye on somebody." Amal blushes.

"Who is it?" I ask. "But tell me only if it's not a secret."

The women all smile and Rima says, "It's a secret but everybody knows."

Rima is waiting for a nod of approval from Amal and when it comes she says, "She's getting engaged to my cousin. He's in the army now."[10]

I ask, "How did you meet?"

Rima doesn't give Amal time to answer. "I told him about her because she's my best friend, even though she comes from another village. Then he went to see her brother, and they arranged a meeting."

The sewing plant sometimes serves as the background for personal affairs that contradict the traditional normative behavior of Arab women.

I ask Alham: "How was your weekend?"

"I sat at home and watched TV and videos, as I don't have any more place for men in my heart," she answers.

Every time I talk to Alham, I am reminded of the story of how she broke up with her boyfriend. Ten years before she had been engaged to be married. The date was set, the hall was rented, a band and a singer were hired. Then Alham called off the wedding. In addition to the shame and the beating she received at the hands of her brother, her father decided that she would never marry.

Sarweh, working behind us, overhears the conversation and joins in, "Who needs men in our lives anyway?"

Alham cuts her off sharply, "What does she know. Nobody was ever interested in her. She's still looking for a little love."

Sarweh ignores Alham's remarks and adds, "Don't believe her, Yisrael, no man wants her either. They say she's bad luck. Two guys went at each other with knives yesterday because of her."

Alham begins shouting in Arabic and Sarweh holds her tongue. Alham continues sewing, ignoring the fact that I am still standing there.

I ask, "So what happened on Friday?"

She glances at me for a second and suddenly stops working. Then, without any restraint, she begins to pour her heart out. I listen to a confusion of words. It is the story of jealousy, the story of a love that has no future. The knife-pulling was incidental.

It is a little difficult to follow the history of the relations between Alham and her two suitors. It seems that she was seeing two men, neither of whom knew about the other one. Latif, one of the suitors, works for a company that provides cleaning services for the plant. That way, apparently, he heard that Alham was seeing someone else. He was thunderstruck and decided to tail her.

"While I was talking to the other guy in front of the house, Latif showed up. His blood was boiling and they began fighting. In the end, Latif pulled out a knife and stabbed the other guy."

I ask her if the police were called in.

"Not on your life!" she says. "They made up between themselves."

"And what did you do?" I ask.

"I ran home," she says.

"So what will happen now?" I persist.

"God is great," she answers. "And I suppose we'll just have to be careful. Ours is a very close-knit society. Whatever you do, somebody's sure to find out, and then everybody talks about it."

She raises her head and glances at me warily, then turns back to her work.

Once she told me that people had been spreading bad rumors about her. Her brothers had threatened to mangle her face.

"When I got home from work," she had explained, "I saw that my father wasn't at home and that my mother was crying and that my sister wasn't saying anything. One of my brothers came in and then another—the one that I helped when he was studying pharmaceuticals in Romania. I used to send him money every month. At first they pretended that nothing was going on. But I was scared. I knew, but I pretended that everything was OK, that I wasn't scared." She had pushed back her hair from her forehead and told me to look, drawing a line with her finger from her forehead down to her left temple. I had looked carefully at what she was trying to show me. I could see a thin, faint line, an almost unnoticeable scar. Only after she drew her finger over it a few times did I really see it. When she was satisfied that I had, she became morose and said, "When they began I told them that they should kill me, that if what people said about me was true, I myself would put a knife in my heart, that if I had disgraced my family they should kill me."

Seamstresses who work more than four or five years in the plant are seen as women who probably will not marry. The work becomes an important aspect of their lives, and they learn to use it to achieve a higher stature, both individually and within the family. Their personal lives are discussed in the plant, and they usually form close bonds with a small group of other women in a similar condition. This informal support group provides these single women solidarity and leverage in negotiation with management and helps to alleviate work-related and personal pressure. Their outlook on male-female relationships and the role of women in their society is cynical. In certain cases, as in Alham's story, they challenge the intolerance of traditional customs and behaviors. In particular, they protest men's lack of trust in women to take care of themselves and their honor. Sometimes they do manage to gain a voice in forwarding their claim for more independence within the community and the family. They, however, do not perceive their agenda of gaining more personal freedom as negating the bases of Arab values in both the personal realm—

chastity and honor—and the social realm—the predominance of the family.

INDIVIDUAL CONSCIOUSNESS

The seamstresses and the supervisors are well aware of their individual rights and duties in the plant. Any infringement of the binding contract between them and the managers with regard to remuneration and status reduces their motivation and stirs up the plant. The next story illustrates this well.

Rosette is an experienced supervisor. She has worked at the plant for nineteen years. She is considered a paragon of professionalism and is known throughout the plant as such. Her practical experience in sewing is enormous and enables her to solve complicated problems, particularly when introducing new products into the plant. Rosette is "married" to her work and well known for her dedication to the plant.

"This is my home. I have given my blood and my soul to the plant." Her contribution to the plant has been recognized for many years. Manager after manager has cultivated her talents, broadened her authority beyond what is usually granted to supervisors, paid her high wages, and chosen her as the Outstanding Division Worker time and again. But Rosette has never been nominated for Outstanding Company Worker. In 1995, the manager of the plant nominated one of the mechanics for this citation and the nomination was accepted. Shimon, the mechanic, was declared Outstanding Company Worker and awarded a certificate, a gold medal, and 1000 NIS. Rosette was deeply hurt; she saw the event as a blow to her own prestige and a belittling of her contribution to the plant. As far as she was concerned, the manager's decision was an act of disrespect, a lack of appreciation for her work, an infringement of their mutual social contract, and a show of unfairness.

"I have been here a long time, I am really good, and no one appreciates me. What they want from me is just work. They chose an Outstanding Company Worker who's got only seven years seniority and doesn't even come from the village. I'm the one who has invested my blood here for the past nineteen years and nobody even looks at me.

The only thing they want from people is work. In Beit Jann, there were supervisors who received Outstanding Company Worker. Are they better than Rosette? What, Beit Jann deserves to get recognition and we don't? I bet they hardly think about our village. If somebody puts his heart and soul into the plant, he's the one who should get the recognition. I help everybody. I'm not talking about the gift and the money. I've got enough. What I want is that we should be respected and appreciated. Last year I got Outstanding Division Worker, and this year I should have gotten Outstanding Company Worker. Today something happened. The Division Head comes into the plant, doesn't look at the staff and the workers, walks straight into the manager's office. Why? Don't the people who do the work around here deserve a single word from him? Comes in, doesn't even say hello, doesn't say a single word, only work. What's going on? Are we from Gaza? Aren't we human beings? I'm sitting down now. I don't feel like working. I don't feel like helping anybody, and believe me, all the supervisors feel exactly the same. If they don't respect us, they won't get any work out of us."

The workers are sensitive to manifestations of appreciation from outside the plant. In particular, they assign importance to the best worker awards. The plant managers nominate candidates according to professional abilities as well as the internal politics of the sewing plant. On the production floor, however, the workers see the award primarily as a recognition of their dedication and the granting of respect. The concern recognition enhances the status of the worker within the plant. Furthermore, the outside recognition gives the women a unique opportunity to draw on an external source in order to cultivate their status. Excellence at work translates into higher status within the family and community. They are concerned more with the public and social recognition of the award and its reflection on the workers' personally, the plant, and the entire community. Thus, Rosette, although talking about the world of work, is actually concerned about the implication of not receiving the award in the sphere of the community. Moreover, there is a hidden competition among the sewing plants that usually expresses itself in comparisons of production performance.[11]

Conflicts in the Plant

HOME AND WORK

At the entrance to the office of the Julis sewing plant are two heavy-set, elegantly mustached men, wearing blue *galabyias* (long robes). They are waiting to talk to the manager in order to inform him that their daughters will have to stop working at noon because of a funeral. The entire village is in mourning, and most of the seamstresses have to participate. They probably won't show up at work the next day either. Weddings, funerals, and the olive harvest cause massive absenteeism. It is the parents and brothers who determine the standards of absenteeism. For them, the needs of the home and of the family supersede those of work. These standards force the managers to confront the male members of the family, and they usually have to comply with the rule of "home before work."

Meir, the manager of the plant, comments, "Their mentality, traditions and customs—it's an ongoing war for us. Like with the Palestinians, the negotiations are always very tough. We often lose when the needs of the plant conflict with cleaning house and cooking, not to speak of times when the mother is sick or the sister needs someone to go shopping with. A wedding, a funeral, the olive harvest, or vows at the grave of Jethro[12]—these are matters over which there simply is no room for compromise."

Eran, the production manager, sits himself down on a chair. "It drives me crazy. You put pressure on the women, force them to work overtime, and then all of a sudden everything gets stuck because they want to go to the funeral."

Eran takes a long drag on his cigarette and blows out a series of smoke rings. "I'm tired of all those hysterical phone calls. Arguing with the parents gives me a headache."

The manager looks at him, "That's what I like about you. You learn fast. Here the family is part of the plant, and if you don't care about your job, just have a good fight with the father and don't show respect for the women."

Meir laughs and recalls how many cups of coffee they had to

drink at the homes of the women after they took them on a trip to Tiberias. The big attraction of the trip was a belly dancer who performed for them on a boat in the Sea of Galilee. We all laugh when he describes the outrage in the village when the families learned what had happened. We laugh a little less when he recalls his conversation with the village delegation who threatened to stop the women from working in the plant because of the management's lack of sensitivity to the mentality of the villagers.

He adds, "I never thought of it in that way. I just wanted to show the women a good time. The way they danced—that was really something. They really had a ball. They still talk about that trip. It was the most exciting thing that has ever happened to them."

Sensitivity to village traditions and values is attained gradually through a process of trial and error. The managers initially attempt to separate work from the community but soon learn the importance of integrating the two. The family subjugates the plant's organization of production, procedures, discipline, and interpersonal relations to the local customs and practices.

Any friction between people from the village and the managers can be extended to challenge the legitimacy of the plant. The friction is an opportunity for expressing dissatisfaction from visible female labor, to which, especially in Druse villages, there is always a group that voices objections to women neglecting home for work. Also, the friction is an avenue for protest for those who see the plant as exploiting their daughter's labor. The managers realize the most susceptible events for friction are those that do not necessarily concern the work itself but are related to the plant's initiatives for enriching working life beyond the work context, such as social gatherings or trips. For the seamstresses, trips to national parks and recreational areas in the Galilee, where they can socialize together, are seen as managerial recognition of work well done and are considered part of their employment conditions. However, these trips contain potential for friction, and the managers are keenly aware of that and always attempt to forestall trouble by taking preventative measures. For example, the managers always invite to the trip someone from the village who is closely related to one of the seamstresses and is well respected.

The next story illustrates the conflict between the managers and the community caused by these trips. When the buses returned from a one-day trip at seven o'clock, there was offensive graffiti spread on the cars of the managers, directed at them personally and at their presence in the village. A quick investigation with the neighbors revealed that it was done by two young men from the village who sometimes work for the seamstresses' driver. The managers decided for the time being not to complain to the police and to ask a few of the supervisors to find out how the village would react to the graffiti. One manager believed the graffiti was the result of a past incident when he forcibly expelled one of these young men for entering the shop floor without permission. As a result, there was a small quarrel and threats. It ended with the young man being fired from his job as assistant to the driver.

The next morning, in the meeting with the supervisors, the incident is discussed. The supervisors claim that the youths were sent by others. Ranya says passionately, "They were sent by those dark forces who don't like the plant being here. They say that the girls coming home from the trip at seven o'clock is disgraceful and suspicious. They hate the plant and always say that it violates the women's modesty and directs them from their duties at home and makes them rebel."

The manager argues and claims that the real reason for the graffiti is personal retaliation against him and the production manager for expelling the young man, and nothing more. The supervisors object. Fahima says, "Don't just find a reason that you're comfortable with. Look beyond your nose. There are people here who don't like us, who will use every opportunity to put us down because they love the money their daughters bring from work, because they don't work, but they hate the fact that their daughter has a say and rebels against them at home. People like that always try to make a fuss of anything they think we are doing wrong. They make a big deal of coming at seven o'clock, which isn't even that late."

The manager consulted with the supervisors about how to handle the situation. They decided not to call the police, which would play into the hands of those who sent the young men by causing embarrassment and hurting the plant. The decision was to send Ahmed, the vice principal at the local school, to speak with the parents of the young men and others who were behind the incident. Ahmed, who is married to Fahima's sister, had been personally invited with his wife to the trip by the manager.

In some cases, however, relations between the sewing plant and the workers challenge the family. The plant and the managers provide economic security and even emotional support, particularly in times of crisis. The workers view the plant and its managers as a means for support during incidents when they confront traditions and conventions that may be injurious to them. These incidents create a burden considered by the managers as a necessary evil and a part of the complex interplay with the workers and their families. The next example illustrates this point.

Five sisters from the Al-Hamuda family work at the plant. The oldest is twenty-two and the youngest, sixteen. They enjoy a certain amount of prestige at the plant as a result of their industriousness and the high quality of their work. Mention of the Al-Hamuda family always elicits compliments from the managers. The father of the family does not work; he is dependent on his daughters and on welfare from National Social Security. The two oldest daughters, Umayma and Lydia, are engaged to men from the village.

When I first hear the story, we are all sitting in the manager's office. Lubna, the fourth daughter, and Tagrid, the youngest, are pale. Lubna's hair is pulled back off her face by a broad brown plastic bow and tied at the top of her head by a black ribbon decorated with buttons to look like diamonds. An attractive woman, she is wearing jeans and a red T-shirt with waves and a sailboat printed on it.

Lubna begins her story, mentioning that the night before, her parents and three older sisters had gone to visit relatives in a nearby village. Only she and Tagrid remained at home.

"Tagrid and I were sitting at home alone when Umayma's fiancé came into the house with one of his cousins. No one else was home, but they still insisted on coming in. So what should we have done, kicked them out? He's my sister's fiancé and he comes over to the house every day. I let them in and they came in and had a cup of coffee."

While they were drinking their coffee, an uncle came in, the father's brother.

"He began to scream at us and wave his hands. He said it was wrong what we were doing and he would tell my father and my father would kill me. He also kicked the guys out. After he left, I was scared something awful and ran over to my grandmother, my mother's mother."

"How come only you ran away?" I ask.

Lubna looked at Tagrid. Then the manager and I looked at Tagrid. She looks younger than her sixteen years. She is thin and has childish features. She has a brown plastic bow holding back her hair, just like her sister's. Her face is expressionless, eyes cast down. She speaks without looking up.

"I'm still little; my father's favorite."

When the family came home and the father heard the story, he lost control and began to beat his wife and daughters.

Tagrid continues, "He screamed and hit us. He also said that Lubna wouldn't have run away unless she had done something bad. Then he said that he would kill her, and he took the ax and sharpened it in front of us and said that he would kill us all." That night the mother and the daughters left the house and went to stay with the mother's sister.

"My mother and my sisters told me that we were not going home again."

Lubna and Tagrid keep looking at each other. They look frightened and unhappy. Lubna says to the manager, "I want to stay with you or with Radi [a Druse mechanic working in the plant who comes from another village]. I'm scared of staying in the village tonight."

The manager looks at her, surprised. He recovers his composure rather quickly, however, and says to her in a fatherly tone, "The best thing for you to do is to stay in the village, not with me or with Radi. Go to some relatives. If your father found out that you stayed with us, he would be after us as well. But don't worry, we here are your family and we always take care of our daughters."

The next day the manager calls all five sisters and the mother to his office. The mother wants to take Lubna away because the father could easily come to the plant. She also offers to work at the plant in Lubna's place. "We trust you," she says to the manager, "now you are like the head of the family."

The manager is somewhat frightened at the responsibility that has suddenly fallen upon him. He says to me, "I like to give the women the feeling that the plant is their home and that we're all like one big family. But this is a very delicate situation. If I interfere, it would be as if I were sticking my nose where it doesn't belong. Yet if their father is really such a firebrand, he might really kill someone—if only because his wife and daughters have washed their dirty laundry in public."

For a couple of days, the plant serves as a kind of safe haven for the sisters and the mother. They work two shifts, from early morning until eight in the evening. After that the manager takes them in his car (after making sure that the father is not lurking around some corner) to their relatives.

Eventually, the sisters and the mother return home. Lubna remains with her aunt. The very night when they are home again, the father loses his temper. Feeling humiliated and injured, he accuses the mother and the sisters of disgracing the family and covering up for Lubna. He beats them all again. The mother takes her daughters and runs away again, this time to the police station in Karmiel, the closest large city in the area. There she lodges a complaint against her husband.

Nasrin, the middle sister, is working in the packaging department. I stand next to her and we talk as she works. She is relaxed, but the events of the past week have left their mark. The deep dark rims around her eyes look as if someone has given her two black eyes. She speaks softly, "The police came and handcuffed my father and took him away. Then because of the whole business, Umayma tried to commit suicide by drinking chlorine. After all, it was her fiancé who caused the whole thing by coming to the house with his cousin. Now she's in the hospital and Lydia is watching over her."

"How are you getting along now?" I ask.

"We're at home for the present. We help one another and we help mother and she helps us." She puckers her lips and I can see that she is on the verge of tears. "I don't know what will happen. I just don't know."

Lubna leans over the sewing machine. Her lips are clenched together and her expression is frozen. She speaks to me unwillingly,

"Because my father threatened me, I told the police that I wasn't ready to give in to him. He's in the wrong. He never works and we have to support him. I'm not going to let him kill me."

The manager of the plant fills himself a glass of water from the cooler. He gulps it down quickly while scanning the production area. I come over to him.

"Have you spoken with Lubna?" he asks.

"According to what she tells me, her father is in prison and there doesn't seem to be any solution in the near future."

"His family wants me to arrange a *sulcha* [a reconciliation]. The father has been humiliated. He has lost the respect of his family. The police have issued a warrant against him, prohibiting him from entering the village. Today they take those things seriously."

"And what does the mother say?" I ask.

"She doesn't know what to do. What's for sure is that the father succeeded in turning them all against him—the fiancés of his daughters and his wife's family. You know, on second thought, I'm not sure that the whole business wasn't planned beforehand."

I look at him questioningly.

"How can you possibly know? Maybe the women organized the visit so that the cousin could meet Lubna and maybe get married. They know that they can fall back on the plant if something goes wrong. But from that to threats of murder . . . "

Before the workday ends, Mayson walks around distributing sweets to the workers, the supervisors, and the managers. Mayson has worked in the factory for three years, saved her money, and is now going to study at a teachers' seminary.

Alya, her supervisor, says, "Despite the fact that she is a good worker and does more than 130 percent of the quota—and top quality, too—I advised her to leave the plant and go study. If we had more women like Mayson, then maybe our children won't turn out like Lubna's father."

As this case shows, the workers extend the definition of a workplace and are able to create a system of obligation whereby the manager is not only an employer but also an active participant in their personal lives. The workers force the managers to enter into patriarchal relationships and to bear the implications. The community considers the role of managers replacing the fathers as a by-product of women taking on wage labor. The Al-Hamuda case exemplifies both the strengths and weaknesses of women in a patriarchal setting, whereby opportunities for gaining more self-identity, autonomy, and control over one's life are reconstructed within a framework of patriarchy. The Al-Hamuda family members do not gain autonomy. Although they shake up their father, they need the manager as a paternal figure to voice their protest to their father. In this case, the father loses his patriarchal authority because he could not face his daughters' criticisms and demands, which were backed by their earning power. In spite of the autonomy gained by work, patriarchy as an institution is not challenged—it is merely reconfigured.

POLITICS AND WORK

Political issues are almost taboo in the plants. Both managers and workers consciously avoid the emotionally charged issue of Israeli-Arab politics. Israel's political agenda is intense, particularly with regard to the relations between Jews and Israeli Arabs and between Israelis and Palestinians. The political atmosphere in Israel is tense, with frequent incidents of friction surrounding issues such as the confiscation of land, Palestinian terrorist activities, politicians' declarations about Arabs, and civil issues related to resource allocation or discrimination. Political echoes can be traced in the plants only on rare occasions. When I asked seamstresses about political issues, I did not get further than praises for the need for peace and an ideal image of Jewish-Arab harmony, of which the plant is supposedly a living example. The practice of removing politics from the shop floor is carefully guarded by both workers and managers. Most attempts to raise political issues are thwarted.

An interesting case in point is that political issues, when they do arise in the plants, are confined to the local Israeli-Arab realm. Tense incidents in the plant involve racial affiliation mainly between Druse and Muslims or between Christians and Muslims, as the next stories illustrate.

It is Memorial Day for soldiers of the Israel Defense Forces, the day when a siren is sounded and the entire country stands at attention for two minutes in memory of the fallen. When the siren is sounded, the Druse women in the plant all stand up, whereas the Muslim women continue to work as usual. Johara, a Druse supervisor, loses her cool.

"I don't get it. The blood rushes to my head when I see them sitting there working instead of standing to attention. It's not that I want them to believe in Memorial Day, but don't forget that many Druse boys are among the fallen, and for this reason they should show us some respect. But even more annoying is that one of the women got up and went to take a drink in the middle and even began laughing." Johara is furious and goes over and turns off her machine. Then she shouts at them that they should stand up and they do. The storm over the standing during the siren does not calm down.

During the lunch break, the Muslim and Druse women continue to exchange bitter words. Johara says to me, "Even though they told me that the Jews had killed their brothers and they didn't want to honor the Jewish dead, I still don't agree with it. I told them that it didn't concern the Jews. The fact that they didn't get up was offensive to the Druse. And that wasn't the first time that I had a confrontation with the Muslims."

I ask her what happened last time.

"The whole plant was collecting money for Druse soldiers to buy them presents and things like that. One of the Muslim women said that she wasn't going to give any money because they were killing her people in the Intifada, in Gaza, and in the territories. So I told her to go home. Not because she didn't want to give money but because she showed disrespect for the Druse."

The intolerance and disrespect shown to fellow workers is more important than the particular political content of the event. What is important in the Druse plant (located in Druse villages) is respect for local conduct in the spirit of "When in Rome, do like the Romans." The interest of the managers in such cases is to remove the political dispute from the plant. They constantly attempt to create a climate of cohesiveness and togetherness that contributes first and foremost to the smooth flow of work.

The second story illustrates the tensions between the Muslims and the Christians. This animosity reflects both cultural differences among these two faiths and their different socioeconomic positions in Israeli society. The Christians, by and large, are urban dwellers, more educated, and more integrated into Israeli society. Their relative socioeconomic position is higher than the Muslims (Lewin-Epstein and Semyonov 1993). The story relates to the trauma experienced by the Arabs of Israel and the Palestinians in the occupied territories following the slaughter of twenty-nine Muslims during prayers at the Grave of the Patriarchs in Hebron.[13]

The day after the massacre, the women at the plant in Nazareth decide to collect money for the families of the victims. The workers' committee approaches the manager and asks permission to put up a notice on the bulletin board that reads as follows:

> The workers of the sewing plant are shocked at the terrible massacre that took place in Hebron and want to express their solidarity with the families of the victims. The murder of innocent people is an unforgivable act of evil perpetrated against the Palestinian people. We condemn it and appeal to all those who love peace and condemn the crime to join us and make a contribution to the families of the victims.

At first the manager tries to dissuade the committee from putting up the notice, but when he realizes that they are absolutely determined to do it, he agrees. That day only funereal music is heard at the plant, interspersed with verses from the Koran.

Amna expresses her feelings. "You see the plant today. All the women have given money. Everyone is depressed. Nobody feels like working. You can see that everyone came in simple clothes and none of the women put on makeup." But there are quite a few Christian women who don't approve of the Muslim protest measures. They refuse to contribute money and ask the manager to stop the gloomy music."

Aysha says, "It is really something terrible, a real catastrophe, but it has nothing to do with the plant. We come here to work, and no one should force politics on us."

I ask if the massacre and the mourning are political.

"Yes," she answers. "The way Amna and her friends are doing it, it's all politics. I really feel bad about what happened. The man who did it is an animal and not a human being. But lots of the women are against collecting money at the plant and putting up a notice. I also don't want to have to listen to music like that and preaching from their religion. They shouldn't bring politics into the plant, and I told that to the manager and he agreed with me."

This case reflects the division between the different religious groups in the Arab society. The Christian women see themselves as more modern, urban, open, and secular. Their political outlook tends to reflect their secularity and their position as what they see an "elite minority" within a minority (Rekhess 1986). Unlike the Christians, the Muslim women in the plant do not differentiate politics from religion and emphasize their solidarity with the Palestinians. The Christians see this approach as the tyranny of the majority. Furthermore, the incident was seen as the Muslim women's attempt to threaten their individuality and self-definition.

In the Israeli environment of constant tension and cleavage, one tragic incident momentarily united all groups. When the Prime Minister of Israel, Yitzhak Rabin, was murdered, the feelings of grief were universal. All the women stood to attention when the siren sounded. Temimeh, the supervisor in the Nazareth plant tells me:

"The atmosphere at the plant was one of deep mourning. We all, Muslims, Christians, Druse, and Jews, felt that a great leader had been killed. We thought of him as everyone's father.

"His death united us all behind our manager. We felt that respecting Rabin's death and the peace he tried to create for us all meant sticking together here as one family. The work went all right and we continued as usual."

Many of the women pasted a sticker on their machines that read "Good-bye, friend."[14]

Conclusion

The setting and the interactions between the workers and the work and the dynamics of constructing shared meaning are illustrated in this chapter. The stories and cases reveal the linkages and divisions between work in the plant and the local environment. The plant reflects a construct built on the foundations of managerial principles of assembly line management and renegotiated Arab worldviews translated into the world of work.

The plant serves as a social arena where the seamstress's dilemmas are presented, examined, and restructured. By simulating familial values in the working life at the plant, the workers, the managers, and the families engage in a constant renegotiation over boundaries and meanings. Within this framework, the manager manipulates the traditional values to build alignment between the needs of production and the workers' worldviews.

CHAPTER 5

The Seamstresses: In Motion Toward Reconstructing Work and Life

For workers who started as teenagers, the Amoskeag symbolized their transition to adulthood. It was tied up with their youth; it was the place where they first learned their jobs, where they became "workers." Commencement of work was a rite of passage, separating the grown-ups from the kids. To even those youngsters who lived with their parents and contributed most of their pay to the family economy, starting work provided a sense of independence. For boys, the beginning of work meant money to buy their first suit, permission to begin smoking and stay out later. For girls, it meant buying a new dress, permission to go to dances and movies, and the right to put up their hair. For both boys and girls it involved joining peer groups of other workers.

—TAMARA HAREVEN
Family Time and Industrial Time

THE SEWING plant is both a workplace that enables the seamstresses to gain income and a meeting place for young women, sometimes from different communities and ethnic groups, who are engaged in developing a network of social relations. The workplace is a refuge from the stifling pressures of the family and a place to establish informal support groups. It is an opportunity to leave the "suffocating four walls of the house" and avoid the fate of sitting at home until they are married.

For most of the seamstresses, working at the plant represents their first interaction with a work organization and its daily procedures and demands. For the first time, the workers are detached from the presence and control of their immediate families. Leaving home for work can be an ordeal for a woman who has never worked before. It takes time to master the sewing technique and understand the quality requirements and proper sewing method.[1] The rigid discipline, uncompromising demand for production and quality, constant pressure to improve, and close supervision are foreign to them.

This chapter describes the relationships between the seamstresses and the managers and supervisors as reflected through the tensions in the plant and the constant negotiation for self-definition and shared meaning. It describes the basic issues that bear upon the working life of the seamstresses inside and outside the plant.

The Meaning of Wage Employment

Taking on wage employment entails entrance into the domain of work, relative independence, and an increased sense of contribution to the family economy. The prevalence of unemployment among Arab men (Atrash 1995)[2] creates a common situation whereby the family depends mainly on the daughters' wages. As this chapter reveals, however, entrance into the world of work does not fundamentally undermine the prevalent power relations, but merely provides the seamstresses with more bargaining power against the patriarchal systems that prevail both at work and at home.

The economic necessity of the family challenges the worldview whereby women should be secluded and subdued (Hijab 1988). According to this worldview, the father should be the main provider. Among the workers, there are many cases where the father is unemployed and the daughters assume the role of breadwinner, thus stripping him of his basic obligation to the family. This contradiction between the dominance of the father and his helplessness in supporting the family modifies to an extent his relationship with his daughters, as described in the story of the Al-Hamuda family in Chapter 4. The decision to seek wage employment has the potential to change the status quo in the family, but it usually takes place with the father's consent, whether open or silent.

Adal says, "My father didn't want me to work in the sewing plant. He told me that he didn't need my money. But I didn't give in. I told him that he was my father and I respected him, and I would do what he wanted me to, but I would respect him more if he let me go to work with my girlfriends. And I told him that it would give him respect too. I told him that I wanted to buy a stove and a refrigerator for my wedding with my own money. So in the end he agreed, and I'm pretty happy here, and my father respects me because I give my mother half of my salary for the house."

Although the daughter's entrance into the workforce challenges the father's role as provider, it does not affect the patriarchal tradition. The father still maintains complete control in matters of female honor, sexuality, marriage, and the division of labor at home, and he often appropriates the income.[3] This dynamic is similar to that described by Wolf (1992) writing on women factory workers in Java[4]:

> It appears that young women's decisions concerning their labor and the returns to it are tolerated to an extent because they can be understood within certain cultural boundaries of female activity. But when a daughter's sexuality or sexual reputation is involved— an arena that extends beyond women's control—parents step in more forcefully, and daughters then obey. (p. 194)

The role of the daughters in supporting the father is justified in terms of the values of mutual responsibility and contribution of all the members to the family's well-being. Taking on wage employment in the plant is not directly linked to family honor nor a threat to the women's virtue. Nonetheless, sometimes the fact that a daughter works may be perceived as a blow to the father's prestige and can create conflicts within the family (Afshar 1991).

At Work but Still at Home

Gender relations at work and their consequences for the home are the subjects of extensive research. This research portrays the workplace as both a springboard for women's autonomy and self-identity and as a new kind of enslavement. Work is considered a sophisticated form of gender subordination that subjugates the women workers to both local patriarchy and global capitalism (Nash and Fernandez-Kelly 1983). The superimposition of work on the reality of the family both reconstructs the interpersonal relationships within the family and modifies perceptions of autonomy and division of labor. This articulation of work as home is illustrated in Mirbat's story.

Mirbat describes the situation in her family. "I could see that things at home were bad, and so I convinced my father that I would work for a year or two until things got better. He agreed, but first he went and spoke with our religious elders about it. I don't quite understand why. The way I see it, working is a secular matter, and the religious elders are not supposed to take sides in secular matters.[5] But because my father's honor was at stake, I didn't say anything. My father understood that if there was no alternative, if he didn't have any employment, then it was only natural that I go to work. I'm the oldest. My brothers and sisters are all still in school, and it's important for me that they finish. It was pretty hard for my father at the beginning because he had nothing to do and just sat at home, and I gave my salary to my mother. My father was full of respect for me and didn't ask me for anything. I gave it all out of my own free will. Even when I bring home only 1500 NIS, it's very important, because it's not only a matter of money. My parents and my brothers and sisters respect me, and even my father is less nervous now because he knows that I'm working in order to help out. He keeps saying that soon he'll go back to work in construction. But even if he does go back to work, I'll continue to work at the sewing plant. Life without work is not life. A woman who sits at home all the time doesn't have much to say about what goes on at home. Since I started working, everybody respects me."

The workaday world at the plant is considered suitable for unmarried women. The hours are long, and overtime and work on Friday are enough to deter married women and their husbands, especially if there are children in the family. The maintenance of a perfect household is considered very important in Druse and Arab families, and devoting herself to this end is the woman's prerogative. Working at the plant for long and exhausting hours is not considered commensurate with a happy married life and a well-kept home. Usually, the first years after marriage are the test period for the woman with regard to her ability to perform her role as homemaker and mother. The need for extra income is not so critical. When couples marry, they have everything they need—the groom provides his bride with a house and furniture, and the bride brings all the appliances.[6] Maintenance costs are usually low, particularly when the extended family lives in the same apartment building.[7] During the years that I spent at the sewing plants, however, more and more married women were taking jobs. They were usually women who had worked at the plant before marriage and continued working until the birth of their first child.

Mahmuda says, "After the wedding, I didn't work. I only helped out my husband's mother. But I didn't want to bake in their mess. I married my husband, not his mother and sisters. When the manager looked for workers, I was happy to come back. Times are hard. Everything costs a lot of money. I want to be able to buy things with my money. If I take money from his family, I'll owe them, and I'm not willing for that to happen. Today I think that a married woman should work and help her husband. They should be equal. If only the husband works and the woman just stays at home and prepares everything for him, he thinks that he is more important than her, that she is in his shadow. If they both earn, she also has a word. It's not that the husband does not consult his wife. I consult my husband with everything. But now that I work and also bring money, we plan together what to do."

Taking on wage employment after marriage is both the decision of the couple and often a part of the husband's family considerations. They take into account the family's economic situation and the status of the son's wife within the extended family. A wife's status is determined by various factors, including her husband's dependence on his parents, the manner in which she places herself in her husband's household, her family background, and her ability to get along with his family and vice versa. There is one distinct case when a married woman's position is almost certainly problematic —when she does not have children. In many such cases, the woman is under heavy pressure from her mother-in-law, and sometimes her husband is not supportive. This situation can lead to alienation, feelings of frustration, and apathy. The story of Miyada demonstrates the difficulties of a woman who has disappointed her husband and his family and receives compassion and understanding at work. The plant becomes the substitute for the family by providing the warmth and support that she does not receive at home.

Miyada's mother died when she was eighteen. Her unemployed father remarried a seventeen-year-old girl. Miyada and her two sisters went to work in the sewing plant, becoming the sole providers of their father's new family. Until age thirty, Miyada worked for her father, who delayed her marriage because of his need for her income. When distant relatives from another village put pressure on him to marry her to their eldest son, he conceded. Miyada moved to the new village and to an even grimmer reality.

"My husband's family is made up of his senile old mother, two daughters, and two sons. All of the children are deaf and dumb. It's not easy living in a family like this. You always have to tell them what's going on. I'm doing it willingly—it's the will of God that they are like this. But it's very difficult for me. Again I find myself giving away all of the money I earn. I've never seen a penny of my salary. I give everything to my husband. I pay for everything, even his cigarettes and health insurance. For five years, a month, and a few days I have lived with them in their house. I count the minutes of every day.

"During the Gulf War I was pregnant. In the news they said that there had to be a sealed room. So they chose my room, even though the house is huge—230 square meters. All day we sat in the sealed room waiting for the scud missiles with the television on and no privacy. We even ate in my room. It was very difficult. I felt like I wanted to run away. One day I couldn't take it anymore, so I told them that there is a rocket coming and they must put on their gas masks. I let them sit like that for more than an hour, just so that I could have a little peace. But the war took its toll—I had a miscarriage. It was my third, and because of this my husband and his family make my life miserable.

"I used to run to my father's house, but they always brought me back. I was very frustrated, and so I went to see the village healer. He told me that I have to change my name. He said, 'With a name like Ichlas there is no chance you will have a baby.' After that I went to work, and I asked my friends to choose a name for me. They chose 'Miyada.' Then I went to each worker, supervisor, and manager and told them that my new name is Miyada and whoever calls me otherwise will see my back. Everybody was very supportive—even the manager—and they started to shout 'Miyada! Miyada!' and told me they were sure that now I would have a baby. The manager even told me that I should try harder. She adds ironically, "I still don't know if he meant with my husband or with work. . . .

"At work everybody was happy for me—for years I had been nervous, quarreling with the girls. Everything used to annoy me. I couldn't stand seeing a pregnant woman or babies. At home, my husband used to beat me, and his relatives would tease me, 'Don't worry, soon the baby will come.' I couldn't stand to be in that house, and I asked the manager to keep me extra hours because he was kind to me and encouraged me with my name change. He encouraged me not to give up and to continue with the war against God until I have a baby."

The seamstress at work represents not only herself but first and foremost her family. The family believes themselves responsible for their daughter's behavior at work and her performance. In the plants there is a saying: "Good workers come from good families" [and vice versa]. According to the workers in the plant, the degree to which a family has educated and instilled values in their daughter expresses itself at work. The symbolic representation of plant equaling family implies behavior toward the manager that mimics behavior in the family toward the father—discipline, subordination, and solidarity. The managers capitalize on this outlook and promote family norms and values as an effective strategy to meet their production goals.

The following statement of Zeda, one of the senior seamstresses, exemplifies this interrelationship between familial and work values, as perceived by the workers:

"Listen, discipline starts at home. She who has received discipline and a good education at home will transport it to work. The first school is the home. Those who don't have discipline, don't have responsibilities, they don't care about their homes, community, and work. Education at home begins at age zero. I can tell when I see new women whether they have it or they don't. I also explain to them what is discipline in the factory and what is proper behavior. I think that she who does not have discipline at work will not succeed in her family life when she gets married.

"Look at me—I came to work for the money and the desire to do something with my life. Now I don't need money—I can sit at home and live off the interest. But the fact that I keep working is part of the discipline. I grew up in a house where they taught me to give, not to take. I'll give you an example. I had the opportunity to go to Eilat with my family. They called the manager and asked him to release me from work. I told the manager, 'Don't agree to let me go, I have a lot of work.'"

Work at the plant is not always complementary to work at home.[8] Zina is the oldest seamstress in the plant. She is married and has four children. After her children grew up she returned to work.

"I work for the children, so that they will not be wanting of anything in life. So that they will wear nice clean clothes and be the best at school. I also work for our new house. Until three years ago I lived with my husband's parents. Now we are moving to our own house. It is important that we have a good house and are not pressured by money constraints. My husband didn't really want me to work. He wanted me to stay home with the children. But he works as a guard and doesn't make much. It's not easy to work and manage a home. I have to feed the children and my husband, and sometimes there are problems if one of the kids is sick."

I ask whether they are considerate at work to the fact that she is married and has children.

"At work they are really OK. I'm *mabsuta, hamdulalla* [satisfied, thank God]. The seamstresses are like my daughters and the supervisor is like my sister. I tell her everything."

"What, for example?" I ask.

She answers without hesitation, "For example, when I fought with my husband when he wanted the duty of husbands and wives and I was too tired. Mona, the supervisor, calmed me down. She gave me a cup of coffee, and she also spoke with my husband. He apologized.

"It is a difficult life. When I say I'm tired from work, my husband says stay at home."

The seamstress is expected to invest much effort at work in order to reach optimal efficiency in both quality and quantity. The integration of home and work is the sole burden of the woman, who has to fully perform her duties both at work and at home. The double responsibilities result in competition between work and home and pressure and stress on the women.

"Believe me," Zina continues, "there is a lot of pressure at work. I have a weak head and a weak heart. I take pills, but I still can't get used to the pressure."

"What is it exactly that you find so oppressive?" I ask.

"It's mostly the manager, who expects us to earn premiums. I can't. The operation is complicated, and I can't do it any faster. My hands don't move as quickly as the other women's. I do as much as I can. But they're telling me all the time that I'm not making enough of an effort. It's true that sometimes I'm thinking of other things. You know. I have problems at home. When I get home I have to take care of the house and my children and husband. I get to bed very late and I just don't have any energy when I get up in the morning. I'm really trying. The work is important to me because I want to give my children everything they want."

For the seamstress working at the plant, performing *extra* work at home is a justifiable excuse for not reaching the production norm. As for the management, work should always come first; only if there are unusual difficulties at home are they willing to be flexible in accommodating the worker's needs, as long as these do not contradict the goals of production. These concessions are given only with regard to specific issues that are focused and defined, such as giving vacation time to take care of sick family members. This kind of help is instrumental and serves the interest of the management in maintaining a loyal and productive workforce. If, however, the problem is continuous and has the potential to regularly disrupt work, the management shows no compassion and the worker is fired.

The work is sometimes viewed as a dead end, a demanding routine, exhausting and monotonous. These built-in difficulties at work become even greater when the socioeconomic status of the seamstress is low and her burden at home is high.

Jihan tells her story. "I find the work very difficult. I get up at 4:30 in the morning, straighten up the house and prepare food for everybody. I have four brothers and two sisters at home. My father is not working, and my mother is sick all the time. Now you can begin to understand why I find it so hard to work. The work is boring. You're doing the same thing over and over again. But I have no alternative. I have to work to support the family. I'm here to earn money, and nothing else here interests me. I'm 24 years old, and I am getting married to a man of 60 with a crazy wife. He's taking her out of the asylum and bringing her home for me to take care of. I don't want to continue working and give all my money to my father and then come home and continue to work. This way at least I'll be working in my own home and not for others. I don't care about his *majnuna* [the lunatic] and his children. I'll have children of my own, and when you have your own children, everything is different."

Satisfaction from Work

Satisfaction is heavily linked to financial remuneration because the workers do not perceive a fair salary and receiving gratification from social relations to be mutually exclusive.[9] With regard to the work itself, there is a complex interrelationship between the basic attributes of work and the seamstresses' perceived satisfaction (Table 3).

As can be seen from Table 3, there is a high consensus that the salary is unsatisfactory, and the seamstresses believe that they are working hard but are not being rewarded properly. With regard to the work itself, in most sewing plants, there is a consensus that the norm is too high. The reason that the seamstresses in Beit Jann and Maghar do not ascribe too much importance to the norm is because most of the departments consist of veteran workers who have been sewing the same products for the past few years. This has enabled them to professionalize and reach high levels of production. The lowest satisfaction from physical conditions is attributed to the food. Seamstresses from most of the plants complain about the repetitive menu.

The work is monotonous and repetitive and is considered uninteresting by the seamstresses in all the plants. The assembly

TABLE 3

Percentage of seamstresses who agreed with statements
related to work satisfaction

Statement	Beit Jan N=109	Kfar Tavor N=120	Julis N=95	Khorfesh N=90	Maghar N=101	Nazareth N=175
The salary is inadequate	89	80	94	93	91	85
The production norm is too high	56	71	72	77	67	73
The physical conditions are adequate (space, light, food)	45	74	48	43	51	83
The work is interesting	49	58	47	42	56	55
The managers treat me well	75	85	83	68	94	87
The supervisors treat me well	75	86	80	78	87	89

SOURCE: Survey carried out on the shop floors, May–August 1995. Response rates were approximately 80 percent of the seamstresses in each plant.

line setting, which is based on specialization, confines the seamstresses to a limited number of operations. The ideology of specialization is considered as a key for high production levels and consequently higher pay. Although the seamstresses tend to prefer specialization, they still assess the work as uninteresting and are not satisfied from it as such. Most plants enjoy relatively high satisfaction from relations with the supervisors and managers, as elaborated upon in Chapters 6 and 7. The high satisfaction in Maghar in this respect can be explained by the familial affinities common between supervisors and the seamstresses in their department.

As has been noted, social relations at work constitute an integral part of the working life. They are the infrastructure for the shared meaning created at work, particularly with regard to the formation of friendships and feelings of solidarity between the workers.

During the lunch break, I sit with a group of seamstresses in the din-ing room discussing issues related to job satisfaction. I ask Nazma, who is considered the leader of the seamstresses, to comment. After considering the subject for a few seconds, she says, "We're pretty happy here because it's not only a job. They make us feel at home. They treat us well, and I have lots of friends here from my village and from other villages. We get to know more people, and we visit them at home, and they come to visit us at home. We take trips together and sometimes we eat out. And if someone gets sick, we all go to visit her. And the plant gives us presents on holidays. Sure, there are some things that are not so great, like the pay. If you meet your quota, the norm of 100 percent, you only make around 1000 NIS a month and even if you're way at the top you don't make more than 1700 or 1800 NIS. That's not enough for what we do. The work is re-ally hard, and the quotas are high. They are getting a lot out of us. There are other problems, like changing the type of merchandise we produce. Some of the products are hard to make, and they keep rais-ing the quotas all the time. Aside from that, the conditions are OK, but we're sick of the food. All the time *hummus* and *felafel*. But what's good is that every worker can go and talk to the manager about anything, even personal problems, and he'll try to help. Of all the plants in the village, this is the best. It's properly organized; you get benefits and compensation."

The seamstresses are well aware of the fact that the work is drudgery and the pay is low. The work itself is not a source of sat-isfaction. On the contrary, it is a source of complaint and discon-tent. Satisfaction is primarily defined through the perceived inter-personal relationships in the plant.

Josephine adds, "Some of the women are unhappy because the work it-self is hard and doesn't go smoothly. There's one woman who catches on quickly but then gets confused and gives up. There's another one who finds it hard at the beginning and can't get used to the work. All she does is think about what's going on at home, and she really doesn't like to work. Then there are those who don't really care because the money goes to their fathers and not to them. Some of the women don't like the way they are treated. If the supervisor gets nervous and begins to shout or say nasty things, they just get up and go home. But if you catch on to the work and have friends here and feel good, so why not keep working, until you get married? What else can you do, sit at home all day long and help your mother? Here at least you're making some money and you can buy things for your wedding."

Anaya comments, "And my parents like the idea that we're supervised here and it's a safe place. The women are picked up and brought back home by car and the gates around the plant are shut, and no woman can just get up and go out without permission. True, we come to work for money, but we also have friends at the plant. It doesn't matter if they're Druse or Muslim or Christian. We're all friends and we like to help each other. We even visit at each other's homes."

At the sewing plant, expressions of job satisfaction derive from the perception of an interrelationship between the nature of work and the nature of the people who perform and manage it. The workplace creates an extension of the social relationships of the workers. These social relationships are an important parameter in determining satisfaction from work. The workers' satisfaction does not derive from factors such as interest in the work and the opportunity for self-fulfillment, but mainly from the linkage to the social sphere of the plant.

Values at Work

In my work at the sewing plants, I was faced with the inevitable and complex interrelationship between the sphere of work and the seamstresses' self-perceptions and values, an interrelationship that is not self-evident to someone who comes from the Western tradition of work values. For the seamstresses, this interrelationship is not unidirectional, in which the work hierarchy determines all aspects of the organization of production. They attempt to lead in those realms in which they have the leverage to do so. Conflicts over production quotas belong to the management domain, whereby each worker has to deal directly with the supervisor and the manager. The worker has no leverage in this domain—if she does not meet standards, she will be sent home. Nonetheless, this is not a clear-cut situation; managers must sometimes compromise and continue to employ below-average workers when there are shortages due to production considerations, such as the need for seamstresses who are polyvalent (can perform multiple functions) or who sew with high quality. As a group, however, the seamstresses enter power conflicts with the management on issues such as overtime, holidays, and food, which are perceived as part of the social sphere and where they have the "home-court advantage."

The everyday occurrences in the plant, both professional and social, provide the content for the conflicts inherent in the process of internalizing values at work. In this process, the seamstresses attempt to instill the values they consider important, whereas the managers appropriate these values and embed them in the organization's goals, codes of behavior, and personal production requirements.

As the next story illustrates, the managers provide practical solutions to problems raised by those beliefs and values that pose a threat to the work process. This reconciliation is done in terms of the tradition and belief itself and gives new meaning to its content within the framework of work.

Rima comes to work one morning but refuses to sit down at the machine to work. The supervisor takes her to the manager, saying, "She refuses to work and refuses to tell me why. She is crying like a baby. Maybe you two can talk to her." The manager asks her how she is.

She begins to wail and the tears soon follow. Her tears apparently console her, for she soon calms down. She sits for a few minutes in silence, frightened and sad. Then she begins to talk:

"I had a dream last night that in a previous existence I was a man who was electrocuted. You know we Druse believe in reincarnation, and now I'm afraid of the machine. I can't go near it."

The manager says to her, "If you were electrocuted in your last incarnation, there's no chance of the same thing happening to you in this one. Every time you die in a different way."

"Are you sure?" she asks.

"I'm sure," he answers and then adds, "Just to make sure I'll get the machinist to install a rubber insulation band between you and the motor. Electricity can't pass through rubber."

"Are you sure?" she asks.

The manager says, "Come with me to the machinist, and we'll fix everything up. The electricity won't reach you."

We go to the machinist, who listens to the story with a serious mien. Then he goes to get an insulation band and installs it between the motor and Rima's chair. When he finishes, Rima scrutinizes the band and then sits down and begins to work.

The manager's authority is comprehensive. The authority of his advice and knowledge stem from his managerial position and from his embodiment in the organization as a benevolent father figure who cares about his family members. These expectations sometimes force the managers to adopt the values and norms considered by the seamstresses in accordance with their perceptions of a good manager. These perceptions correspond to the seamstresses' priorities, beliefs, values, and interests.

One morning I come to work and find none of the managers in the office. When I ask Amira where the managers are, she answers, "My family is in a meeting with the head of the division."

TABLE 4
Seamstresses' salary allocations (percentages)

	Beit Jan N=109	Kfar Tavor N=120	Julis N=95	Khorfesh N=90	Maghar N=101	Nazareth N=175
Gives full salary to the family	35	30	51	39	39	23
Splits the salary with the family*	52	38	39	43	44	39
Keeps all of the salary for herself	13	32	10	18	17	38
Total	100	100	100	100	100	100

*Excluding the reception of pocket spending money.
SOURCE: Survey carried out on the shop floors, May–August 1995. Response rates were approximately 80 percent of the seamstresses in each plant.

The Income Determinant

The issue of how wages are allocated between the workers and their families represents the degree of the workers' autonomy. The seamstresses' wages are controlled by the father if he is unemployed or if the large number of children at home makes one wage earner insufficient to meet the family's needs. Usually, however, the wages are distributed in a way that takes into consideration the needs of the family and of the seamstresses, as illustrated in Table 4.

As Table 4 shows, the predominant pattern among the workers in all the plants is to give the entire salary to the parents or to split it with them. All the workers live with their families and feel obliged to contribute to the household economy.[11] The high rate of seamstresses who keep their own wages in Nazareth reflects the urban nature of the plant and the relative independence of its seamstresses. Many of the seamstresses at Kfar Tavor are older and unmarried and are more involved in managing their households. Although they contribute to their families, they consider control over their wages a main source of their independence.

Working implies having enough money to furnish their homes when it is time to marry and buy appliances. The workers also attend to their personal needs and buy clothes and jewelry. Sometimes they save for trips abroad, supporting family members in higher education and furnishing or renovating their houses. The pursuit of a higher standard of living has given greater legitimization to the idea of women working outside the home (Al-Haj 1987, 1988).

Rulla says, "For some women, money is the most important thing. True, they have friends here and they're treated well, but what's really important is the money. They need money to buy clothes, to help out at home, or to go study. Some women come to work against their will. You can tell from their homes which of the women are good seamstresses. If their fathers take all their money, then they really have no motivation to work.[12] They don't get anything out of it. Maybe they get 50 NIS a month pocket money. But what can you do with 50 NIS nowadays? You can hardly buy a blouse with it. Women today have much greater needs, and 50 NIS is just a drop in the bucket. Here in the plant the women who need the money work really hard. If the situation at home is all right and their salary goes into their own bank account, then they'll work very hard. They want to buy gold jewelry or take a trip to Egypt. And if the situation at home is really bad, they'll work hard because they need every penny to buy food for the family. Nowadays the economic situation is tough. Everything is expensive and every penny counts. The women who come to work know that in order to make money they have to produce, and produce high-quality merchandise. Otherwise, it's a waste of time to get up in the morning."

Seamstresses evaluate the fairness of their salaries by comparing their pay slips with others'. This comparison takes into account hours spent at work, quality, and, of course, amount produced. If their pay reflects their perception of what they deserve, then the salary is considered fair. If not, the workers will show their dissatisfaction either through immediate absenteeism or in lowering their production level. Generally, their perception of fairness responds to their own subjective criteria, not to the official methods of calculating salaries.

Furthermore, the managers usually have the power to manually interfere with the seamstresses' salaries. They can add or subtract at will, regardless of production level. The manager interferes mainly when a seamstress is stellar in a certain department or when a seamstress shows consistent improvement. Through this intervention, the manager addresses the expectations of the seamstresses regarding a fair salary, even if it does not correspond to their official wages.

The direct influence of the manager on the seamstress's salary is a manipulative tool in forwarding his interests. Because the manager can bypass the official pay system, he is able to manipulate the seamstresses' salaries to enhance his power over them. The seamstress is practically helpless in situations in which the rationale of giving or taking is intentionally blurred. This show of power is nothing but crude manipulation and creates an environment of favoritism to the point of causing intentional friction between workers. The managers use their right of intervention in the salary as a means for reward and punishment. The workers adopt a strategy of protest, or voice (Hirschman 1970). They ascertain that the only avenue for voicing their dissatisfaction with the managerial intervention is through protest, either through absenteeism or by insisting that the manager reassess their pay slips.

The seamstresses sometimes recruit the managers to help them protect some of their earnings when the father seizes their entire salary. The next story illustrates such an incident.

Maha is a particularly nimble worker, and her vitality at the machine always attracts a lot of attention. When it becomes known that she is planning to leave the plant, the manager asks me to talk to her. During the course of our conversation, she exhibits her natural friendliness, but she is decisive and full of self-confidence.

"I'm leaving," she says, "because I'm fed up. It's as simple as that. I'm just fed up with the work. When I first came, I was quite young."

"How old were you?" I ask.

"Sixteen. My father didn't force me to work, but I was really bored at home. One day a friend of mine invited me to come to the plant with her to work. She told me we had lots of friends there, that the work was all right, and that they treated the women well. So I went. Meanwhile, the situation at home deteriorated, and my father sent my sister to work as well. Everything that we earned went straight to our father.[13] I didn't get anything. I was young and didn't understand very much, and my father said that I had to help out at home. But I'm fed up now. I've been working for three years, and I haven't bought myself a single outfit. I asked my father to give me at least 50 NIS a month for myself, but he said that we couldn't afford it. Aside from that, he always examines the stub of my paycheck to make sure that I'm not cheating."

I ask her if she thought that sitting at home would be better. "And besides, wouldn't your father force you to go to work if he needed the money?"

She gives me an impish smile. "Look," she says, "I went to the manager and told him what my problem is. I said to him that he could give me some of my earnings for myself and the rest put on the stub of the paycheck for my father. He said he couldn't do anything like that, so I told him that I was leaving. He understands my problem and suggested the following: leave work for a month or so. This will put pressure on my father who needs the money, and after a month he figured that my father will send me back to work and this time let me keep a little for myself. Whenever I feel ready and want to come back, he will accept me. So, I'm going to leave now. My father will hit the ceiling, but he won't touch me, and I'll stay at home for a month or two. Afterward, he'll see that he needs the money and he'll let me go back to work, but he'll agree to give me my 50 NIS a month."

And that is exactly how it works out. Maha leaves the job for three months. When she comes back, I ask her if she worked things out with her father.

"Sure," she says, "just like I told you. See my new blouse. I bought it with my own money."

I ask, "What about the manager's money?"

Maha smiles to herself secretly but does not answer.

The seamstresses see cooperation with the managers as important. Although the plant is in many senses a simulation of the home, the seamstresses seize opportunities that enable them to enhance their self-interest in terms of autonomy and expression, which are manifested in the control of at least some of the money earned. Although the seamstresses are in management's grip, they can manipulate the situation in a way that their personal needs take precedence over the family.

Work and Health

Health is always on the seamstresses' minds. According to the seamstresses, an unhealthy or physically weak woman cannot properly fulfill her role as mother and wife. Women in the plant perceive their work as unhealthy—they report back problems caused by prolonged sitting, their legs and waists hurt, the dust irritates their eyes and breathing, and the noise gives them headaches. This anxiety about health expresses itself in physical and psychological aspects at the sewing plant (Robert 1983; Vinet et al. 1989).[14] The seamstresses consume massive amounts of aspirin for almost any problem. There is a ritualized procedure whereby the managers control the cure: the aspirin. The perception of health is strongly connected to absenteeism, because illness is the most legitimate reason for missing work. Sometimes this legitimization leads to a self-fulfilling prophecy whereby a seamstress who does not feel like going to work becomes sick. The frequent absenteeism due to sickness is in contrast to Robert's (1983) account of factories in newly industrialized countries, whereby "workers hesitate to stay away from their work, even when sick, due to the fear of losing their employment" (p. 31). Managerial acceptance of sickness as a legitimate excuse to miss work is a manifestation of the shared meaning that is created in the plants. In this case, managers accept local perceptions, practices, and definitions regarding sickness and health.

Health problems are loosely defined—almost every personal problem becomes a health problem that prevents coming to work. As Uda openly admits:

"The women are ready to stay home for any old reason—they have their period, a headache, or they have to help their mothers. There's no problem getting a note from the doctor. There are some women—you won't believe it—who are afraid to take pills for a headache because they're afraid that it will prevent them from becoming pregnant. They would rather stay at home and bring a note from the doctor. The manager gets really angry but what can he do?"

Although the manager generally complies with the sick notes, he does try to curtail the phenomenon by speaking to the families or personally going to the sick woman and pleading with her to work. In one of the plants, for example, the manager attempted to curtail his workers' frequent absences by coming to an agreement with the village doctor to strengthen his criteria for illness. As the manager comments:

"I visit the doctor occasionally and make sure to give him a nice package of underwear for him and his sons."

Apart from the common health complaints, the most alarming hazard related to work at the sewing plant is the perception of the connection between work in high-pressure industrial settings and fertility.

For more than an hour, Sami tries to convince Saida not to quit. "Do you have problems with work?"

She answers, "No, everything is fine." She anticipates his next question and continues, "The salary is fine, the managers and supervisors treat me fine, and I have lots of friends in the plant. I even meet with them after work, when I go to their family weddings."

"Then why are you leaving? I know that your family needs the money."

Saida lowers her eyes. He keeps pushing her until, with sudden determination, she answers emotionally, "I'm afraid that if I work here, I'll have trouble getting pregnant. I know the story of Affifeh who works here and can't get pregnant. Me and Samir, my fiancé, decided that I should stop working. I want many children."

Sami gets angry, not so much from Saida's belief that the work influences fertility but from the insinuation that Affifeh's barrenness relates to her working at the plant. He attacks her, "You don't know what you are talking about. Everybody in the village knows that it's not Affifeh's problem but her husband's. Don't be primitive. Look at Faiza, she's been working here for ten years and has six children. On the contrary, working at the plant makes you more fertile."

Saida is not convinced; she simply stops reacting and puckers her lips.

The concern for fertility is prominent, as the women's social status and self-fulfillment still stem mainly from having children and taking care of a family (Moghadam 1993). Any situation that poses a (real or potential) threat to the woman's fertility and health must be avoided. Saida's claim is common—many fathers I talked to during my years at the sewing plants expressed their concern for the health of their daughters. Their logic is that the hard work at the sewing plant deteriorates the physical condition of their daughters, which consequently can harm their ability to conceive.

In those families for whom preserving the health of their daughters is a major concern, the sisters or the mother exempt the worker from housework. As Suna says,

---

"My parents are concerned about my health and understand how hard I work. They don't even ask me to help. Lots of the women help out after work, cleaning the house and cooking and taking care of the younger kids. I'm treated like a princess. My mother says that I work hard enough at the plant and should take a rest once I get home, to maintain my good health. She makes me my dinner and spoils me. I don't do anything, maybe read a book or watch television or, what I like best, meet with my friends. In the winter, it's harder. So I watch television and talk to my brothers and sisters. I think it should be like that because the work at the plant is really exhausting. You've seen how many women practically fall asleep at the machines. They're dead tired because they're working all day here, and the rest of the time they're working at home."

Work and Private Life

The women at the sewing plant come from a tradition-bound society in which the basic values of family honor in general and the honor of women in particular are still held (Fernea 1985). The sewing plant is a forum for women in which the internal contradictions between the customs and traditions of their world and their personal desires, dreams, and fantasies can be discussed, commented upon, and evaluated. In the plants, the women can attain various perspectives on their private lives. There are the views of their peers, who come from various villages and traditions—Muslim, Christian, and Druse; the supervisors, who are usually older and more experienced and who are also part of the village world; and the managers, who present the perspective of the Jewish male. Among themselves, the women expose their private lives within a group of friends, although the gossip soon spreads to everybody.[15] The stories regarding private lives and delicate personal matters sometimes require personal and material support. This support is given by everybody—peers, the supervisors, and the managers.

Because the overwhelming majority of the women have just reached maturity, the personal and social issues consuming most of their attention are matchmaking, the choice of a mate, and establishing a family. The sewing plant plays a role in these dramas.

Rigid tradition often creates cruel situations, and the women view the plant as a refuge, a haven where they can unburden their most intimate problems and find sympathy and even operative assistance.

Personal events affect the ability of the women to work. At the plant, a personal crisis in the life of one woman becomes public domain. There is almost no such thing as a secret. The woman's personal distress usually leads to a decline in her productivity. A sudden drop in output is a kind of public declaration of a crisis. The support she receives from her supervisor and management is intended to show sympathy and help restore her former level of production.

Sub'hia has undergone a religious transformation. She dresses with extreme modesty, always wearing a gray dress and covering her head with a white kerchief. She is 25 years old and has already worked at the plant for eight years. She comes from a large family in which there are nine children; two of them are already married, and the rest still live at home. Her father left home after falling in love with a neighbor and moving in with her. There was an enormous scandal in the wake of the affair, after which the father completely severed his relations with his family and cut off his contribution to their upkeep. Sub'hia is the sole supporter of the family. In addition to her job, she also uses her own car to drive other women from the village to work. Sub'hia was engaged to her cousin (her father's brother's son), but the engagement was broken off.[16]

"For two years I was engaged. I loved him and he loved me, but his mother began to spread stories about me—that I go around with other men. Believe me, it's all a lie. How can anyone go around with other men in a small village like ours? Everybody knows everything about everybody else. Besides, I work all day at the plant, and after work I have to help my mother at home with the younger children. I told my fiancé to speak to his mother and tell her not to ruin our lives. He told me that he loved me, but he is weak, very weak. He said he talked to his mother, but in fact he didn't. He told me that he loves me and wants to marry me but that he is afraid of his mother. And she influenced him and went around telling lies about me. In the end, I couldn't take it anymore. I was fed up. I told him—it's either me or your mother: choose. Again he told me that he loves me and wants me, but in the end his mother won. So before they could do anything, I told him I wanted a divorce. His family wanted us simply to call it off and separate, but I insisted on a religious ceremony, a legally certified divorce."

Sub'hia had been suffering from the moment she decided to annul the betrothal. She went through a period of deep depression. She couldn't sleep at night, and she went around work like a sleepwalker.

"The women and the managers saved my life. They helped me; they had nothing but kind words for me. They encouraged me to stick to my decision."

Sub'hia remained firm even though her former fiancé promised her the world. Her story became the concern of the entire plant. Every move she made was the result of consultation with her supervisors and the manager. The manager financed her legal advice. He also went to speak with her mother and sisters and encouraged them to support Sub'hia in her decision. The manager continued to support Sub'hia after the breakup not only at the plant, but also by financing a computer course that had been her well-known dream. When a new potential groom, a distant relative from Jordan, asked for her hand, the manager encouraged her to get married even though it meant losing her as a seamstress.

The well-publicized support of the manager earned him much respect and loyalty. As he expresses it:

"When I helped Sub'hia, I thought about her tough position. But I knew that all of the seamstresses were testing my behavior. If I hadn't helped, her production would have gone down, and also I gained a good name both in the factory and in the villages nearby. Lots of women who came to seek work, when I asked them 'Why did you choose this plant?' said that they had heard good things about me."

Compassionate behavior with the women is not confined to a personal level. It is also diffused throughout the social domain of the plant, consequently transcending and transforming into the plant's legends and myths. The interrelationship between the workers and the managers takes the form of a trade-off, whereby helping the women in their personal matters creates an advantage for the managers on the shop floor. The ability of the sewing plant as a work organization to embrace the personal and social content of the world of the seamstresses is a cornerstone of its organizational culture.

The seamstresses sense that in matters of marriage, whatever happens is their destiny, and they have no court of appeal, as Sana's story illustrates.

"I was engaged in a *badal*, a double betrothal.[17] My brother was engaged to my fiancé's sister. That was the decision. The two families are related. The father of my fiancé is my father's cousin. At first, I didn't really agree. I didn't want to be married off like that, but my brother was so much in love with his fiancé that in the end I agreed."

I ask Sana why she had to agree. Couldn't her brother have gotten married anyhow, leaving her to marry someone else, of her own choice?

Sana replies in what I would call a patient and didactic tone of voice: "The woman's father would not agree to do it otherwise. He

said that either he marries both his son and daughter to us or there's
no deal. So I agreed, at the beginning for my brother. He was really in
love with the woman. The whole village knew that—you can ask the
women here. Two years ago there was a road accident. My brother and
my fiancé's brother were killed. After the accident, my father went to
his cousin and asked him if they wanted to cancel my engagement because there could be no *badal*. My fiancé didn't agree. He said he
loved me, and despite the accident he wanted us to get married. At
first his family agreed, but after a while his father came back and said
he wanted another *badal* between my third brother, Hamid, and my
dead brother's fiancée. Hamid refused. He said he didn't want to marry
someone who was meant to be his brother's wife."

I ask why. Sana goes on, "He said a lot of things about her, even
that she had the evil eye and that he was afraid. But the truth is that
he didn't think she could love him after she had been so in love with
his brother. I think he was right. Nobody wants to be second fiddle,
especially in love. She would marry him and think about his dead
brother all the time. What kind of life would that be?"

I ask her if the woman had agreed to marry Hamid.

"With them they can't say no to their father. What he wants is
what counts."

I then ask her what about her own fiancé.

Sana takes a deep breath, thinks for a moment, and answers me
dryly. "There was nothing much to do. His family said either a *badal*
or everything's off. I think my brother was right. You can't marry a
woman who was so much in love with another man, especially your
own brother who you also loved. He would spend his whole life being
jealous."

"And your fiancé agreed?" I ask her.

"No. At first he said that he didn't agree and didn't care what his
family said. He said he would marry me because he loved me. But his
father put a lot of pressure on him, and in the end he agreed to cancel
our engagement. And you know what?" her voice changes. "Before I
got engaged to him, there was someone else who wanted me, and I really liked him. Now he's already married and my fiancé is getting
married because they arranged another *badal*. In the end, with two
men wanting to marry me, I'm left holding the bag. Meanwhile, I'm
working, I'm helping my own family, and I'm saving money. I don't
intend to give up work. If you want to fight, you have to have something other than your family. Then your fight is more respected. And

here I can consult with my friends. And I'm making money. Maybe I'll take a trip to Egypt or buy a car or get stuff for my wedding, whenever that will be. There are plenty of *badals* around."

A year later Sana got married, in another *badal*, and left work.

Personal difficulties at home also influence behavior at work. The seamstresses and supervisors show compassion for a seamstress in need. They try to create a supportive environment by helping her with her quotas and advocate her case to the managers. There are, however, extreme situations where personal problems interfere with work for a long period. In the next story, the manager's inclination is to fire the seamstress, but social pressure from the supervisors and seamstresses changes his instrumental approach to a more humane one.

Lina is a married seamstress who has been working for almost seven years in the sewing plant. She has always been considered a good seamstress, one who meets all her norms and premiums. For more than a month, her performance has declined below the norm, and the manager is considering firing her.

She says, "For the last five years I worked at 120 pace. I hardly missed a day of work. Now that I'm having a hard time, the managers forget that I used to be good. They just say, 'If you can't do 120, go home.' Or they say, 'You're good; there's no reason you shouldn't be able to do as much as you want.' I've been here a while and I know their methods. But things happen in life, even outside of work. It has an effect. I can hardly work. All the time I have tears at work, even from my hands."

I ask her, "What has happened?"

She pulls back some hair from her forehead and tells her story. "When I was young, I was in love with someone. He was handsome, and when he visited me, he spoke to me very nicely. I felt that he understood me and would be a considerate husband, because I am a nervous person. I told my parents that I want him and he wants me. But they wanted my brother to marry first. Then it all began. My brother's bride's family said that they will only agree to let their daughter marry my brother if their son married me, *yaani* [as in] *badal*. I didn't want to make trouble. I didn't want to ruin my brother's life for my own, so I agreed. I agreed and got married, but my heart stayed with my love. It was very hard, but I didn't have a choice. I fight a lot with my husband. He feels I'm not with him. The only light in my life is my little girl. The situation is bad, and my brother also is having problems with his wife. I told my brother that if he divorces her, I'll do *davka* [purposefully]."

I ask what she means.

"With us in a *badal*, if my brother gets divorced from his wife, he takes with him the sister's husband, you know, my husband. If my brother gets a divorce, I'll stand on my head and do *davka*. So that he'll be *baasa* [miserable]. Even though I don't love my husband, I won't leave him. When I wanted to be happy [by marrying her love], my brother made me *baasa* [by forcing her into a *badal*]. Now I'll do him *baasa*. He wants to get a divorce and marry a young woman. And me? Go back to my parents' house and serve his new wife? I won't have it. My life is not great now, but why make it worse?"[18]

She looks at me as if suddenly remembering and adds, "We had a terrible fight, my husband and I. I can't sleep with him anymore. So he behaved badly—he took me by force. Because of my daughter, I stayed quiet. Because of her, I'm willing to suffer." She took her wallet out of her smock and withdrew a picture of herself with her daughter against a stone wall. "Anaya. She is my eyes; she is my sunshine. Now you understand why I have a hard time at work. I think about it all the time." Her voice revealed deep suffering. "I want to stay at work; it's the only thing I have left. If I stay at home, I'll die. If the manager tells me to leave, I'll commit suicide. I can't take more."

A delegation of seamstresses and supervisors bring Lina's case to the manager and say they will be accountable for her. What she misses, they will make up for her. The manager exhibits generosity and agrees. Later, when the delegation leaves, he says, "The women here have it hard. The men don't care—what they want they take. Her husband doesn't work. He's frustrated and takes it all out on her. She is a good worker, and I know she'll come around. If you want to work here, you need to understand these situations and be generous. It's a good policy, good public relations in the plant and in the community.

At one point, I wanted to speak with her husband, but Najah, her supervisor, warned me. She said, 'Don't interfere. Her husband is hot blooded. If he learns what she's saying about him, he'll kill her.'"

The plant is perceived as a second home, a Japanese-style workplace that promises long-term commitment even after a worker leaves (Lincoln and Kalleberg 1990). There is a legacy of taking care of the women even when they leave. This tradition is a managerial strategy for presenting the benevolence of the plants, because the villages are relatively closed societies in which information is available to everyone. Ex-seamstresses advocate on behalf of the plant, help recruit workers, and promote the plant's reputation.

Conflict with Management

The seamstresses constantly examine the behavior of the supervisors and managers toward them. Every gesture, style of expression, comment, or reply is internalized and analyzed. The daily behavior of the managers and the workers themselves is of considerable importance in defining the quality of work life in the plant. The seamstresses are extremely sensitive to the display of respect and fairness, although there may not be complete agreement on all sides as to what exactly these terms signify. Misunderstandings on this matter often result in tensions and conflict.

Sometimes these tensions and conflicts derive from reasons not relating to the work itself. The cause of the conflict can stem from the social relations between families and the community, but its implication on the seamstresses enters the realm of the plant. Although the managers claim to understand the worldview of the seamstresses and know how to manipulate it, they are oblivious to it when it implies disturbing the organization of production.

One of the seamstresses, Rima, told me the next story, illustrating this point.

"Yesterday morning I came late and one of the production managers raised his voice at me. Afterward I had to wait a long time at the door of his office before he gave me my punch card.[19] I hadn't done anything wrong, but the production manager said that I was lazy and made problems and was always looking for ways not to work. This all happened because the other day I didn't want to move to Samia's department [Samia is the supervisor of the folding department]. They wanted me to help with the folding, but I didn't want to. I told them that I would go home, but I didn't want to do that kind of work. I always agreed to help, and I always helped because I am very good at all kinds of sewing—I am ambidextrous—but I didn't agree to this. So Samia told him that I didn't want to because I was lazy and think only of myself. The manager told me either to do the work I was told to or to go home. That was at two o'clock, and I sat outside and waited until 4:30. I cried a lot, and a lot of my friends who saw me on their way to the bathroom or to get a drink told me that I was right. The manager and the supervisor didn't want to listen to me. The manager just kept saying 'work or go home.' I told my father that I wasn't going back to work even if we needed the money. My father said that they had insulted me and that I shouldn't go back. Last night Muna, my supervisor, called me and told me to come to work today. Because I respect her, I came. The production manager didn't say a word to me. Neither did Samia. Anyhow, I'm not interested in talking to them because they insulted me without even asking me why I didn't want to do the work.

"You see, it sticks with you all the time. It's like a bad boy whose father hammers a nail in the wall because he did something bad and says that until he does something good, he won't take out the nail. And then the boy does something good and the father pulls out the nail, but . . . " and she breaks out crying again, "the hole in the wall is always there. Even if the manager knows that I'm a good worker and that I help everyone, he'll still always remember what happened."

"Why didn't you want to help Samia in the folding department?" I ask her.

"She wanted me to sit next to Raja."

"But Raja is your cousin and you've always been good friends."

"That's true. I even brought her here to work. But there's a problem. My brother and her brother owned a truck together and they had a fight, and now there's a problem between the families. Because of that Raja and I had a fight, and we haven't been talking for a couple of days. Samia knew all about it, but she wanted me to sit next to Raja on purpose. She didn't tell the production manager that I had a problem. She only said that I didn't want to help. That's when he became angry with me and said that I was no good."

The seamstresses sometimes see the supervisors and managers as a single front that always backs each other up. Conflicts with the supervisor are usually solved within the department. If, however, the seamstress or supervisor decides to involve the manager, this involvement is restricted to the actual matter at hand, without exposing the personal issues that surround the problem. In cases of disputes, personal motivation that is not directly related to the work is considered unacceptable by the managers. The managers, however, exhibit reconciliatory tactics "like a father who is pacifying his quarreling children."

Soha has quarreled with her supervisor, Majda. At the inquiry of the production manager, Soha claims, "She told me that I have no brains in front of all the other women. She always insults me in front of them." Majda, the supervisor, does not even bother to deny it: "Soha has no discipline; she is a bad influence on the other women." Exchanges like this continue for a while until the production manager decides to cut the argument between the two women and says to Soha, "It doesn't matter what the supervisor says, you shouldn't reply by shouting at her. You should wait until after work and then talk to her. Now apologize and go back to your workstation."

Soha says, "I'm not going to apologize."

The production manager replies, "Then you'll not go back to work." All this time Majda is indifferent. Soha does not return to her workstation. For the rest of the morning she sits in the lobby.

When Soha leaves, the production manager is agitated about being manipulated by both Soha and Majda. He grumbles to Majda, "I'm backing you, although you shouldn't have insulted her in the first place. She understands very well that both of us were wrong in asking her to apologize."

Majda ignores his words and just insists that Soha is a bad example to the other seamstresses. During the break, the seamstresses surround Soha and legitimize her reaction. A few of them go to the general manager and complain about Majda. The manager brings the production manager, Majda, and Soha together, and after hearing the allegations, he ignores the details of the event and comments, "It is not honorable that in our plant people yell at each other and insult each other. It shames us all." Majda continues to be indifferent. Soha smiles; she realizes her victory. The manager concludes with the oft-repeated cliché, "In our plant, we are together; we are one family. It is dishonorable that these situations occur—for us, the managers, for the supervisors, and for the seamstresses." It is clear to everyone in the office that the incident is over, and Soha proudly goes back to her workstation. Majda goes after her. When both leave, the manager says, "Sometimes the women are smarter than all of us. They know how to manipulate the supervisors, and even us, to get what they want."

The seamstresses are not passive acceptors of the rules of behavior at work, and they constantly examine the work values and norms that the management promotes. This story illustrates how the manager has no choice but to take on the role of an all-embracing patron, not taking a real stance but speaking in slogans. The manager essentially gives up his role of authority and transfers the responsibility to the supervisor, who has to confront the workers and the department on their own terms. The supervisor has the formal victory, whereas the seamstresses win a moral victory, and the manager's paternal stance only illustrates his lack of sensitivity to the social life in the plant.

There are cases in which a group of seamstresses provoke the manager in an attempt to extract a reaction from him that corresponds to their point of view and interests. If the manager perceives that the seamstresses have crossed a line, he is unwilling to negotiate because it would undermine his authority and dominant role in the plant as patron, father, and despot. The frequency of such conflicts between managers and workers is rather low. The supervisor and the production manager serve as a buffer and handle most of the discipline problems in the production line. Additionally, the managers themselves refrain from open conflict with the seamstresses. When unsolvable conflict occurs, it usually involves the outside environment: the family or the community, as the next story illustrates.

During 1996, the sewing plants undergo a difficult period. A few of them are closed down. The seamstresses who want to keep working are scattered among other plants of the concern. A group of nine seamstresses from one village find themselves more than an hour's ride away from their new workplace. They reach an informal agreement with the plant manager, however, that he will not keep them extra hours. This agreement is of course breached after a few weeks when there is an urgent order. The manager convenes this group of seamstresses and explains to them the urgency of the order. He asks for their cooperation and they silently accept. The manager also asks the driver to wait the extra two hours. At four o'clock, however, when the regular working day is finished, the group of seamstresses stop working, signal the driver, and get on the minibus. The production manager is alarmed and tries to get them off the bus, but his efforts are in vain. The manager interferes and says, "She who does not get off the bus to return to work is fired." None of the women move.

One of them, Hanan, a quality controller, says, "You promised, and you broke your promise. If we work extra hours, we'll get home at 7:30—and we still have work to do at home."

The manager is very agitated and says, "You should have come to me first and not just gone to the bus. Now get back to work."

There is a deep silence for a few seconds. Hanan says, "You are the manager, and we respect you, but we are going home."

The manager says, "If you go home, don't come back tomorrow," and leaves. One of the women wants to stay. The driver, however, persuades her to go along with her friends. They all leave.

The seamstresses' leaving was possible because the manager did not keep his word, thus breaking the accepted behavioral norms in the plant and hurting the basic tenets of shared meaning. Not keeping his promise released the seamstresses from loyalty to the manager.

Conclusion

The role of the seamstresses in negotiating the shared meaning that constitutes the work culture in the plants is illustrated and analyzed in the specific ways in which the seamstresses interpret and give meaning to their work on the shop floor. In this process, the seamstresses are not passive agents. They constantly negotiate with the managers and supervisors to express their points of view and thus create a possibility for self-definition at work. The seamstresses are daughters in patriarchal relations both at home and at work. They continuously attempt to redefine notions of gender, rights and obligations, autonomy, and behavior at work in terms of their private sphere. Making sense of family values on the shop floor serves as a mechanism that mediates between their life in the plant and their life at home. By relating to the supervisors and managers as patriarchs and matriarchs, the seamstresses import moral sentiments and behavior embedded in the home to work. These familial attributes of the organizational culture are not ideal. Their manifestation in the plant is as a set of complex, sometimes self-contradicting, and interlocking activities and processes that guide behavior and that stimulate conflict and negotiation on the shop floor.

CHAPTER 6

The Supervisors: Go-Betweens

But when I lie in my bed at night, I have only one
thought: 'Almighty God,' I think to myself, 'help me to
give absolute satisfaction to my superiors!' (I think of
nothing else.) Whether they choose to reward me or not,
of course, that's their affair. (If I can see a clean, well
cared for town, the convicts properly looked after, not too
many drunks in the streets—there's the satisfaction of a
job well done. What more could I want?) I'm not after
honours and decorations . . . ! Of course, that sort of thing
has its attractions, but as the poet says, compared to the
joys of a job well done, everything else is dust and ashes!

—N.V. GOGOL
The Government Inspector

THE POSITION of departmental supervisor is held by women
only. All the supervisors are promoted from the rank and file of the
plant. Most of these women are in their twenties and thirties or, in
a few cases, in their forties. Most of the supervisors are unmarried
and live with their families, and their economic contribution to
the home is long lasting. They do not have a common educational
background. Some have completed only elementary school, others
are high school graduates, and yet others have acquired professional training in accounting, secretarial work, or sewing. Most of
the supervisors come from the village where the plant is located. In
Nazareth and Kfar Tavor, they come from different communities.
In sewing plants located in Druse villages, such as Beit Jann and

Julis, they are mainly Druse; in mixed communities, such as Maghar, there are Muslim, Druse, and Christian supervisors; in Nazareth there are Christians and Muslims, and in Kfar Tavor there are only Muslim supervisors. The religious affiliations of the supervisors reflect the demographic composition of the plants.

The supervisors manage departments of thirty to seventy seamstresses. The departments are responsible either for specific operations or products. The management is integrative and extended; the supervisors manage both the production and the seamstresses. The supervisors are also the representatives of the managers and the plant in the community, and their role extends beyond the sphere of work and into the personal lives of the workers at home. This chapter aims to characterize the intricate and complex role of the supervisors. It reveals the double meanings and ambivalence in the supervisors' lives and work and their contribution to the process of creating shared meaning in the plant. It shows how the supervisors construct their role and their self in the plant, taking into account the demands and rules of work as well as the values, practices, and worldview of the community. Furthermore, this chapter elaborates on the role of the supervisor as mediator.

Essence of the Role

The supervisors deal with the multiple aspects of running a sewing department. Its day-to-day management requires good human relations skills and professionalism.The supervisor must understand the needs of the concern: its goals, priorities, operational principles, values, and norms. The supervisors view themselves as managers working under pressure, required to provide quick answers to pressing problems while meeting clearly defined overall goals.

The supervisors serve as mediators in the plant. First, the supervisors are the instructors in the plant and are the ones who teach the seamstresses the basic techniques of sewing. They convey to the workers the rules, procedures, hierarchy, authority, and appropriate behavior of the plant in all aspects of production. Second, the supervisors translate and interpret the two different sets

of meanings, values, assumptions, and practices that the seamstresses and the managers have, creating a common language and
an open channel of communication. The need for interpreting
managerial policies leads supervisors to develop a system of informal accommodations that flexibly reconcile with shop floor constraints (Thurley and Wirdenius 1973). Third, the supervisors are
mediators between the seamstresses and their families regarding
incidents and behavior at work. Fourth, the supervisors mediate
between the plant and the community, mainly advocating for the
plant after controversial events, such as in the case of Lyla described in the Chapter 1. They convey the mood, attitude, and
feelings of the community to the managers of the plants.

The supervisor's job is rooted, first and foremost, in her great
sense of commitment and responsibility to her work. The sewing
plant is her arena for self-realization, achievement, and the development of her career, especially because a number of the supervisors do not see themselves as potential wives and mothers.

Nehaye tells me, "The work is very hard because you have to work
with the women and, at the same time, make sure that there is a high
level of production. Sometimes there are lots of problems with the
machines or with the raw materials, and everything falls on the supervisor's shoulders. Not to mention that problems of discipline with the
women also take up a lot of time. Sometimes one of the seamstresses
is your cousin or maybe even your sister and you have to yell at her.
You can't show favoritism. At home is one thing—work is something
else. Very often you have to stand up for your department and fight
with everyone else, even with the managers and the machinists to ensure that the department comes out as well as possible. But what can
I tell you? The work gives me a lot of satisfaction. I'm not ashamed to
tell you that my job is my life. What else do I have? I don't have a husband, I don't have children. At work I get a lot of respect, and I can really show what I'm worth here. And at home I'm the main provider,
helping my sister buy clothes, my brother, who is studying to be a
dentist in Romania, and my other brother pay off his mortgage."

The unmarried supervisors, who have no obligations of raising a family, shift the balance of their self-realization from the private sphere to the public sphere of work. Their role at work becomes a simulation of patriarchal relations at home, whereby the supervisors embrace a version of the father, mother, and older sister. As "fathers" they are managers, as "mothers" they care and mediate with the managers, and as "older sisters" they are the friends of the workers. It is the work that provides them with self-esteem and prestige, because they become one of the main breadwinners in their families. Their strength in the family increases, especially in decision-making matters regarding household issues. The interface between these roles is sometimes a problematic endeavor that creates tension between the supervisors and either the seamstresses or the managers, who require them to continuously reconstruct their role and self.

The supervisors must first of all be excellent seamstresses, familiar with both sewing techniques and production details. Aida describes the supervisor's characteristics:

"A good supervisor is first of all a good seamstress; that's why she was promoted. She knows all the sewing operations and gets everything ready in time—thread, fabric, elastic. She knows what someone needs without waiting to be told. She knows that a woman who is finishing one job has to have more work waiting, even before she finishes. She knows how to fix the machine, how to let women work by themselves. A good supervisor knows how to introduce new merchandise and new lines into the department. She has to be independent, and she has to have her own methods."

The emphasis on professionalism is an important aspect of the supervisors' role. Supervisors consider themselves facilitators in addition to being managers. Their main goal is to help and serve the seamstresses and to ensure the flow of work, which is key for high production. In this sense, the supervisor is a field manager, who apart from managing and supervising has substantial physical work to do. She must constantly provide work to the seamstresses and, simultaneously, continuously control and monitor the production level. In addition, she must solve production problems as they arise. The flow of work has multiple facets—constantly coaching the workers, ensuring the smoothness of the production process, and meeting the department's production and quality requirements. This means that the supervisors must maintain tight control of their departments, in both production and human relation terms.[1]

The supervisor must invest extensive professional and managerial efforts to attain a stable department. The supervisors train their seamstresses and build up their departments over a long time period, encouraging the workers to raise their output, maintain high quality, and show sewing flexibility in a variety of items. A well-functioning department has a balanced workforce that enables the supervisor to manage production and quality with maximum results.

Fatma describes her system of management as follows. "The supervisor is both mother and sister to the seamstresses in the sewing plant. She is the link between them and the manager. She is responsible for production, quality, and raw materials. She is required to break in new women and make sure that production never lags. First of all, a good supervisor never loses her temper. She listens to what the women have to say and tries to understand their problems, whether they are related to work or to their private lives. She is, in fact, more like a friend than a boss.[2] The supervisor has to have an overview of the situation. It doesn't make any difference if the woman is working at a machine and the supervisor is doing some other kind of work. They are both here to work. The supervisor has to have a very good grasp of exactly what is going on in every part of her department. She has to listen carefully to what the manager has to say. She has to check out the merchandise in accordance with the proper forms and production schedules. A good supervisor has to be very conscientious about quality when there are problems with merchandise that is sent back from central quality control."

The central managerial aspect in the plant is meeting departmental production goals, and this serves as the criterion by which supervisors are evaluated. It is the source of their bonuses and premiums. Their ability to succeed depends on an ongoing track record of high quality and production levels. Achievement of this track record ensures them high esteem at work and in the community.

Relations Between the Supervisor and the Seamstresses

The relationship between the supervisors and the seamstresses is multidimensional. The double meaning of the supervisors' role is an integral part of their interpersonal relationships with the seamstresses. On one hand, they are managers who exercise authority over the workers, command them, and scold them, if necessary. On the other hand, they are often members of their workers' families or are personal friends. The boundary of this ambivalence tends to be manifested at work.

Noal, a supervisor, comments, "The supervisor has to know how to be a friend to the women. She has to be like the manager, whose word is law but who at the same time has a sympathetic ear for their problems. But she has to attempt to keep work problems separate from their problems at home. She has, first and foremost, to understand the women and try to help them in every way possible, like their friends. The women will do everything for a supervisor they like. It is very important to train them properly from the beginning, to educate them, to explain everything to them very clearly and in detail. In this respect the supervisor is like a mother to them. The women come to me with all their problems, professional and personal. I have 38 women in my department, Bedouins and *Fallahim* [farmers] from a number of villages. There are not too many differences among the women. They are all more or less alike. You have to treat them all the same way, regardless of their religion or the kind of village they come from."

The relationship between the supervisors and the seamstresses is seen in familial and emotive terms. The supervisors "take care of the women," the women "love" the supervisor. Demonstrations of affection are as common as crossed voices and angry looks. An expectation of mutual consideration exists alongside the acceptance of authority.

Raja tells me, "We yell at the women if we have to. People get angry at times, but if the supervisor makes a mistake, it's up to her to apologize to the women. A few months ago, I was in a terrible state because of personal problems. I had tears in my eyes all the time. I spoke to the women and told them that I was having some trouble and needed their help. I asked them to try and work quietly and stop bothering me with all kinds of nonsense. It really helped."

"How did the women take it?" I ask.

"Most of them knew my story and helped me. I have really good relations with my workers. They tell me all about their problems with their families and with their boyfriends. I feel like their mother or sister. I don't want to feel like their boss. I want them to know and to feel that I'm just like them, working in the department—no different."

The supervisors have a wide repertoire of managerial styles. One style is authoritative, although most prefer a more warm and "feminine" style. The seamstresses obey because of their personal loyalty, commitment, and intense emotions toward the supervisors. This "feminine" management is accompanied, however, by authoritative measures. The seamstresses' main loyalty is to the supervisors, not to the work per se.[3]

The relationships between the supervisors and the seam-stresses are reciprocal but also complex. The supervisors tend to present these relationships as dyadic, obliging both sides equally. In practice, however, this perceived mutuality is not always congruent. The relationship between the supervisors and the seam-stresses can be described as a mentoring relationship, whereby the supervisors serve functional and psychological roles. Their functional roles include coaching and protecting their workers. The psychological role includes personal support, friendship, acceptance, counseling, and role modeling.

The issue of fairness is also a part of the supervisors' managerial style. In spite of the fact that the supervisor may come from the family or *hamula* of some of her workers, she cannot allow herself to show them the slightest partiality. She has great potential power to help or harm the workers individually, with regard both to work and to relations with the senior management. As long as she remains aware of the extent of her power, she is also aware that the only way she can preserve feelings of fellowship and unity among the women is by scrupulous impartiality. It is usually women from the supervisor's own family or *hamula* who complain that they are treated unfairly.

As one of the supervisors, Hoda, states, "It is important for me to demonstrate the same attitude toward all the women. They can feel if they are being discriminated against. Once I saw one of the women from my *hamula* sitting and crying all the time. I went over to her and asked her very tactfully what was wrong and offered her some advice. The other women declared that I was showing favoritism, and I had to make it clear to them that they were all equal in my eyes, all one family. But regardless of what I do, there are always those who claim that I am partial to the women from my own family and my own village. It's important to give them the feeling that their supervisor is a good person who is ready to help them, regardless of what village they come from."

Embracing both the authoritative and hierarchical aspects of work, while complementing them with emotions and feelings of friendship and togetherness, enables the supervisors to use a wide range of tactics and pressure on the workers. These can be either formal or informal, thus embodying both the managerial and familial value systems.

Munira tells me, "You treat the women well without yelling at them and then everything goes smoothly. You have to have good work relations, to be a friend to all of them. Work is work, and if everything is going well, the supervisor is like a sister or friend. But if there is trouble with quality or quantity or with discipline, I have to deal with it. For example, there was a seamstress who promised to work on Friday and didn't show up. Then she was asked to work overtime and she refused. I took the problem to the manager, who threatened the woman. The next day the seamstress took sick leave because she didn't feel like working. So I asked the manager to let me handle the case. I didn't let her come to work until she agreed to sign a form, agreeing to work on Fridays and overtime and quit taking unnecessary sick leave. Since then, I've had no problems with that seamstress."

One integral aspect of the supervisor's job is outside the physical boundaries of the plant—in the homes of the seamstresses. A supervisor regularly visits the women at home and knows their families. The families recognize the supervisor's authority as representative of the plant and see her as the guarantor of their daughter's interests—health and honor. They are prepared to discuss and decide with her various issues pertaining to their daughter's work. She also serves as a channel of information for family members on a variety of subjects concerning work, such as possible overtime, management plans, and activities of the plant for the benefit of the village, spiced, perhaps, with a little gossip.

The supervisors are attentive to the complex issues associated with the seamstresses' entry into wage labor, especially in terms of the relationship with their fathers. They were in the same position once, they come from the same community and set of assumptions, and their relative experience in these matters qualifies them to address new issues in the workers' lives. The supervisors sometimes serve as mediators and advocates for seamstresses on internal familial matters.

Jihan tells me, "One of the women bought herself a new blouse and a pair of pants. When her friend saw her, she went out and bought the exact same outfit—to show that they were good friends. Then the second woman's father began to beat her up. Why? Because he said that she had to give her money to the family and save up to buy things for her wedding. The woman was angry at her father and angry at the whole family. That's bad. So she asked me to go and talk to her father. I told her I was ready on condition that her father also agreed. At first he refused. But then my brother, who knows him, spoke with him and told him that this way he was ruining his daughter, that his sister, who was her supervisor, would solve the problem. So he said that because he respects my brother, he would agree to talk to me. I came to their house and we sat around drinking coffee and talking, and in the end the woman agreed that she wouldn't buy things just for the fun of it and would give her paycheck to the family. Her father agreed to give her 100 NIS a month for pocket money. I told him that if the woman never saw any of the money she earned, she would stop working hard and wouldn't have any reason to earn premiums."

The supervisors also mediate between the needs of the plant and the needs of the families of the seamstresses. This mediation is necessary because of the frequent tensions between the family and work regarding overtime and low pay. The family sees the supervisor in multiple roles—as a member of their social group, as women, and as managers in the plant—in that order. This means that she is expected to give precedence to the community and the family over the workplace. The supervisors realize that they are forced to walk on a very tight rope. In their interactions with the families of the seamstress, however, the interests of the work are primary.

Supervisors and Managers

In the plant's hierarchical structure, precise status differences exist between supervisors and managers with regard to function, responsibility, and authority. Nevertheless, the position of the supervisors in the overall structure is closer to that of the managers than to that of the seamstresses. The supervisors are expected to present managerial competency even though they do not have a formal management education.

The supervisors enjoy relative autonomy in managing their departments within a necessary consensus with the managers. According to Su'ad:

"The managers usually rely on the supervisor. They give her the right to manage the department the way she sees fit, providing she delivers the goods. But it's not as if the managers and the supervisors function separately. We work together and our goals are achieved together. If, for instance, the managers don't pay enough attention to quality, neither will the supervisors. If the supervisors and the managers don't meet together regularly to decide how to work together, there will be problems. The supervisors don't always understand exactly what the managers want from them. Every manager has his own system, and even though we may be experienced supervisors, we still have to get used to every new manager and his methods. There is nothing that can be done about this. We stay in the same job for years, doing the same thing over and over again. Managers come and go. We even teach them a thing or two when they're just getting started, and once they learn they start telling us what to do and how to do it and begin changing things that we've been doing for years. That's why they are managers. But the supervisor is always the manager's right hand and has to help him in everything, especially with the women. A good supervisor takes a big load off the manager's mind."

The supervisors, who are the most stable group in the plant, retain the shared meaning of work values, norms, and practices, both those of the managers and those of the seamstresses. Managers come and go, and it is the supervisors who are the bearers of the guidelines for behavior under the various circumstances and events at the plant. They constantly incorporate the managerial system into the seamstresses' outlook. The supervisors embody both sets of rules, procedures, norms, and behavior and translate them into practical behavior as a mechanism for absorbing conflict and delineating moral codes at the plants.

The supervisors accept the manager as the highest professional authority, aware that he is working under constraints dictated to him by the division. They also accept that he has a broad grasp of the overall operation of the plant, whereas they themselves focus largely on the running of their own departments. Thus, in the daily reality of the sewing plant, only the manager can really judge if one department has to relinquish some of its workers or machines for the benefit of the plant as a whole, a situation that may cause tension between the supervisor and the manager. This kind of conflict happens from time to time. The manager has to weigh his general priorities and those of the plant against the priorities and schedules of the supervisors and their individual departments. This may adversely affect the achievements of a particular department. Zohara comments on this issue.

"If I have to send some of my seamstresses to another department, it will be to my disadvantage, since I will certainly not be able to fulfill my work schedule."

In situations of this sort, the supervisor may feel that the manager's decision is directed against her personally and arbitrarily. Loyalty to the manager is one of the central values in the supervisor's job as well as one of the central facets of managerial strategy. Loyalty is understood on a personal level; reciprocity is an integral component. A manager who undermines the authority of a supervisor in the running of her department is perceived as breaking the rules of decency and loyalty that are the cornerstone of the managerial system in the sewing plants.

The loyalty of each supervisor to her department and to her workers is a sensitive matter and has little relation to the needs of other departments in the plant. For example, the level and quality of production determines the supervisor's personal evaluation and salary. If, however, the manager withdraws one of the supervisors' seamstresses from the production line because of an urgent need elsewhere, the performance of her department is immediately affected. The supervisor is torn between her loyalties to the department and to the performance of the plant as a whole. This tension cannot be avoided and embodies the inner contradiction entailed in performing the job of supervisor.

Another source of tension between the supervisors and the managers is the disruption of the solidarity and togetherness developed by the supervisors and their workers. The supervisors work hard to build a sense of unity and accountability within the department (one way is through departmental celebrations of seamstresses' personal events, such as birthdays and engagement parties). Achieving departmental unity and solidarity takes a long time and requires an emotional investment and physical energy. Any disruption of the departmental flow of work, particularly by a manager's intervention in the supervisor's department against her will, is perceived as a blow to the supervisor, a threat to the stability of her department, and disregard for the efforts she has invested. Disruptions hurt the department's ability to meet production goals and maintain a sense of excellence and thus present an infringement of the principle of equality between the supervisors. Salweh's story illustrates the deep sense of loyalty the supervisors have to their departments.

"My department is set up to produce 1500 pairs of boxer shorts with Lycra elastic bands. I have two women who know how to sew the Lycra but only one machine for it. So I asked for another machine. Eran, the production manager, told me there was another machine in Rudeina's department and I should transfer the woman there. I thought that the woman should be working for me on the boxers, but they told me that she would be working for Rudeina, and I didn't agree. I'm not ready to train a woman in order for her to work for another department. Then I'll be stuck. The other day they brought me Cacharel [a European brand] shirts for finishing. They shouldn't have done that. Rudeina's department was doing that, and they brought her another product. Whoever sewed the shirts from the beginning should do the finishing as well. But the production manager didn't want to make it hard for the women in her department, so instead he made it hard for me and my department. They're out to get us and I don't know why. I just don't have any luck. My department is my first priority. If I give a woman to Rudeina's department, I'll be hurting my own department; the merchandise will suffer and our output will fall."

In conflicts in which the manager undermines the supervisor's authority, she meets with her department and expresses loyalty to her workers. The department, for her, is the source of loyalty, unity, solidarity, and mutual assistance. This reality leads to managerial ambiguities, whereby the supervisor takes a stand in favor of her department and the manager takes a stand in favor of the plant. In the background are not only departmental cohesiveness and the message she wants to send to the workers of protecting them at all costs, but also concern for professional performance. If her department is hurt, she will not make her production goals and will be accountable to the manager. This type of dispute often becomes a social drama: the supervisor receives emotional support and high esteem from her workers, but they end up dealing with inconveniences when she ultimately has to comply with the manager.

The managers of the sewing plants want to maintain a core of experienced department supervisors, capable of independent action insofar as it is possible. Some supervisors are extremely professional in their work and highly motivated, so much so that the managers have little need to interfere with department management. Moreover, the supervisors would view such interference as a personal affront. In this respect, the hierarchical divisions of authority between managers and supervisors become somewhat indistinct, and supervisors are able to acquire significant power. This power expresses itself in having a free hand in the department, as long as production and quality goals are met.

The autonomous management of a department by a supervisor, however, is conditioned by a high level of personal loyalty to the manager; the two are mutually interdependent. The loyalty is on a personal level and involves full agreement on the part of the supervisor to the methods, goals, and needs of the manager. The supervisor must conform to the manager's views, styles, and priorities in order to gain autonomy in running her department. Supervisors do not necessarily see this type of relationship with the manager as an advantage, because it creates more friction within the department. Taking an a priori promanagerial stance implies that the supervisor has relinquished her function as a spokesperson and advocate for her workers. Few supervisors agree to uncritically identify with the manager, because eventually it lessens their independence, autonomy, and bargaining power with the workers.

The supervisors expect managers to recognize their professionalism and exhibit reciprocity in their relationships. Ignoring the supervisors' experience and their role as facilitators of the production process is seen as breaching the implicit contract between them and the managers. The entire value system developed in the sewing plants is echoed in this bond. The supervisor is the extension of the manager, the mediator and translator of the manager's outlook and worldview, and executor of the manager's work plan. The relationship must be harmonious and reflect deep understanding and trust.

The managers have differentiated attitudes toward the various supervisors. They grant considerable autonomy to those who are professional, have proved themselves at work, and obey the manager unquestioningly. These supervisors give up resources of their departments without fearing a loss of status. They are pillars of the plant and enjoy high status with the manager at work. The manager consults with them and respects their advice. They are the legacy of the plant, those who for years participate in reshaping and renegotiating all aspects of work and life on the shop floor.

New supervisors have a more fragile relationship with the managers. They have to deal with their lack of professional management skills and the difficulties of performing all their professional-organizational duties. Furthermore, their dyadic relations with the managers have not yet crystallized.[4] At times they are hesitant about approaching a manager to clarify an issue, simply because in their former position in the plant they had no direct access to him. Establishing a close working relationship with the managers is part of the supervisor's job. This relationship ensures that the managers will actively support the supervisor and back her in all of her departmental matters. This support is a prerequisite for success.

Supervisors and the Concern

For most of the supervisors, the concern has no direct impact on their work. Their frame of reference is their department. This perception stems from their minimal tangible connection with the concern, except for the occasional visits of one of the directors and the rare extension course they take at the division center in Karmiel.[5]

The supervisors' connection to the concern is seen mainly through team meetings with functionaries from the division, who pass on information about the obligations to fulfill orders, raise quality levels, or meet production schedules. The concern managers consider the supervisors as those who have direct influence on the quality of the merchandise, which gives the concern its competitive edge in the international market. The supervisors accompany visits by customer representatives who want to check the quality of the merchandise. Such visits instill in the supervisors a sense of pride that they belong to a large concern with an outstanding international reputation. This feeling is reinforced when they make visits, from time to time, to sister plants or participate in yearly events arranged by the concern for all of its employees.

During the course of time, the concern has acquired a good reputation among the Arab and Druse villagers because of the way it ensures the women's safety and good name. It has become known as a firm that accepts the special cultural and behavioral norms of the seamstresses as part of its organizational culture. Many of the supervisors told me that they came to work at these plants because "they were the only places where their parents would let them work." Many said that they would recommend "only this concern" to their sisters or relatives who wanted to work in industry "because it shows respect for all the communities and their customs."

Smooth operation of the sewing plants depends on smooth planning and logistics, cutting, delivery, and inventory management. If this support is not provided on time or with the needed quality, the plant cannot meet its production goals. This creates pressure on the supervisors because it is beyond their ability to influence. Although it is perceived as the prerogative of the managers, the supervisors are the ones who face the consequences of logistical problems. For example, when materials do not arrive or are damaged, the managers must deal with the supervisors' justified claims regarding their inability to meet their goals. This raises tensions, and confrontations are likely because the supervisors are frustrated by what appears to be the managers' blind support of the concern.

Flora, a supervisor, is extremely frustrated. She goes to the manager and tells him that she has failed in her role and is quitting. Dror, the manager, tries to persuade her that she is a good supervisor and shows her graphs and data proving that her output, quality, and absenteeism are the best in the plant. Flora is not convinced.

"There is too much pressure. I can't take it anymore. Especially the new product of Marks and Spencer. It is made of thin material that curls up. All the women are depressed—they can't reach their norm and there are quality problems. Then their salaries will be low and they'll come to me with complaints. I don't have energy anymore. I want to leave. This problem with the raw material is hurting my department."

Dror backs Flora up and says that he has talked to the cutting manager and the division manager, but they don't understand. To placate her, he suggests that she write a letter to the division manager. She likes the idea and says, "I'll write. But it's the last chance. If it doesn't work, then I'm leaving and *hallas* [the end]."

Flora writes the following letter:

A Letter to the Division Manager About Raw Materials:

I would like to notify you in this letter about the condition of the raw materials in the last period which is getting gradually worse. There are problems that repeat themselves— cutting, asymmetry, unequal parts, the material curls up, the color tones are not uniform. Imagine to yourself the pressure on me and my department. Every morning we come to work with enthusiasm. We begin to work and suddenly encounter a catastrophic problem that messes us up for the whole day. The department and I get into a lot of pressure and the seamstresses take advantage of this. On one hand, we have quantity and quality obligations. On the other hand, problems with the raw materials hurt us from all sides. The seamstresses have to cut and sort and waste productive time. I understand that the raw material can't be perfect. But you'll agree with me that there's a limit. I want you to understand the pressure on me. All the seamstresses are on my case. The plant is meant to produce underwear, not problems. The customer should be satisfied with our products. I occasionally get material that is garbage—forgive the expression—and we all know that from garbage you can only make garbage. Even though we try our hardest, it's hard to overcome the problems if they repeat themselves.

> *Hoping that you will help us,*
> *Flora M.*
> *Maghar Sewing Plant*

The manager never passed the letter to the concern. He had only wanted Flora to stay at work and used the letter to appease her. Flora did not know the aftermath of the letter; the manager had no intention to pass it over. It was used as a tactic for presenting a "common front" against the division and a show of solidarity between the manager and the supervisor. Eventually this line of product ended and a new line that did not curl up was given to Flora's department.

Conflicts over Backing

The supervisors expect the backing of the managers in issues related to decision making in the department.

One day toward noon, Amneh sees that she doesn't have enough fabric to finish making one of the products. She decides to send four of the women home. The production manager is not at the plant that morning, and when he returns toward the end of the day, Amneh tells him what she has done. Incensed, he tells her that she should have checked with the manager whether they could have been of some use in another department. Amneh is offended.

"Not only did he shout at me, he didn't help me. Perhaps I made a mistake, but it's his job to explain things to me and not to shout at me. I'm fed up with that sort of behavior. If that's the way he acts, then he doesn't care a straw for me. If he doesn't agree with the way I do things, I can stay home. I've got everything I need at home. Let him give me official notice and I'll say 'Bye, see you.' He thinks he's the only one who knows anything; nobody else understands anything. Maybe I did make a mistake, but that's no way to behave. I can't get used to that. At home my brothers all have the highest respect for me. My mother waits at home for me till five o'clock and doesn't eat a thing until I'm back from work. He yelled at me for letting the women go home instead of making sure that there was enough fabric. What does he think? Let him shout at his wife, Mr. Manager."

Offending the supervisors breaches their perception of reciprocity.[6] When a supervisor's interpretation of events is not ac-

cepted or when a manager scolds her, she has a choice. If she cate-
gorizes the insult as a severe breach of reciprocity, she can resort
to a solution of exit—leaving work. If she complies, she can use
her voice to defend her position and point of view, thus reiterating
the norms and values of the work. The next story illustrates the
latter option. The story illustrates how professional and personal
backing play a role in managerial methods. Any departure from
these norms is immediately grasped as a lack of respect and leads
to a breakdown in relations.

Najah has worked as a supervisor for fifteen years. "The whole mess
started when the division quality controller stopped the work of Fahimeh, the other quality controller. She [the division quality con-
troller] said that Fahimeh approves defective merchandise. I went over
to her and she showed me an example. I thought it looked fine. I told
her that I thought we could continue anyway, but we had better go
and talk to Rami. We came to the office, you know, in a friendly way.
I showed him the merchandise, and I said to him, 'Take the underwear
and see if there's a problem and tell me if we can continue to work.' I
was really sure that he would agree with me because we had had the
same problem a month before and then Rami had agreed that we
could continue. So Rami looked at the underwear and Fahimeh asked
him to give her permission to continue. He said it was no good. I explained to him that we had a problem sewing the legs.

"Fuad, the production manager, saw that there was going to be an
explosion and walked out of the office. Believe me, if he had stayed
on, nothing would have happened. But he didn't want to take sides in
the argument, and so he pretended that he had something urgent to
do and left. I told Rami that I couldn't go on like this, and he answered me in an angry tone that I shouldn't think I was doing him a
favor. That's what he said after I'd been working under pressure for
months, working overtime without end and working Fridays until
two in the afternoon. He was the one that was holding up the smooth
flow of work. I told him thanks a lot if that's the way you thank me
for all the work I've invested. You're trampling on everything and I
don't like it."

She looked at me and then she lowered her large brown eyes and spoke softly.

"I took off my smock."

I looked at her with surprise and she smiled. "You know that I took off my smock, so why are you looking at me like that?"

Taking off your smock at the sewing plant is equivalent to saying, "I quit." It is a symbolic act of resistance usually performed in the presence of the worker and the manager and is considered a burning insult to the management. A woman who takes off her smock in front of everyone is, in effect, declaring that she has lost faith in the management. The managers, too, see this act as a particularly vehement form of protest.

"It makes my blood boil," Rami tells me, "to see a worker take off her smock so boldly. It's like a rebellion. If a woman or particularly a supervisor, who is an example to everybody, does that—I'll kick her out of the plant. I never want to see her again. At that point I don't care what happened or who was right. A woman who takes off her smock in front of everybody is disgracing the plant. It's like putting a stigma on the plant and its managers. It's a vote of no confidence in the managerial abilities of the supervisors and me, in our ability to solve the problems of the seamstresses. That's perhaps the most important point of all—personal management. All the time I am trying to get it home to them that the manager solves all their problems—at work and outside of work. The manager is a fair person, doesn't play favorites and doesn't hand out demerits. When one of them takes off her smock, it means she isn't giving the manager a chance, that she doesn't believe in him."

The manager must be sensitive to the style and content of using his authority toward the supervisors. The content of the hierarchy is not pure control; it is mellowed and inserted with meanings of compassion, consideration, and friendship. If the manager ignores these new contents and resorts only to authoritative justifications and displays of power, then he openly changes the rules of the game and the supervisor has no avenue but to quit. Nonetheless, the conflict is open to negotiation.

"What happened after you took off your smock?" I ask Najah.

"Fuad grabbed me on the stairs and asked me to stay. I was burning up inside. Nobody appreciates what you do. Rami had to show that he's a man, so he wanted me on my knees, and that's just not my style. I stayed at home for three days. Rami called me up at home and asked me to come back. I told him I wasn't coming. If you want, I said, you can come over here and we'll have a cup of coffee. He said, you come for a cup of coffee, and after that I'll come to you for a cup of coffee. I didn't want to insult him, so I came for a cup of coffee.

"After three days, my friends from the department told me that they missed me and I shouldn't leave them. I still don't respect Rami, but I decided to return to work for my workers."

Najah's story reveals the drama behind the intricate relationship between the managers and the supervisors. The game has distinct rules. The manager is entitled to dispute the supervisor's decisions within a prescribed framework as long as he maintains respect. For the supervisor, it is important that the form of the manager's expressions still preserves her status as part of management. Only then can the supervisor affiliate with the manager despite their difference of opinion, thus strengthening her organizational self.[7] Confronting her with a decision that contradicts her professional judgment led Najah to take a symbolic act in front of the whole plant. This bold gesture was aimed directly at the manager and challenged his legitimacy, power, and proficiency. Although the manager had the power to fire the supervisor, he lost the battle in the moral field.

The managers try to avoid prolonged conflict because they have little leverage in risking the cooperation of the supervisors. In such conflicts, the supervisors implicitly remind the manager that he must resort to a course of action and behavior that saves the face of both sides. These conflicts illustrate the limit of the managers' power and how their misuse of it can adversely affect them.

The managers' tendency to see the plant as one integrated system and base their decisions on the interest of the entire plant often collides with the supervisors' territoriality and desire to preserve the integrity of their departments. Flexibility is an issue that often causes friction, particularly during times of changing products and styles from one season to another. For the managers, the change in the seasons is a time for reorganizing the assembly lines, mobilizing seamstresses within and between departments. The basic criteria for mobility relate to the seamstresses' qualifications, abilities, flexibility, and proficiency. Although reorganization is accepted by the supervisors, friction and complaints are part of the ritual. The supervisor must tackle a practical problem—how to explain the transfer of seamstresses to other departments. These transfers are characterized by mini crises in which seamstresses cry, yell, and threaten to leave work, and supervisors quarrel with managers.

Iman's department is strong and coherent. The relationships between the seamstresses are friendly; they spend time together outside of work and attend each others' celebrations. With the coming of the summer season, the managers decide to reorganize the department. Iman complains bitterly and objects, crying and claiming that it is not fair. "I've been working many years to train my workers, and now they are taking them from me." As a protest, she decides to take a special vacation, claiming that she has to help her sister who had just given birth. The manager apparently is quite satisfied with her decision and uses the opportunity to personally reorganize the department. When Iman returns to work three days later, she finds an already established new reality. She bursts into the manager's office and lays down her protests.

The manager lets her blow off her steam and then says, "I have learned an old Arab proverb, 'He who is in the market is the one who buys and sells.' You were not here, so I changed your department." Iman is speechless and leaves the office.

When I ask her why she let the manager reorganize her department, she comments, "I did it on purpose. I wanted him to be the bad guy. Now the whole plant knows that he took advantage of my absence to make these changes. Nobody blames me for cooperating with him. I retained my reputation of taking care first and foremost of my workers."

The option of exit can be seen as a resistance strategy to the manager's policies, particularly the apparently arbitrary decision-making process. For Iman, it is an active option that sends a message of noncompliance to both the manager and her workers. Although she does not have the power to curb the manager's decision, she does not accept its rationality either. She takes a definitive stand and supports the integrity of her department.

Equality and Equity Equal Honor and Respect

One important aspect of the relationship between managers and supervisors is the maintenance and preservation of a sense of equity among the supervisors, on both formal and informal levels. Although in practice there is a differentiation between more senior professional supervisors and newer supervisors, managers attempt to preserve the ideology of no discrimination. The supervisors believe that they all perform the same job, all put their best into it, all are loyal to the concern and to the manager, and all demonstrate an equal level of commitment.[8] The supervisors are sensitive to the managers' attitude toward them because, unlike the seamstresses, they see their jobs as careers, as a way of life. Thus, the patriarchal relations between supervisors and managers on the shop floor reflect the power of the managers over the supervisors' income, labor, and status at work (Walby 1990). Any favoritism immediately generates the feeling that alien interests are intruding into proper management.[9]

In my years of fieldwork in the plants, I came to see the terms *respect* and *honor* in the vocabulary of the Arab and Druse supervisors as having several levels of meaning. They mean respecting a woman's modesty in intersexual contacts; respecting her hierarchical position as supervisor; respecting her as a human being; and, finally, refraining from introducing irrelevant matters into her relations with the managers.

Respect is an important code of behavior in the plant. It mainly entails saving face in public.

Fatma tells me, "The managers are sometimes good and sometimes bad. Sometimes the manager will shout at the supervisors in front of the women, even though he has an office and certainly knows how to talk nicely. He yells about trivial things. He tells you all the time that if you want to work, that's fine, and if not, he can find someone like you for 1000 NIS a month. That's a blow to the supervisor's self-respect."

"Did this ever happen to you?" I ask.

"It happened just once and I didn't want to come back to work. I'm not used to being shouted at, not by my father and not by my brother. I even said that to my husband before we got engaged."

Maintaining honor and respect is an important code of behavior regarding the manager's respect of each supervisor relative to the others. Yosra's perspective illustrates the importance of honor and respect through a nondiscriminatory approach.

"Sometimes I feel that I am not respected by the managers. A couple of days ago I was sitting and drinking coffee and the manager came by and shouted at me. Once he didn't even wish me a happy holiday. Sometimes they discriminate between one supervisor and the next. There are supervisors who can sit down to eat breakfast for as long as they want. And they spend a lot of time in the manager's office. There are others who are treated like donkeys—work horses. There is a problem like that here. If the manager doesn't treat us all equally, then we don't get to know exactly what is going on, and then there are problems with the supervisor's work. She doesn't know ahead of time what has to be done and can't plan properly, and later they complain about her. I don't need to have a personal relationship with the manager. I only want him to pay me properly and to pay all the supervisors the same, and let me know what is being planned. I also want to have my say, not everything decided for me. The manager should give the supervisors a better feeling. They shouldn't get excited over stupid things. They should talk to us."

The breach of honor creeps into conflicts at work, mainly regarding differing interpretations of meanings. The supervisors and the managers are members of different cultures and attribute divergent meanings to gestures and language. Ignoring this difference accentuates conflict beyond its concrete content.

Sana tells me, "I had a problem with the production manager and he accused me of something unfairly. He took me to his office and began to shout at me, using words I never heard before in my whole life. Nobody ever spoke to me like that. And I couldn't answer him back because he's a man and I'm a woman, and besides, I never used words like that in my life.

"I asked him how he wanted me to go back to work after he had insulted me like that. He told me that if I didn't go back to work I'd be out of a job in five minutes. I told him that if he wanted to fire me he didn't have to look for flimsy excuses. I also asked him if he had ever asked me to do something that I didn't do. I told him that I wanted him to respect me, not to shout at me and that I was ready to go back to the machine I worked at seven years ago. So he said that I should go home, and he wasn't giving me any severance pay. I went to the general manager and told him what happened and he begged me not to decide on the spot but to go home and calm down and think it over."

The general manager sits with the production manager and Sana and discusses with them "the words." The production manager claims that there is no actual meaning behind those words—they are just manners of speaking. They both try to explain to Sana the nature and meaning of Hebrew slang. Sana listens patiently and just nods her head. She scolds, "These words insult me personally. They insult all the women in the plant. You are guests in the village, you should behave yourself."

The manager looks at her and then says to the production manager, "Here respect to the supervisor is more important than work. Among ourselves it's okay to use these words, but with Sana we will use Sabbath words." They all smile.

Wages and Remuneration

The supervisors see the issue of salary as problematic, and it is always on their agenda in deliberations with the managers, because wages are not commensurate with their responsibilities. This is particularly evident when compared with the earnings of the seamstresses. An experienced supervisor, with years of seniority, makes only a few hundred NIS more than a good seamstress. The supervisor cannot advance in the management hierarchy, but there is a wide range of jobs she can fulfill at the supervisory level. She can be in charge of a large department that sews elaborate products; she can be responsible for packaging; she can serve as chief quality controller for the plant or as chief instructor. Although all these jobs require a good deal of professional expertise, the responsibilities they entail are not reflected in the basic wage.

The managers have the prerogative of determining bonuses and premiums for the supervisors above their low basic wage, and this extra money becomes an important component of their take-home pay. Before the passing of the minimum wage law in 1996, the average basic wage of a supervisor came to about 1600 NIS a month. A quality controller earned a premium of 40 to 50 hours' pay, and more demanding jobs earned the supervisor another 60 to 80 hours' pay. A quality controller thus earned between 1900 and 2100 NIS a month, and a supervisor earned between 2300 and 2500 NIS a month. This salary is in accordance with the collective agreement, with differentiation dependent on seniority. Since the passing of the minimum wage law, supervisors receive the same basic salary as the seamstresses and depend on management bonuses to supplement and raise their income above the average seamstress's salary. The concern prefers to use managerial bonuses instead of raising their basic salary; this way the social benefits remain the same as before the passing of the law. Customarily, there is an annual increment according to seniority level, but the difference in pay between one level and the next is almost negligible. These increments, therefore, are not viewed as either a form of remuneration or a professional promotion.

The management is well aware of the problem and seeks various means to raise wages. Bonuses may be given for special effort. Additionally, if one of the supervisors has a car, she may earn additional money by driving the women to and from work.

The supervisors always present their view that their contribution is higher than their pay and blame the concern for lacking gratitude. The managers attempt to justify the supervisors' relatively low wages by pointing to the low profitability of the textile industry in general and the ever-present threat of international competition from countries in which wages are much lower. They repeatedly cite the example that a supervisor in the concern's plant in Egypt earns $120 a month, whereas in Israel she earns about $800.

With all the complaining, dissatisfaction from salaries is never translated into group action or group demands for a raise. The supervisors discuss their bonuses individually with the managers. It is assumed, for the most part, that the concern is tight-fisted and that the managers have little leeway to be generous with compensation. As far as the supervisors are concerned, it is a situation they have to live with.

The managers themselves try to maintain a balanced policy with regard to the remuneration of the supervisors. The more experienced and the more capable among them receive a higher wage than those just starting in the job, because of both seniority and larger bonuses and premiums. The supervisors acknowledge the existence of an informal wage scale, whose standards are strictly adhered to. In theory, the salaries of the supervisors are their own private business, but, in practice, each of them knows what the others are earning. If one of them gets too far ahead with bonuses and premiums, there will be a long line of supervisors at the manager's door petitioning for their rights. Money is the surest sign of a supervisor's worth, beyond the attention or kind words given her by the management.

Ivtesam shares with me her feelings on the subject.

"The managers get ahead, but the supervisors stay in the same place. You think that if you have a lot of seniority you're really making progress. But it's not so. A supervisor with seniority doesn't have any advantage. I'd like to know why we don't get ahead, why we're practically in the same place we started from. What is 2300 NIS for a supervisor who has worked for more than ten years? The supervisor does all the work and in the end she goes home empty handed. The supervisor has all the trouble but she only gets *grushim* [10] They don't see us as managers, like them. We are not more than the seamstresses to them, Arab village women."

The issue of remuneration emphasizes the inequalities inherent in the entire textile industry in the Arab villages. Even though the supervisors' contribution is recognized, they are still not considered full-fledged managers in the concern. The fact that they are supervisors does not fundamentally change their income, only their responsibility. In this sense, the exploitation of the supervisors is strongly apparent. The managers draw them into the realm of management, but with regard to remuneration they are confined to the realm of the seamstresses.

Relations Among the Supervisors

The value of teamwork is considered the key to success at the plant.[11] At the plants, team-related values are harmony, reciprocity, and recognition of achievement. When teams do not operate in accordance with these values, the climate of the plant is hostile. Hostility is felt among the seamstresses, between the seamstresses and the supervisors, and among the supervisors. Furthermore, the discord spills over into relations outside the plant and affects personal friendships.

The range of relations among the supervisors is large and runs along a continuum from deep friendship, to solidarity and mutual esteem at work, to dislike, to hatred. Most of the conflicts among the supervisors simmer for some time under the surface. Those involved are usually not interested in bringing them into the open and thus generating an open crisis at the plant. But if a conflict does erupt—and it is not important how trivial its source —it does not take long before it engulfs everyone in its wake—in the plant and at home in the village. Such a conflict requires the interference of a moderator, and it is usually the manager who tries to resolve the conflict through arbitration and compromise. He must intervene and intervene boldly if he is to get the plant back on track.

The next story illustrates a case of an all-out war taking place in the wake of a conflict between two of the supervisors, Suha and Johara. The two had worked together at the plant in the same capacity for a long time. One might say that there was a certain symmetry between them. They were both highly esteemed by the manager of the plant and both ran large departments producing similar kinds of merchandise. It was as if there were an unwritten agreement between them. They presented a united front to the manager, to the other supervisors, and to the seamstresses and appeared to be good friends. The manager, for his part, was careful to preserve their status as senior supervisors and never showed favoritism, either in his personal relations with each or at team meetings. The united front burst wide open the day that Suha decided that the time was ripe for her to take professional precedence over her erstwhile colleague.

Suha had to sew samples of a product on a machine that belonged to Johara's department and asked permission from the manager to take the machine. She did not bother to mention the fact that the machine belonged to the department of another supervisor. This is the way Suha saw it.

"We had a fight over a certain problem. Once I had a single-needle job to do. I went to Jacob, the manager, and asked for a single-needle machine. He said, okay, there's no problem. The machine was in the blouse section of Johara's department and I saw that nobody was using it. Jacob was in the dining room, so I decided that I would take the machine and put a woman to work, and when he finished eating I would tell him about it. Johara saw that one of my seamstresses was working at the machine and lost her temper. She threw a spool of cotton at the woman and nearly hit her in the eye. I saw the whole thing and I told Johara she should be ashamed of herself. [Suha also added an epithet but refused to tell me exactly which one.] Johara began to scream insults at me and I answered her back. She has a sister, Feize, who works in her department as a quality controller. Feize saw us quarreling and came over and began to hit me with her shoe from behind. Some of the women from my department also came over and told her that she should be ashamed of herself, doing something like that. In a few minutes all the women from the two departments were shouting at each other. There were even women with sisters and cousins in the other department who were shouting at each other and it was a big mess until the manager turned up.

"I left the department and went home. My quality controllers told Jacob that they didn't agree that I should stay home while Johara continued working. They said that if he didn't send her home they would all walk out. He told Naif, the driver, to take Johara home. I told my parents and my brother what happened. My brother went to the plant and told Jacob that if Johara and her sister came back to work they would be dead for what they did."

Jacob was in a dilemma. Although he wanted to end the fracas, arrange a *sulha* [reconciliation], and get the plant back into working order, with both supervisors working, he could not ignore the fact that Suha was from one of the most respected families in the village, whereas Johara came from another village altogether. Suha's father and brother spoke with the village elders, and consequently a delegation arrived at the plant and bluntly presented to the manager an ultimatum: either fire Johara and her sister or all the women from the village will leave the plant.

Jacob had no choice. He insisted, however, on handling the matter in his own way. First, he suspended both supervisors and Feize from work for two weeks. After this cooling-down period, Jacob decided that Suha would come back to work and Johara and Feize would be transferred to another plant of the concern.

Suha says, "When I came back to the plant I told Jacob that he hadn't behaved properly. She should have been kicked out of the concern altogether. She was always opening her mouth at me because she was jealous, and no matter how much I felt sorry for her, she always crossed me. She thought that she was better than me. That she deserved the same as me. I was a supervisor in the plant when she still worked for me as a seamstress. I'm stronger and smarter than she is. If you put her and a snake in the same pit, the snake will run away."

The aftermath of this conflict[12] became one of the myths of the sewing plants. The plant underwent many changes. The structure of the departments changed as a result of changes in product lines, causing the breaking of large departments into smaller ones. With time, Johara's and Suha's seamstresses were dispersed among the new smaller departments. Many got married and left. From the original labor force in the plant who were a part of the conflict, only a few dozen remained. The story continues to circulate, however, in the plant. Seamstresses and supervisors still identify themselves with either Suha's or Johara's party, even new seamstresses who did not work at the plant at the time of the quarrel. Apparently Suha and Johara represent diverging work philosophies. Suha's approach represents a more considerate and consensual management style that prioritizes the benefit of the plant as a whole. Her party consists mainly of village women. Johara's tradition, still proudly represented by a few supervisors, entails uncompromised departmental coherence. They are territorial about their departments and guard their boundaries carefully.[13]

The conflicts between supervisors are multilayered. Regardless of where conflicts begin, they tend to accumulate additional issues related to style of work, personal matters, and familial or community matters. These conflicts create camps in the plant. When friends or relatives belong to different camps, tensions may arise, and efforts at a *sulha* are made. The workers realize that conflict is never distinct, but wide and multidimensional.

Conclusion

Supervisors are in a unique position in the sewing plants. They rise from the rank and file of the shop floor to being in charge of a department. The primary attribute of their work is full responsibility for their department in organizing its production and managing the seamstresses. They play the role of mediator between the managers and the workers, particularly in crisis situations. They serve both sides as cultural interpreter. They advocate for the workers' demands before the management and, in turn, translate the management's point of view into a language comprehensible to the workers.

The affinity of the supervisors to the cultural traditions of the workers and their ability to adapt them to the demands of work in the plant enable them to translate the meanings and recast content into the social relations of production. The supervisors see themselves as gatekeepers and mediators, the ones capable of preserving and interpreting managerial and local sets of cultural values and bridging between them. In their mediating role, supervisors find themselves in a self-contradictory position. Although they are expected to be loyal to the management, they still feel responsibility toward the seamstresses they manage. They have to solve this inherent dissonance by recognizing this conflict and sometimes bearing its consequences.

The work enlarges the supervisors' personal and professional horizons and contributes to their sense of independence. They believe that they have greater control over their own lives. Being a manager at work develops a sense of self-importance and expresses itself in their relative independence from their families and increased power within them.

CHAPTER 7

The Managers: Embodying a Double System

And in examining their life and deeds it will be seen that
they owed nothing to fortune but the opportunity which
gave them matter to be shaped into what form they
thought fit; and without that opportunity their powers
would have been wasted, and without their powers the
opportunity would have come in vain.

— MACHIAVELLI
The Prince

MOST OF the managers and production managers in the sewing
plants are in their early thirties and do not have formal education
in textiles.[1] They are required, however, to have some training in
industrial engineering and management or in associated fields.
When they are accepted to their jobs, they undergo interorganiza-
tional training, spending a few weeks with significant units such
as the cloth plants, product development, cutting, production planning, and storehouses. After this training period, they are assigned
to a sewing plant as a junior production manager and do the rest of
their learning on the job, coached by the managers. They are chosen primarily on the basis of an estimation of their potential managerial and leadership skills. One of the important criteria for selection is command experience as officers in the Israeli army. The
managers are usually recruited from outside the concern, although
occasionally junior industrial engineers working in development
and production planning in the division headquarters request to be

transferred to production in the sewing plants. Career opportunities in production are relatively limited. Usually one has to work as a production manager for three to five years before becoming a plant manager. Managers are male and the majority are Jewish, although there are a number of Druse and Muslims among them.

The managers of the plants see themselves as unique among managers in the textile industry. Professionally, they are no different from other managers of labor-intensive factories. They operate, however, in a different cultural environment than other labor-intensive factories in the Jewish sector. The needs of the family and the community must be taken into account in managerial considerations. Management is not restricted to the four walls of the plant but extends into the homes of the workers, either through visits made by the managers after regular work hours or through the fathers and brothers who visit the plant.

The most common management model integrates the local values of the family into an instrumental management policy, imitating the familial environment, including its kinship hierarchy, to coincide with work in the plant (Leiter, Schulman, and Zingraff 1992; Moghadam 1993).[2] Managers structure their relationships with the seamstresses and the supervisors and the normative behavior in the plant in accordance with their perception of the male-female relationship in Arab society. This relationship is marked by male domination, gender-based division of labor, and familial values of accountability and solidarity. This chapter reveals the strategy of the managers, the patterns of their interactions with the supervisors and seamstresses, and their managerial style and methods as they participate in shaping the work culture of the plant.

Worldview Transformed into Strategy

The managers of the sewing plants plan their work, first and foremost, in accordance with the aims of the concern. The concern dictates production goals and quality levels, supply schedules, control, and accounting. It is the concern that decides the type of merchandise to be produced and wage policy. Nonetheless, the managers determine the type of managerial system most suited to the specific circumstances in which they work. Although there are, of course, differences in style among the various managers, the principles of the management system are more or less the same in all of the plants. On the declarative level, the managers stress both their commitment to the production goals and working in an environment of mutual respect, trust, and cooperation.[3] This strategy, although generally proved as an effective and fair management system, lends itself to manipulation, control, and subjugation of the workforce.

The role of the managers is integrative and entails multifaceted responsibilities. Because of the particular labor force in the Galilee sewing plants, the manager has to construct a managerial system that takes into account the production process in addition to the worldview of the Arab seamstresses.

David, a production manager, says, "You have to give the women a good feeling, the feeling that they matter to you. The main difficulty with the Arab workers is that they don't come to work only in order to make money. So you have to look for what it is that motivates them. Here the women come to work also to be with their friends. Remuneration alone is not the whole story. First of all, the seamstresses give most of their earnings to their fathers. Of the 1000 NIS they make, they are left with maybe 200 NIS. The fathers also decide when the women will come to work and when they will stay away for long periods. The olive harvest takes a month. If there is a wedding in the family, they'll take two weeks off in order to help in the preparations. Apart from that, the Arab woman helps out with household chores, which means that she is tired at work. Her dependence on the family is a very influential factor. It's enough for anyone in the family to fall ill for the woman to stay at home and take her mother's place. The home has first priority. Work comes second."

The intrusion of the domestic domain into the world of work is characterized by an attempt at isomorphism by which the management adapts familial patterns, including structure, values, norms, and worldview, to the sphere of work. Ongoing events in the plant, work procedures, issues of discipline, and interpersonal relationships are all explained and interpreted by the managers and the workers within the context of local meanings. For the managers, it is the best strategy for control and assurance of creating the conditions for smooth production.

The managers try to adapt normative behavior at home into the behavioral requirements of the shop floor. The managers identify those attributes in the social relations and family organization that have a direct bearing on the work process. The creation of shared meaning from the adaptation of local behavior and norms means that the managers and the workers must comply with their ideal manifestations. Thus, for example, the manager should respect his workers and show kindness and tolerance toward them. If the manager loses his temper and shouts, he apparently breaks the code of the shared meaning. This creates a conflict and a process of negotiation whereby the content of the shared meaning is modified, either in favor of the manager or in favor of the worker. Thus, the manager who shouts can apologize if he is convinced that he is wrong, or the seamstresses can accept his aberrant behavior.

This conflict and negotiation is a process of redefinition of relationships on the shop floor. Through this mechanism, values are transformed and shaped into the domain of work.

David continues, "You've got to understand the mentality of the people here and it's not that easy. If you don't understand the way they think, if you don't understand their customs, then you're in trouble. For example, there are some things that have an entirely different significance for them than they have for us. If you tell one of the women that she is being insolent, it's a dirty word, and chances are she won't show up for work again. You have to remember never to touch them and you can't even shake hands with a religious Druse woman. But you have to demonstrate your authority. You have to stand up for whatever managerial decisions you make and not let them think that you are someone who compromises. You have to let them feel like they are still at home. At home and here, the man has the last word. But you have to be flexible. For example, one of the Druse women wanted a day off to attend her brother's induction ceremony into the army. I told her it was all right but that she would have to work overtime on some other occasion."

The managers promote the ideology of workers and managers as a single family. In their managerial strategy, there is no differentiation between the workers' private and work lives. They perceive each one as the extension of the other, representing the same social realms. While working in the plant, I continuously had the impression that I was not the only anthropologist on the shop floor. I was occasionally astonished at how managers applied tactics and behavior similar to an anthropologist conducting field research, in spite of their different objectives.

By their apparent understanding of the workers' worldview and adapting to the local values and norms, the managers achieve a certain degree of flexibility in their daily management. It grants them greater maneuverability in expressing control and exercising unequal power relations in the plant, because they can implement patriarchal relationships. The essence of this managerial strategy maintains asymmetrical hierarchical relationships in terms of work and in terms of the social hierarchy. These dual dimensions are the key strategies for manipulating the workers on the shop floor. The reconstruction of patriarchal relationships creates a strong organizational culture as a means of normative control, which complements formal and remunerative forms of control.

Fostering Commitment and Cooperation

The managers endorse values of respect for seniority and compliance. The managers harness and manipulate these values and embed them in the seamstresses' personal commitment to production goals. This personal commitment expresses itself in various aspects—identification with the workplace, dedication to the work itself, and a sense of belonging to a distinct social group.[4]

The managers foster commitment through the workers' moral involvement, which is "based on internalization of norms and identification with authority" (Etzioni 1961, p. 10–11). By presenting the production needs and management concerns as part of the seamstresses' motivation, the managers are able to mobilize for both continuous progress in production level and special efforts in times of pressure. Managers attempt to cultivate mutual loyalty and fairness and draw on these to legitimate their demand for high performance levels and a willingness to mobilize in times of urgent needs by working extra hours.[5]

Ofer, the production manager of the Nazareth plant, remarks, "You have to motivate the seamstresses. If I have an urgent order, I raise the problem with them about how much we have to sew and what it means in terms of overtime. They know my record—I show loyalty, and they show loyalty. We show loyalty to each other. This is what leads to commitment. Your attitude toward the seamstresses is what makes all the difference. When I was just starting, I wasn't aware of this. I came from the army, where I was used to giving orders. Aside from that, I was convinced that one workplace was just like another. You work for your salary and everyone does his or her job. But I soon learned that what really counted here was your personal relationship to them, showing them consideration, showing them you cared about them. There was a woman here whose brother was in a road accident. The next day I told her that I had arranged for one of the company cars to take her and her parents to the hospital to visit her brother. Believe me, she didn't stop crying and her production went up by 10 percent. Naturally, everybody in the department and in the plant and in the community heard about it—that gave me lots of points."

These claims of mutual give and take and apparent reciprocity are part of a calculated strategy. They manifest the blunt usage of the personal sphere to promote production goals. The management's espoused values emphasize the importance of interpersonal relationships and the need to create a situation of personal dependence and commitment that borders on emotional blackmail. Consideration of personal problems is more than a gesture of goodwill. It is a managerial tactic for obtaining commitment to work.

Exploiting internal family hierarchical relationships, particularly the roles of the father and brother, helps promote managerial values emphasizing working in harmony, mutual assistance, mutual responsibility, and teamwork. This ideology reflects the organizational and functional reality prevailing in the sewing plants in all aspects of the relationship between managers and seamstresses. It is reflected in the way in which the managers imbue the women with the central values of the work culture and manipulate these values for their own needs. The managers knowingly use the principles of cooperation and involvement, translating them into the language and grammar of the workers. This provides assurance that an atmosphere of mutual responsibility and commitment prevails, its aim being, ultimately, to reach high standards of production and quality.

Zohar, the manager of Beit Jann, expresses himself: "In all matters relating to cooperation in the plant, it is the manager who is at the helm, directing the work and making sure that everyone is working together. The seamstresses here are professional, but if there is no one leading the team and giving them the feeling that 'we're all in this together,' the plant will suffer and there will be a decline in output and quality. Underlying the principle of teamwork is the philosophy that we are all committed and all have a common goal, and it is important for all of us to identify with the goal and with the company."

The managers correlate commitment with cooperation and mutual aid. This linkage expresses the familial values of cohesion and teamwork. By promoting these values, the managers curb possible interruptions of the flow of the production process. Any disruption causes delays and consequent losses in production level. Emphasis on cooperation and mutual aid allows for production flexibility. This flexibility manifests itself in the ability to open production bottlenecks through the mobilization of workers and concerted efforts. The managers give utmost importance to cooperation between departments in the form of helping with either the work itself or with the labor.

Sabi, the manager of the Nazareth plant, comments on the issue. "I speak to the seamstresses and the supervisors all the time, trying to get across the idea of cooperation, because inconsiderateness shows its ugly head in so many ways. I'll give you an example. When a quality controller is not interested in helping the seamstress improve her work but just gloats over her mistakes—that's inconsiderateness. Or when a supervisor and a machinist quarrel over something and then blame it on the seamstress, who has no idea what they are talking about, that's also inconsiderateness. Or when two supervisors compete among themselves over machines or seamstresses—that's non-cooperation. I keep stressing how important it is for everyone to be an example in his or her personal relations in order to promote cooperation and mutual assistance. I asked all the supervisors to prepare a joint program for improving the quality of needlework in the plant. I emphasized the importance of teamwork in solving problems. It's important for me that the supervisors and the seamstresses realize that they also have an influence on the character of the plant. They think that the plant is commitment to the manager, but I tell them that the way people look at me is the way they look at them, too—the way they look at *us*."

The values of cooperation and commitment are interdependent. Cooperation has concrete meaning on the shop floor as the mobilization of effort and time for a common purpose, mostly raising production levels. Cooperation has various dimensions within the department and between departments. It is a precondition for achieving the plant's goals. Cooperation and commitment can be on the individual level, as in working harder and extra hours, or on the departmental level, as when a department does the work of another. Both cases involve going beyond the call of duty. The two values of cooperation and commitment comply with the meanings of the plant and the Arab family.

Socialization of Supervisors

The managers see themselves and the supervisors as the bearers of the organization's values of cooperation, teamwork, and accountability. The manager is the guide and coach; his aim is to instill the values, work methods, and the priorities within the production process.

Even, the plant manager in Maghar, says, "I work closely with the supervisors and back them up. This doesn't mean that there isn't friction at times, particularly because of the demands I make. There are some things about which I won't compromise."

"Like what?" I ask.

"First of all, the attitude to the seamstresses. Sometimes the supervisors insult them by yelling at them or even, in extreme cases, cursing them. I refuse to let something like that pass; otherwise it would spread like wildfire."

Although the managers adhere to the principle of backing the supervisors, they preserve a unified concept of norms and behavior. The essence of creating shared meaning is in its uniformity, whereby behavioral codes oblige everyone at the plant. This uniformity is a barrier to conflict and minimizes renegotiation, which is a deviation from the ideal concept of the work culture as a familial culture.

"Together with the supervisors, I make sure that the sewing instructions are absolutely clear. I want the sewing to be 100 percent professional. I want them to be able to read the instructions on the kit and turn out a product the way it's supposed to be. Furthermore, I give the supervisors a lot of autonomy. Here the departments are highly crystallized. The supervisors and the seamstresses from their departments even meet together on holidays for a good time."

The managers usually try to create a process of socialization whereby the supervisors become the managers' extensions. This socialization process aims to create a sense of common goals and behavior and establish homogeneity in the management system.

"Here it is important to stress that 'together' implies responsibility. You find that the team at the plant shows a lot of concern for everybody and everything, but there is still a difference between showing concern and shouldering responsibility. There are those who just go about their own business, and there are others who try to keep the whole picture in focus. This means that the supervisor doesn't only entrench herself in the needs of her own department but has an overall view of the needs of the plant as a whole. When there are conflicts among the supervisors or between the supervisors and the managers, the whole plant suffers. When I first came here, I did a lot of 'softening up' in order to diminish those intramural conflicts. The team began to understand that what I wanted was full cooperation, including both give and take. The more crystallized the team, the better the plant operates."

Empowerment of the supervisor is considered a key management value because of the intricate integration between the work process and discipline and the necessity of considering the normative behavior and values of the seamstresses. This socialization combines the basic behavioral vocabulary of industrial production, including obligation, subordination, and norms about absenteeism and tardiness. Socialization is an ongoing process. It is embedded into the various organizational and production procedures. The managers heavily emphasize firmly establishing it in recruiting and training newcomers.[6]

Even continues, "The first thing I look for among the supervisors is a high level of commitment to work, a real concern for what is going on around them and not just an eye for their own work. Of course, I also want a high level of leadership skills. Flexibility is also important. A good supervisor has to be capable of performing a number of different functions. She must also have the ability to learn. Bad management of the seamstresses can close down a plant. But I also teach the supervisors to smooth out the rough spots."

"What does that mean?" I inquire.

"It means giving in some places in return for not giving in others. I'll give you an example. When a seamstress insists on going out in the middle of work in order to take care of some personal matters, the team has standing orders not to refuse automatically. You have to let her out sometimes in order to increase her sense of future commitment to the supervisor and to the department. There will always be overtime and special efforts and demands for a higher level of output. The team crystallizes work methods—how to introduce new items into the production line and how to produce the separate parts of each piece of merchandise. We have a lot of meetings on these subjects, with the machinists as well, so that we can create a common language and the supervisors can learn from one another. But the emphasis is always on improving efficiency and quality. One other important point in crystallizing the team is never to show favoritism. Never show a preference for one supervisor over another. That would be a time bomb, especially in a plant where the supervisors come from different religious and ethnic communities."

From the manager's point of view, the supervisors must combine professional and interpersonal skills that can alleviate tensions and conflicts and enable them to respond quickly to events on the shop floor. An important management value is demonstrating authority. The managers find it difficult to shape Arab women because of their inexperience in all matters relating to the world of work. In this area, the managers attribute to the supervisors an added value as insiders and mediators. The supervisors can both relate to the seamstresses and their families and exhibit authority in the familiar paternalistic manner.

"The supervisors are the manager's implementing arm, at his bid and command. Good supervisors exercise complete control over the seamstresses, have a good grasp of what is necessary on the production floor, and leave the manager enough time to deal with the division and other outside connections. I give the supervisors a free hand in dealing with the seamstresses. I intervene only rarely. The supervisor has to be *the* authority in the department. I don't interfere with her methods. I just want to see results. I don't go into the departments frequently because when I do, the supervisors seem to fade into the background and it turns into a kind of confrontation between me and the seamstresses. The advantage of my system is that the supervisor gets experience in a large variety of situations and has to find solutions for the problems that crop up. The ability of the supervisor to deal with the seamstresses by herself leaves me free to deal with other problems and to concentrate on getting results."

The process of socialization to the management system is aimed to alleviate the load of the manager and cushion him against matters he considers soft and culturally bound. The managers are managing in an unstable environment in which work values are reconstructed and reinterpreted. The basic rudiments of Arab and Druse culture, emphasizing fairness, solidarity, and togetherness (Halabi 1997), are constantly manipulated by both the managers and the workers, and the managers need the supervisors as close allies in this process.

Male Managers, Female Workers: A Managerial Style

Relations between the manager and the workers extend over a long continuum. At one end is the system of hierarchy. In this system, the manager is the highest professional authority, putting the final stamp of approval on professional issues. At the other end of the continuum are the interpersonal relations. The manager is involved in numerous aspects of the seamstress's private life and in her relations with and within her family. Life after work hours is intricately connected with the world of work. The managers themselves see their involvement in the women's' private lives as part of their job, ensuring the effective and loyal cooperation of the women at work. Helping them solve personal problems can minimize damage to the smooth running of the plant. This is particularly true in cases of financial distress in the family, and the management has established a number of mechanisms for dealing with such contingencies. The plant has a fund for providing loans on exceptionally easy terms and helps finance hired laborers to work in place of the women during the olive harvest.

The managers often advise the women about problems within the family, lend them support, and sometimes mediate between them and their families. The meaning of confidence expresses itself in an intimate relationship between the managers and the workers and increases the dependence of the workers on the managers, often obscuring the boundaries between their work world and their private world.

The managers' claim of the Arab male role legitimates their interference with the workers' affairs both in the plant and outside. The managers appropriate patriarchal relations in the private sphere and transfer them to the domain of work. The ramifications of such interference can be crucial to the workers and require the manager to exercise utmost sensitivity. He must behave within and internalize the framework of the Arab values and norms. As an outsider, he must exhibit respect and understanding of the complex interrelationship between the worker and her family, the importance of the father to the family, and the constraints of both the father and his daughter with regard to latent and manifest behavior. When assuming the role of the father, the manager must identify the boundaries of how far he can practice paternalism without undermining the father's authority and the women's restrictive code of behavior. Managers playing the role of patriarch, therefore, risk being trespassers, as illustrated by the next story.

Firuz, a quality controller, developed an intimate friendship with Yussuf, who works as a production planner in the cutting department. It began innocently—in the capacity of her job she consulted Yussuf about quality issues. From there things moved rapidly. Firuz and Yussuf fell in love and decided to marry. They were afraid, however, that if Firuz announced their intentions to her father as a matter of fact, he would be outraged because of Firuz's having a secret affair. He might forbid the wedding and accuse Firuz of hurting the family's honor. The consequence of this accusation can be extremely grave.[7] Firuz decided to consult the manager.

"Firuz came and asked me about the guy. Innocently. But I already realized what was going on, even though I didn't know the details. I told her that Yussuf is an *Al Ha'kefak* [swell] guy. He comes from a good family; his sisters are teachers. He is enlightened, not ancient [traditional]." After she heard the manager's positive opinion of Yussuf, Firuz went straight to the point and asked the manager to speak with her father.

"She asked me to speak about the matter to her father, to convince him to approve the relationship and meet Yussuf's family. I was in a dilemma—this had never happened to me before. All I needed was for people to know that there are affairs in my factory. How many women do you think will show up for work the day after such news breaks out? First I wanted to make sure the story between them was serious. I started creating situations that allowed them to be together, like in the joint trip of the sewing plant and the cutting room, I seated Firuz's department next to the cutting department. They had lunch together. . . . There were a few other small chances for them to talk.

"Since I saw that they are serious, I decided I'll talk to the father."

We come to Firuz's family house. The manager approaches Ali, Firuz's father, in the most direct way possible and says, "I came to talk to you about your daughter."

At first Ali thinks the manager had come to complain about Firuz in matters of work. He immediately replies, "What did she do? Did she do something wrong at work? Just tell me and I'll take care of it."

The manager lets him finish his sentence and says, "God forbid. You know that Firuz is one of my best workers. I care about her and her work."

Ali replies, "I know you, you're OK. You're like my son. . . . "

The manager interrupts him and says, "You're right. I care about your daughter's life and future, and if you see me like your son, I see her like my sister." In the same breath he adds, "In fact, I want to introduce her to someone. With your permission, of course, they should not meet without that."

Ali is shocked. The manager continues, "He's an educated guy from a good family."

Ali asks, "Where do you know him from?"

The manager says, "He's the only single man who works in the plant. All the rest are married. He's a really good worker. I send him to courses and training. He's very motivated. He has a good heart, he's a family man. I am interfering because I think that they are well suited. Firuz is also educated and has a good heart. It's important to me that it works because it would do good for them and for me as well. Just as your daughter helped me in tough times at work, I feel like I owe her something back. And a groom is a gift for life." The manager continues as if the whole thing had been decided upon. "I'll take them to the Acre Beach for their engagement pictures.[8] I also suggest that you meet his family. We can all meet at a restaurant. You pick the place— Italian, Middle Eastern, Chinese—it's on me."

There is a short silence. I look at Ali's tense face as he digests the manager's speech. The manager, on the other hand, is cool. He says, "Firuz doesn't know about this. No one does. They all work in the same factory, and they know each other in their work capacity. He gives her technical solutions, and she succeeds because of him."

Ali comes to his senses and says, "Fifty-five years I have been working with Jews, and I have never seen someone like you. You give me your word of honor. Don't tell her about this conversation. If she has enough blood in her veins, she will speak to me and then I'll talk to you."

Two weeks after the incident, Firuz leaves work. Her father, insulted by the manager assuming his role, decides to not approve the marriage. To ensure that the relationship not develop without his permission, he forces his daughter to quit. The manager sadly comments, "I only meant well. They look at me as a father in this plant. Maybe I took it too seriously."

One notable component of the system of manager-worker relations is the use and abuse made by the managers of the model of male-female relationships prevalent in the woman's family. The manager's aim is to establish a direct relationship, insofar as it is possible, in which the woman will love, honor, and respect him; work for him unconditionally; and maintain industrial harmony in the plant. Creating this bond on a personal level has instrumental significance. The managers use their power in the plant to create virtual intimate relationships with their workers. Furthermore, they use deception by taking advantage of these interpersonal relationships as a mechanism for control and achieving production goals.

In a system wherein a limited number of men manage a large number of women, the male-female factor is highly conspicuous.[9] The women evaluate the managers not only by their managerial abilities but also by their personalities and their masculinity. From their perspective, a manager who treats the women respectfully and is attentive to their problems and fair in his judgments represents the accepted normative behavior of men. The managers' exhibits of attention, however, go beyond the formal normative behavior at work. These shows of affection are mainly instrumental, the result of calculated behavior aimed at generating motivation to work.

One of the managers, Ilan, describes the male-female element of his managerial strategy as follows: "To tell you the truth, my own approach is, I think, unique. My basic premise is that the women are motivated by a certain sexual tension. I have 170 seamstresses under me, most of them young, unmarried women, and I am well aware of how they look at me. By generating a sort of undercurrent of sexual tension, I ultimately get what I want—a commitment to work."

I ask Ilan what he meant by that and how, exactly, he goes about it, considering all the taboos prevalent in Arab society.

"I maintain professional relations with the women in an atmosphere of intimacy. When I have something to say to one of them, I will address her personally, especially if I want immediate results. I will look her straight in the eye, maybe put my hand on her shoulder, but I will never violate their moral code."

"Is touching a woman's shoulder permissible?" I ask.

"It is. Don't forget, I'm her older brother, I'm the manager. But I don't go any further than that. It begins and ends with giving her my undivided attention."

"And how does she respond?"

"The woman responds immediately and is usually ready to meet your demands for overtime or greater productivity. I pay great attention to them and never overlook a new outfit or a new hairdo. I personally ask them how they are and frequently arrange for personal interviews with them to show that I care. If you can succeed in maintaining this kind of tension over a long period of time, the women will respond in kind for just as long."

The managers create sexual tension to foster a sense of obligation to them and consequently to the work. There is a kind of code that develops between the manager and the seamstress. You take an interest in her, you are her patron. The sexual element is implicit in the words she uses: "I respect you, you are like my brother, you're my eyes," and so on. For the managers, it is important not to show favorites.

"That's why I usually pay attention to those with a forlorn look about them. They are usually the older, unmarried women, who are not particularly attractive. They develop a kind of dependency on me, and with them the system gives the best results. A good-looking woman knows her own worth and has a developed ego. But an indifferent looking woman who is eminently capable needs a little help in building her ego. She'll never disappoint you. Because of this, the ugly women are all my best friends. None of them ever let me down. There have been almost impossible situations in which the department was down on me and yet 'my women' succeeded in convincing all the others to stay and work overtime—even till ten at night. And ultimately, they're the ones who become dominant in the department and set the tone. All the other women know that they have a special relation with the manager that can be of use to them as well. I play their game and I help the other women, but I never fail to mention that I do it because of 'my women.' In short, I create a dominant group on the line through personal relations with them, and they get my ideas across to the others. In return for their help, I give them a good feeling, a lot of respect and almost whatever else they want."

This crude manipulation of women who normally are not allowed to interact with male nonfamily members is a well-known game in the plant, which in a few cases verges on sexual harassment (Terpstra and Baker 1991).[10] The managers attempt, however, to control the amount of personal affection because it can easily become a double-edged sword. In many cases, the manipulation is reversed and the manager finds himself manipulated by the woman who is the object of his personal attention. A manager who brings himself to this position cannot refuse the woman's requests, even if they are unreasonable (such as unjustified absenteeism and long breaks). Seamstresses who receive this kind of attention desire visible gestures of affection (such as casual conversation in the workstation), impairing the credibility of the manager in the eyes of the other seamstresses and contradicting the perception of impartiality. Furthermore, excessive attention to a particular group of women can harm cohesion and interpersonal harmony in the departments and sometimes undermine the supervisor's authority.

The possibility of sexual ties between a manager and his employees springs from the fact that the male-female situation in the plants does contain the potential for the breakdown of moral codes. In order for such a relationship to develop, the manager must take a risk and exercise his power directly on the women. These situations are problematic for interrelationships at work because they lead to manipulations and conflicts that create tension at the plant, as the following story illustrates.

After the ring of the bell signaling the end of break, Janette, a supervisor, continues to drink coffee and smoke for a few minutes. It has been her habit for quite a while. She sits in the production manager's office, which overlooks the production floor, and leisurely smokes and smiles at her department, enjoying this blunt manifestation of autonomy. Rami, the manager, and Yossi, his production manager, are sitting in the main office in embarrassment, but they do not dare say anything to Janette.

Eventually Rami says, "I'm fed up with her; it's been like this for two weeks. What does she think, that just because we are fond of her we will let her keep making fools of us in front of the whole sewing plant?"

He gets up and goes to the production manager's room. For a few minutes shouts can be heard, and then Janette goes back to her department. Later, I speak with Janette about the matter.

She says, "Rami shouldn't make himself all holy and protecting the honor of the women. Suddenly he's a hero and shouting at me. I know him—all men are alike. He leaves me extra hours and then takes me back to the village in his car. That's how it is with managers. The manager before Rami also spoiled me and got me presents and gave me things at work. Once I asked him what does he want that he treats me so nice. He said that he loved me and that was it, and he didn't want anything. He just kept telling me how sexy I looked, what great perfume I was wearing, and things like that. I don't have a problem going with someone I like. I told Rami that when we sat after work in a coffee shop on the Sea of Galilee."

I look at her with surprise. Although I know that Janette is fairly independent because she has limited family control (her father died, her married brother left the village, and she lives with her old mother),

I had not realized that the gossip in the plant regarding her relationship with the manager is true. Stories of intimate relationships between managers and supervisors circulate rarely and are regarded as an off-shoot of the intimacy between managers and workers.

Janette continues, "We went to this coffee shop so we could talk. The manager told me he was under pressure, and he wanted me to help him at work. But I don't believe men—they only want one thing. To use the girl and then throw her. At first they are willing to do everything and spoil you, but they only have one thing in their head. After that they don't respect you. I don't believe them. They always blame the woman and say that I am lying. Who do you think they'll believe, me or the manager? Then I'll have *fadichot* [embarrassments] in the village and my brother will come and beat me." She thinks for a while and adds, "I think that tomorrow I will not put on makeup, I'll wear clothes like the religious ones, and I won't do my hair at all."

Janette's story exemplifies a rather rare incident of crossing boundaries. It accentuates the weak position of women in the plant and the potential for exploitation. I am not referring to forced exploitation, but to a dependency derived from unequal power relations. Breaking the normative codes of behavior toward the workers is a risky enterprise. Crossing the line is threatening, not to the managers personally, but to the plant in terms of its legitimacy in the community. Pseudointimate relationships are mainly expressed through gestures of affection, attention, and respect. When the managers attempt to capitalize on this relationship as a managerial strategy, it becomes transparent to the other workers and eventually presents a problem because individual relationships counter the advocated work values of togetherness, fairness, and equality. The treatment of sexuality in the plants is embedded in the cultural norms of the host communities. For example, in the case of Trinidad textile plants (Yelvington 1996), male-female relationships also adhere to local norms of acceptability that, unlike the Galilee case, involve an open and flirtatious discourse of male-female sexuality. Although the cases are on extreme opposite poles of a continuum—sexual segregation in

Galilee as opposed to openness in male-female relationships in the
Caribbean—in both cases the sexual undercurrent serves as a managerial technique for control.

Perspectives of the Seamstresses

The managers of the sewing plants view the work values of
their workers in instrumental terms. For the managers, the personality and characteristics of the workers are relevant in terms of
their capacity to work well. An ideal worker is young, unmarried,
comes from a remote village, and is religious. In recruiting new
workers, the manager does not ask questions about the newcomer's expectations of work or take an interest in her as an individual. He tries to map her background in order to assess her fit-
ness and likelihood to endure at work. For example, he asks
whether she is engaged to be married, how many siblings she has,
whether the father works, whether she has finished school, and so
on. These questions paint a picture that allow the managers to
gauge the worker's potential. The ideal worker, one likely to produce highly, is about seventeen or eighteen, will marry at age
twenty-two, and will work for about four years to save up for her
wedding. This "shopping list" presents the managers' superficial
and stereotyped approach to their workers.

Sammy, one of the managers, explains, "The Arab women are really
great. The profile of the women working in the textile industry is as
follows: they are young, they have good human qualities, they are
well-coordinated and so can operate the machines. They are quick to
catch on and can switch from one product to another without any difficulty. They are obedient and have a work ethic. You can give them
orders and they will follow them unstintingly. They are not rebellious
and are impervious to change. The major challenge in management,
however, is the women themselves. You have to be very careful because one wrong word, uttered in a moment of anger, can be cata-

strophic for production. One woman will get up and go home and all the others will be demoralized. You have to watch your tongue. You have to appear to them as a highly respected man who always keeps his word."

The fact that the managers must be considerate of the women and the culture they represent—taking great care never to humiliate them or hurt their feelings—generates rules of behavior at work. These rules of the game provide definitions and meaning for behavior on the shop floor and within the social realm of the plant. Their breach leads to a crisis situation in the plant that adversely affects work relations and the work itself.

Disgracing a seamstress in public by shouting at her or scolding her is considered insulting. In both Druse and Arab societies, speaking nicely in public is a value related to loyalty and integrity (Halabi 1997). Managers sometimes lose control and use insults to shake up a seamstress who has strayed off course, mainly regarding meeting production quotas. These incidents create considerable tension in the plant and can incite open hostility toward the manager. The next example illustrates the meaning that the seamstresses attribute to such displays.

"Shut up and work!" shouts one of the production managers at a seamstress who is talking while she works. Immediately there is discomfort on the floor. Most of the women become morose, as if the insult were directed at them all. Finally, one of them can no longer contain her feelings and says to the production manager:

"How can you talk to her like that? Doesn't she have parents? Isn't she a decent person? All she did was ask her friend for a package of material. You guys, you're not human. We're working nine hours at the machine. We don't eat and we don't drink, and you don't even let us breathe."

As already noted, the rules of the game must be scrupulously observed. Respect for the women and exhibiting sensitivity to their feelings, along with restraint in chastising them in public, are not values in themselves but essential features of the work culture and the principles of management. If they are disregarded, communication between managers and seamstresses would break down and mutual trust cease to exist. The manager would lose respect in the eyes of the seamstresses, and his professional abilities, leadership qualities, and authority would be called into question. In short, the very foundations of work at the plant would founder.

Misbehavior at the plant is seen by the management in terms borrowed from the world of the Arab family. This applies to the definition of rights and obligations at work, as, for example, with the issue of absenteeism.

At a meeting with the women in the dining room, in the wake of a steep increase in absenteeism due to illness, Oded, the manager of the plant, raises the issue.

"Absenteeism hurts the plant. Last month we had 17 percent absenteeism. We lost a lot of production. We all realize this. A woman who stays home hurts herself and her good name as well as hurting the plant and our obligations to our customers. If there is a lot of absenteeism, we simply can't fulfill our quotas on time. The woman also hurts her friends who have to stay on and work overtime because of her. Of course there are good reasons for staying home. Being really sick is one of them. But to pretend to be sick and to bring a note for a day or two's absence—I can't agree to that. Some of the women who stayed home without a good reason said they were sorry and signed a paper saying they wouldn't do it again. Anyone who is tired, we can talk about it. You all know that Afifa wasn't feeling well and wanted to rest a little. She came to see me and not only did I give her a couple of days off, but I myself drove her home." Samira, one of the supervisors, began to applaud, and the other women joined in.

The managers integrate two sets of values—work and family—whereby the content of each must be translated into a common understanding and shared meaning. Ultimately, these two sets reflect power inequalities, hierarchy, and normative control. The content of values such as respect, reciprocity, consideration of individual needs, and personal attention have a double implication. First, on the personal level, the manager's perspective on the workers is that they must be treated kindly, reflecting the seamstresses' perception of good behavior. Second, these values are also adapted into the domain of work, becoming a system of normative control and an underlying common management system.

Labor Relations

The sewing plants' location in the midst of the Arab community provides a steady flow of labor, but also exposes them to local political forces. The sewing plants are vulnerable to political manipulation. Although they are economically important to the community, they have their own Achilles' heel that ensues from their position as a capitalist enterprise identified with Jewish economic domination. Furthermore, the vulnerability of the workers and their dependence on the plant are also sources of discontent.

The next incident is an example of the intermingling of local politics and work, disguised as a labor relations dispute. It is an attempt to manipulate the managers and the seamstresses for gaining political capital at the expense of the plant. This political gain portrays the plant as unreliable and uncaring and accuses it of bluntly breaching workers' rights. The incident began with a letter to the concern manager signed by 90 of the 180 workers in the plant.

Dear Sir,

We, the undersigned, work in a sewing plant owned by you. We are writing you in order to bring to your attention the terrible working conditions we face. In our plant work 180

workers, most with seniority of over five years. We work in
terrible conditions and feel that we are being taken advantage
of. We are made to work many overtime hours as well as
Fridays, in spite of the fact that our working day is already nine
hours long. Our production quotas are high compared to the
rest of the industry and we work rapidly. Still we have high
motivation and work ethic.

Sir, what we get in return is not what we deserve. We do
not receive the legal minimum wage, but much less, and we are
not appropriately compensated for our overtime. We are forced
to work on holidays, sometimes without adequate pay. We do
not receive decent uniforms. What we get are reprimands and
threats.

Sir, we are still human, and we cannot accept this
situation. We demand action to repair this damage without
delay.

> *Names and Signatures*
> *cc: Minister of Labor and Social Affairs*
> *The manager of the plant*
> *General secretary of the 'Histadrut' [General Labor Union]*

The letter paints a picture of the plant as violating the law and
basic principles of labor relations. Furthermore, it accuses the
plant of breaching the principle of fairness. The letter presents a
contrast. On one side are the workers, who have high morale and
motivation. On the other side is the plant, which is violating the
law by not paying them minimum wage or overtime and holiday
rates. The plant also offends the honor of the workers by not giving them decent clothing, only reprimands and threats.

The trigger for the incident was a meeting with the representative of the DFP, the Democratic Front for Peace and Equality
(the former Communist party), in one of the seamstresses' houses
in order to gain support for the DFP in the General Labor Union's
upcoming elections.[11] A second meeting was scheduled, to which
the DFP representative did not arrive. In his absence, Ribchi, who
is known in the village for his militant spirit and political aspira-
tions, led the meeting. Ribchi's two sisters work in the plant, as

did his wife before giving birth. He assumed his authority based on his public position in the village as chairman of the Released Soldiers Organization.[12]

Ribchi encouraged the seamstresses in the meeting to fight for the improvement of their working conditions and persuaded them to give their consent to write the letter. His sisters collected signatures from the workers even before the letter was written. The ninety workers who signed had not read the letter and did not know its contents. The signatures were collected on a separate piece of paper and later attached to the letter.

In the aftermath of the incident, Ribchi told me that the letter was a spontaneous move. Being a husband of a former seamstress and a brother to two workers, he deeply felt the need to fight for their rights. He says:

"I am the true representative of the young Druse. I believe that Israeli society neglects and discriminates against the Druse. The plant represents Israeli society and it doesn't matter that it does good to the village. For me it is a symbol for exploitation, and that is why I fought against it." He adds, "I do not deny my political aspiration, and I hope this will not interfere with my candidacy for the security officer of the village."

The representative of the local branch of the *Histadrut*, the national labor union, was not aware of what was going on. When the letter came to light, he saw it as an outside intrusion in the affairs of the village. He wrote a letter to the general secretary of the *Histadrut*:

When I heard about the seamstresses' letter I spoke with the plant manager and demanded an immediate meeting with the workers' committee in the plant to clear up the matter. When I read it I was amazed and I knew it was a political matter. I talked to the workers and they told me they signed a blank piece of paper and did not know what it was all about. It turned out that it began right before the elections for the union, at a meeting arranged by a DFP member. I would like to bring to your attention his irresponsible behavior. Finally, I would like to mention that the sewing plant has always respected the collective agreement. The management cooperated with us on numerous occasions including our demands for severance payments for seamstresses who left and other issues.

The representative does not mention Ribchi. He tells me:

"I believe that we should wash our own dirty laundry." He begins aggressive advocacy for the plant, canvassing from house to house, speaking with families and community leaders. He tries to persuade them to ignore the incident and cool Ribchi's involvement with the plant.

The manager of the plant assesses the explosive potential of the affair and embarks on a series of steps aimed at damage control. He comments, "I was amazed at the letter and its distortion of the truth. When I talked to the workers, they made it clear that they are satisfied at work, except for the low pay. The letter was a warning signal—a red light. I knew that I had to deal with the incident and not ignore the letter; otherwise it would be admitting its accusations to the workers, their families, and the community. The damage from this letter affects the seamstresses and their willingness to excel, as well as the image of the plant in the community. A bad image in the community makes recruitment hard and increases voluntary turnover."

Initially, the manager gathers the workers' committee, a group of four seamstresses elected by their co-workers mainly for the purpose of organizing social events in the plant. Using the committee as representative of the "authentic" voice of the workers, the manager asks its members to speak with the seamstresses who had signed the letter. They find out that the seamstresses know nothing of the content of the letter and had not requested that Ribchi write it. They want the committee to clear the matter with the manager, but claim that the low salary bothers them, and they want the manager's help in the matter. The committee decides to write a letter to the manager of the concern, denying the accusations in the original letter and revealing the deception involved:

> *We, the undersigned, the workers' committee in the plant, upon learning of the affair and following an investigation, have found no ground to the claims specified in letter that hurt the good name of the plant. The seamstresses have been cheated by an outside force. They signed a blank piece of paper and did not know the content of the letter. Please consider the letter and its claims obsolete.*
>
> *With highest respect,*
> *The Workers' Committee*
> *cc: Minister of Labor and Social Affairs*
> *The manager of the plant*
> *General secretary of the 'Histadrut' [General Labor Union]*

When the dust settles, I ask the manager to comment on the incident. He says, "To sum up the matter, I decided to do two things. First, I rewarded the committee for their support and shortened overtime hours for a month. This was done with the agreement of the division manager. Second, I met with Ribchi after others had softened him up. He denied everything and said the letter was a misunderstanding, that he didn't even write it. We reached an agreement that Ribchi will be the public's representative at the plant, that he can come in any time to check on the working conditions himself. He has political aims and wants to appear concerned about the workers. I even supported him in his candidacy for the position of security officer, which he eventually got. He took back all the accusations in the letter except for the salary issue.

"What I learned from the incident is that what the other managers say is true. We are blade runners, we always depend on the *meshugas* [crazies] of the community. If you are not careful, they can finish you. It's important for the plant to maintain steady contact with the families and work to create trust. We have to establish reciprocity with the community. We contribute and help the village: we donate chairs and scraps of cloth to the preschools. But we expect in return that the community will be committed to the plant and its reputation and help the plant when necessary. The workers' families have to lobby for the plant in the community."

The managers are constantly in a position where they have to cater to and be receptive to the trends and ambiance of the community. Many of them spend a good part of their time strengthening their contacts with community leaders and being involved in community life.

Managers, Family, and Community

The relations between the managers of the plants and the families of the seamstresses—particularly fathers and brothers—are informal and personal. The family's involvement relates to matters pertaining both to the woman's behavior and the protection of her rights. In this respect, male members of the family see themselves as representatives of the community, authorized to make sure that the plant is behaving properly. Because of this, the plant has an open-door policy with regard to members of the family. Fathers and brothers may come to the manager's office with their complaints, questions, or requests and expect a fair hearing. The manager can also pass on, through male members of the family, his own requests of the woman with regard to absenteeism, discipline, output, and the quality of her work. In the context of the patriarchy of the family, expressed in its accountability for its members, if the woman behaves badly in some way, it reflects on the honor of the family as a whole (Kandiyoti 1988).

The managers' attempts to create a family-like climate in the plant do not mean that the plant performs the functions of the family. The usage of the family in the plant is metaphorical. It reflects an attempt to create relations of production in which the obligations of the workers and their work values replicate kinship bonds. The managers' attempt to present the plant as an ideal type of familial organization is a cover-up for employing effective control mechanisms based on authority, close supervision, loyalty, and discipline. The process is one of selective adaptation of acceptable social norms and transference to the domain of work.

The plants in the villages are dependent to some extent on the families of the workers. If relations between the manager and the village and family are good, then he can depend on having a stable workforce. An open line of communication with the fathers and brothers prevents the woman from leaving work unexpectedly. As noted, managing a plant entails, inter alia, ongoing negotiations between the manager and the male members of the seamstress's family. The managers attempt to establish a division of roles with the father, who intervenes when the daughter is not doing her work properly. The manager, in turn, is responsible for the safety and well-being of the daughter. These rules of the game give the family the right to interfere with the ongoing processes of the plant. The manager is aware of this price he must pay, as pointed out by Oren, the manager of Hurfeish.

"The fathers feel they have the right to come to the plant and make demands on the manager. They want the woman released for a day for all kinds of reasons, from helping out at home to fulfilling a vow to visit the grave of some holy man. You don't have an alternative if you want to maintain good relations with the parents and the community. I use the father or the brother if I have problems with the woman over discipline or chronic absenteeism. I invite him to the office and explain to him the problem and then warn the woman in his presence. The same when there are problems with her level of production. The father is ashamed of his daughter, and you can believe me, it has a very good effect on her."

"Doesn't the father feel offended?" I ask.

"Not at all. On the contrary. He wants to be involved. He feels responsible for what his daughter does, not only at home but in the plant as well. Also, don't forget that most of the money that the woman earns goes straight to the father, so he wants to get involved and make sure his daughter gets all the money she deserves."

Relations with the family add a significant burden to the job of the manager, especially when there are seemingly irreconcilable differences. Sometimes there are conflicts of interest between the managers and the fathers, when the fathers attempt to subdue the managers by invoking the power of the community. One of the managers, Dror, tells the next story.

"Amina wanted to stop work, but she also wanted to get severance pay.[13] So she started making all kinds of intentional slips. Her output declined. She didn't pay attention to quality, and she began to stay away from work more and more. I told her she could go—but she wasn't getting any severance pay. She wasn't prepared for this, and one day her father showed up. He was very nice at the beginning and tried to convince me just to give her severance pay and let it go at that. He also said it wasn't worth it for me to make a big deal out of it. It would be better for my reputation in the village if I gave in. I was against the idea in principle and thought that if I gave in to her my reputation in the village would suffer. So we played ping-pong for a while. He tried all sorts of things, some of them not so pleasant, such as convincing other families to withdraw their daughters from work and also influencing the mayor not to pave the road by the plant. But I still refused. One day he asked me what was his daughter doing that was so bad that I wasn't ready to give her severance pay. I told him that she was sabotaging the work and murdering the merchandise. He turned blue in the face and began to shout that what I was saying was nonsense, that you couldn't murder rags. I told him that maybe it was nonsense to him, but it was my living and I didn't intend to give her severance pay if she left. So he decided to try something else and began to spread a rumor in the village that Amina was getting married. Now, the law does not require that we give severance pay to a woman who is getting married, but it is our custom here to give it to them anyway. It's like a wedding present from us, a sign of our appreciation for the women who worked here. I had no intention of discontinuing the custom just because of her. Still, I wanted to find out if the story was really true. I asked around the village and discovered that it was a trumped-up story, so when the father called me I told him off in no uncertain terms. His reply to me was really heartwarming: he hoped that all the money I saved on her severance pay would go to pay my doctor bills!"

The managers are often in uncomfortable positions within the community. The manager's relations with the families are superimposed on his relations with the community. In a conflict with a family, the family often recruits other families to pressure the manager, stressing the plant's guest status in the village. The plant is continuously put to the test. A manager who stands firm can usually overcome this pressure because the plant tends to be an important source of income in the community.

Mutual relations between the plant and the families are multifaceted. The managers are expected to fulfill their part of the responsibility and in cases of mishap to deal with it appropriately and report to the family and community. Any unusual event implying a violation of behavioral norms that is connected somehow to the plant—even if it took place outside of working hours—will result in serious sanctions against the plant. The family will assume that the manager is not taking his personal responsibility for the women seriously. The most common sanction is, of course, to take the women out of the plant, because it is now considered the site of possible future difficulties. This is a very serious sanction because it damages the reputation of the plant and adversely affects the willingness of others in the community to let their daughters work there.

As for the family, cooperation with the managers provides them with a sense of involvement and influence in the plant's decision making; this element becomes part of the rules of the game. Maintaining these rules enables the parents to preserve their status as those who have a say in everything connected with their daughter's work.

A manager considered trustworthy by the families and sensitive to their problems enjoys full cooperation. This trust is reflected in the ease with which new members of the extended family are recruited for work. The plants usually suffer from a labor shortage because of the relatively high turnover, and a manager who enjoys the families' trust benefits in this respect.

The intensity of family involvement in the plant depends to a large extent on the location of the plant. If the plant is situated in a city (such as Nazareth) or in an industrial area (such as Kfar

Tavor), both somewhat distant from the women's homes, involvement is low key. But if the plant is situated within the confines of the village, access is a simple matter and family involvement is much greater. In these situations, formal relations develop with the community as well. The plant participates in community projects such as providing uniforms for the local soccer team or donating equipment and materials to the local school or kindergarten.

The managers try to maintain good relations with the heads of local councils, representatives of the local trade unions, and important community and religious notables. During visits to their employees or to the village elders, the managers always stress the commitment of the plant to the welfare of the community.

I accompany Zohar, the plant manager from Beit Jann, on a visit to Farid, one of the village notables. We go though the narrow lanes leading to his house. Inside the house, we sit in easy chairs. Zohar says, "We employ 190 women in the sewing plant, and if there were any more available, we would employ them as well. We're even ready to employ married women and introduce a late shift—if there are candidates."

Farid says, "It's hard to get working women in the village. There are other sewing plants without enough working hands."

Zohar persists, "We're the largest plant in the village, and the women working for us enjoy ideal working conditions. You know us well. We take good care of the women. You can't compare conditions in our plant with those of the smaller sewing shops."

Farid looks at him as if to say "I've heard that one before." Then he says, "That's true, but the salaries are low. The parents are interested in money." He continues talking, mainly about the role of the plant in the life of the village.

"We do appreciate the concern and its owners. We let the plant into the village some twenty years ago. We know each other well. We even agreed twenty years ago that our women would go from here to Nazareth to learn the sewing trade. All the managers who work in the plant here know the families and come to all our celebrations. That helps convince the families. They know the manager and are willing to entrust their daughters to him. They believe that he'll take care of them and their health." Zohar nods in agreement, and so do I.

Farid also nods and then continues, "But the work is hard, and the women work too hard, and then it's hard for them to help at home. There shouldn't be so much overtime and work on Fridays." He hesitates for a moment and then goes on, "The plant should listen to the parents about that."

Zohar replies, "We respect the families and take their needs into consideration. We even have an open day at the plant for the parents. Without their cooperation we wouldn't have succeeded the way we have. But even you'll agree with me, Farid, that there are certain limits, that the parents shouldn't interfere in the management of the plant and my decisions as manager."

Farid agrees with Zohar and adds, "I wouldn't let them interfere in my plant, but cooperation with the families is important. Work should be work, but work is also like in the family. At work the manager is the father, but he has to cooperate with the other father after work."

As this dialogue illustrates, the plant is under the continuous scrutiny of the community. There is a realization among the community that the plant is exploiting the cheap labor of the women and their limited employment opportunities. Although the fathers continuously complain about the low salaries of their daughters, they see it as the price paid for insisting on the segregation of women. In spite of rhetoric by both the fathers and the managers, the fathers do not empower the managers to be fathers at work. They do not see the plant as the extension of the family that the managers attempt to advocate. What they do expect, however, is accountability.

As Nabil, one of the fathers, comments:

"The plant is not family. It never was and never will be. It is just a workplace. The managers are not fathers. When the woman says to the manager that he is like a father, it is just a figure of speech. There is nothing behind it but the showing of respect. What I expect from the manager is responsibility, that he take good care of our daughters

and pay them on time. I expect him to keep the plant free of gossip
and out of reach of outsiders."

The involvement of the managers in the life of the villages is
extensive and in many cases they have to walk a tight rope. They
are caught in squabbles between the religious groups and the
clans, and if they pay too much attention to one side, they are immediately accused of showing favoritism.

"You have to know exactly what is going on in local politics," Amos,
the manager of Julis, says. "It took me a long time to understand this.
Because of local politics, a lot of women left the plant. They interpreted my behavior as being of benefit to their enemies."

He shuffles through the papers on his desk and hands me a note
written by one of the seamstresses.

> *To the Manager of the Plant:*
>
> *For more than four years I have worked at your plant
> diligently and loyally. Until the last elections[14] I felt I was
> being treated well at the plant. But after the last elections
> to the village council and especially the skirmishes between
> the various clans in the village, I began to feel the flak at
> work. I began to feel that everybody was against me at the
> plant and, therefore, I decided to write a letter of resignation
> in order to prevent any unpleasantness. I wish you all good luck
> at the plant and in your private lives. At the same time
> I would like to get my severance pay and all the rights coming
> to me because of the reasons mentioned above. Thank you
> for all your help.*

Amos was livid with anger when he received the letter, seeing it
as a personal attack, as if he had shown partiality to one of the clans.

In the Arab villages, local elections clearly define two rival sides that reflect familial ties (Reiter and Aharoni 1992). The plants, which consist of women from various *hamulas*, are often swept into the local rivalries. The managers try to distance the plant from the pre-election campaign and curtail any attempt to hold a political discussion in the plant. After every election, however, there are usually fights between the losing and winning sides. The losing side always blames the winners for cheating and distorting the results. The aftermath of elections spills over to the plant, and sometimes it is unbearable for a seamstress from one side (usually the losing side) to work in the company of the others.

I ask Amos how, despite everything, he prevents friction between the women from the various communities and clans.

He replies, "When there are a number of different ethnic or religious communities represented in the plants, the management tries to maintain status quo between them. If in one village the Druse are in the majority, for example, then most of the supervisors and seamstresses in that plant will be Druse. There was one case in which not a single supervisor was Muslim, despite the fact that 30 percent of the seamstresses were. I use a different system. I encourage self-determination. We are a mixed plant with Druse, Muslim, and a few Christian workers. The important thing is that mutual respect prevails among them all. I don't want a situation in which the word religion or ethnicity will be a dirty word in the plant. On the contrary, I encourage the supervisors and the seamstresses to be proud of their origins. If, for example, the supervisor has a Druse holiday, I encourage her to take a day off, even if the rest of the department goes on working. I don't want anyone to feel that there is a confrontation between the plant and the family over a holiday. Beyond that, they all know that they come to the plant to work and not to engage in politics and altercations. The minute you ignore the subject altogether, you create an atmosphere of alienation and separateness. You have to deal with the subject and expose them all to the holidays and customs of the others."

The managers in the plants encourage pluralism, not so much because of humanistic reasons, but because it creates an organizational climate of tolerance and consideration that is instrumental to managerial control and compatible with manifested values of the work culture.

Conclusion

The managers of the plants consciously recognize the need to manage the sewing plants within a framework that takes into consideration the local culture. They realize that to successfully manage a sewing plant and meet the stringent production requirements, they must create a work culture with shared meanings that derive from both the local and the managerial domains. The plant is part of the community, and the managers restructure their managerial strategy in accordance with the male members of the family.

Managing the plant is a continuous process of carrying out production requirements and goals. The manager's ability to fulfill these goals depends not only on coordinating logistic and technological aspects, but mainly on managing the seamstresses and supervisors. The styles of management concentrate on those aspects that have utmost relevance to the seamstresses' performance. Thus, the management system recognizes the importance of manipulating the local values to meet formal requirements. Elements from Arab culture are appropriated and injected into the patriarchal relations between the managers and the workers. This patriarchal relationship of managerial domination on the shop floor is twofold: the managers simulate the role of the father, and they exercise their control and enhance their workers' dependency on them at work.

CHAPTER 8

Out with the Old and In with the Hi-Tex

Within the factory, every proletarian is led to conceive
himself as inseparable from his work-mates; how could
the raw material piled up in the warehouses come to
circulate in the world as an object of use to man in
society, if a single link were missing from the system of
labour in industrial production? The more the proletarian
specializes in a particular professional task, the more
conscious he becomes of how indispensable his compan-
ions are; the more he feels himself as one cell within a
coherent body, possessed of an inner unity and cohesion;
the more he feels the needs for order, method, precision;
the more he feels the need for the whole world to become
like a vast factory where he works; the more he feels the
need for the order, precision and method which are the
life-blood of the factory to be projected out into the
system of relations that links one factory to another,
one city to another, one nation to another.

—ANTONIO GRAMSCI
"The Factory Worker"

The late 1990s signified a transformation in the Galilee's textile
industry. Four of its eight plants were closed—Beit Jann, Kfar Tavor, Shfaram, and Maghar—and hundreds of seamstresses were
laid off. The transformation was triggered by the Israeli economy's
increasing integration with and dependence on the world market.
The concern had faced increasing operational costs of its plants in
Israel as a result of fluctuating exchange rates, rising costs of raw

materials, and rising minimum wages. Furthermore, the concern's production systems proved vulnerable, as labor-intensive, low-skilled, low-wage producers from the Far East, Eastern Europe, and northern Africa began to compete vigorously in its traditional market. Geopolitical changes in the Middle East, mainly the peace treaties with Egypt and Jordan, created new opportunities for the concern, particularly in relocating its production facilities. In Egypt and Jordan, the concern pursued the availability of labor that is ten times cheaper than in Israel.

The chairman of the concern explains:

"The salary of a worker in the Galilee is $1000 a month, as opposed to $100 a month in the neighboring alternative. The basic industries need to change radically if we want to survive. In a country exposed to international competition and trade, our only chance is openness to the world. Israeli companies should become more global and produce in countries with a competitive advantage in labor and integrate this advantage in the organization and the knowledge of the company in Israel. The globalization should be not only in production, but also in our marketing and integration in the financial world."

The relocation influenced the concern's organization of production in Israel. Whereas the mass assembly lines moved abroad, in Israel the concern reshuffled its organization of production according to a new strategy it termed *hi-tex*. The connotation of this term is an industry that is clean, modern, efficient, sophisticated, and innovative, as opposed to the former low-skilled system of standardized mass production.[1]

Hi-Tex

Hi-tex refers to organizing the textile industry in an innovative manner in terms of designs, fabrics, and products, and the organization of production. The concern realizes that the hi-tex strategy will enable it to compete effectively by increasing the shelf life of its products. It estimates that each new generation of products will give it a relative advantage and a degree of exclusivity in the world market for two to four years, before being replicated by competitors from the Far East.[2]

Whereas the sewing plants used to produce large quantities of a limited range of products, such as slips, underwear, and boxer shorts, they now have to produce, on reconfigured production lines, a larger variety of products and designs, including undershirts, pajamas, robes, bras, and fashionable lingerie. Furthermore, the products themselves have become more innovative, including combinations of colors, motifs, complicated stitches, and mostly a variety of sophisticated fabrics. These changes in product design have been followed by a modification of production lines. The plants have resorted to a more flexible system of production that is based mainly on (1) technological developments such as automated sewing machines based on electronic microprocessor technology and partially computerizing the shop floor and (2) modifying the system of production to fit smaller batches of products while employing a modular production system that requires more skilled seamstresses who should master a variety of sewing operations and handle different sewing machines (Dunlap and Weil 1996).

The long standardized assembly lines that produce relatively simple products were moved to Egypt and Jordan. As Shmuel, one of the division managers, says:

"It is only natural that we have moved the long lines of simple underwear to Egypt. These products are simple to sew, and it is easy to teach the Egyptian seamstresses, so they easily reach a high rate of production. The learning curve, or the adaptation period, for these products is very short, and the technology involved in making them is simpler. The work in Egypt resembles what we had here just before moving there. We are replicating our old system of production. In this system, what you need is good supervision and a constant flow of fresh and young seamstresses at low cost, and this is what we find in

Egypt. Here in Israel we emphasize the advantage of introducing seamless technology and our own fabrics and designs. Furthermore, we are entering products we haven't produced, including women's undergarments such as robes and bras."

In the sewing plants that have remained in the Galilee, the concern has attempted to install a flexible production system that is more responsive to the demands of the complicated products and in accordance with the more stringent requirements of customers. The backbone of this system is a combination of automated seamless machines and more rigorous procedures of production and quality. However, hi-tex does not represent a radical departure from the assembly line system that had prevailed in the plant. Rather, it represents a coexistence of rigid, hierarchical standardized assembly lines with flexible specialization and new forms of organizing the production (Sayer 1989; Vallas 1999; Wood 1993). Although the sewing plants preserve the assembly lines, these lines have become considerably shorter. Whereas previously each department would sew one main function, and the product progressively moved from one department to another, now each department assembles the entire product.

A few plants have tried sociotechnical solutions such as self-regulating work groups (Pasmore 1988), but these attempts were abandoned because of complications. For example, workers have difficulties regulating their own pace needed to meet predetermined group quotas. It is difficult to motivate workers on the principles of team-based remuneration, because this "democracy" of evaluating teams as opposed to individuals discourages the highly skilled workers. There are also problems that relate to the basic assumptions of teamwork, such as the need for less supervision and the ability of the team to manage itself.

The attempt to develop automation encountered difficulties. The concern apparently decided that the advantages of automation in increasing control and improving coordination were too expensive and marginal. It prefers the traditional system of supervisors who closely oversee the shop floor. Furthermore, automation of the sewing machines is rather limited in potential. As Taplin (1995) writes:

> It is difficult to automate garment assembly because fabric is limp. Some peripheral operations such as pleating, hemming, needle positioning, and thread cutting have been automated but nothing has yet replaced the sewing machine as the primary assembly tool. Here, operators pass material through sewing machines; repetitive tasks that nevertheless defy automation because the fabric has to be individually positioned. (p. 422)

The new technology introduced by the concern consists of mainly seamless technology. Although it enhanced efficiency and quality, it also called for greater maintenance and mechanical support. There is a need for constant maintenance and resetting of the machines according to the different needs of the products and fabrics. In the sewing plants that have introduced seamless technology, there is a new differentiation of workers—those who work on the automated machines, which require less skill and professionalism, and those who work on more complicated products and operations, which require high proficiency. In the latter operations, the learning curve is longer, and sewing a product can take up to eight minutes, as opposed to three minutes for producing a slip. Among the latter types of workers, the notion of sewing as temporary work is being replaced with a need for a solid professional workforce that achieves high mastery in its profession.

As Ronen, the manager of the Nazareth plant, describes:

"When I came to manage Nazareth after Maghar closed down, I came to a different sewing plant. As you see, we are sewing about twenty different products, from undergarments to pajamas and cloth slippers. Each product is very demanding. It requires a lot of expertise from the seamstresses and it takes a lot of time. The quality demands are also sky high. It's not like old times, when you had one type of slip with one color and one size for each department and you could get to production levels of up to 200. Now you have to be very careful on the sewing of each product. I have to be more professional, the mechanics have to be more professional, and the supervisors have to be more professional.

Now we don't give up our seamstresses so easily. We don't want high turnover of the seamstresses like in the past. Once they acquire skills, we want to keep them. We worry about the next generation."

The hi-tex sewing plants, although fewer and smaller, have changed their composition and the characteristics of their labor force. Although the majority are still single daughters, in the sewing plant in Nazareth, for example, there are more married women and new immigrants from the former Soviet Union.

The flexible organization of production for the hi-tex products includes more vertical integration between the sewing plants and the division headquarters. The sewing plants shifted from being relatively autonomous entities, whereby managers control every aspect of production, to being more dependent on headquarters. This dependence is particularly acute with respect to planning, technical support, and quality.

With the Law of Minimum Wages, which increased the seamstresses' salaries by more than 30 percent, and its mechanism of annual reconfiguration (according to the average salary in the economy), work in the sewing plants has become more attractive. Moreover, high unemployment in Israel (averaging 11 percent in 1998), has made work in the sewing plants more precious.

Additionally, I detect a trend toward a change in paradigms in the organizational culture from family to hi-tex. While the family paradigm reflects the clan work culture described in this book, the hi-tex paradigm emphasizes both hierarchy and market orientations (Cameron and Freeman 1991). The familial climate of the plant has changed to a more business-like setting. The work has become more formal.

Moshe, one of the managers, expresses the new sentiment:

"I don't approve anymore of the idea of the managers humbling themselves before the women. It's a new time. We have a developed folklore that tells us that managers have to be on the same level as the workers to get results. You know the story of the manager who got down on his knees on the production floor and begged one of the seamstresses to produce her daily quota just for him. All that emotional blackmail is beside the point. That's not management. At first I was also like that because they told me that's how it works. The approach was to get to know the women, to visit them at their homes, to ask them how they felt, to take an interest in them and in their clothes, to be their shrink, to flatter their fathers. But the old system got on my nerves. The parents would come to the plant with all kinds of demands. 'Let her off today, her mother doesn't feel well,' and all sorts of bull like that. The stupid idea that the women work for the managers is out. I tell all the seamstresses and especially the new ones: 'Here we work for money.' They come to work and they get paid for working. That's the bottom line."

The rules of the game in the plant have become more concrete and in accordance with the demands of work. There is greater emphasis on hierarchy and authority and intolerance of breaches of discipline and inability to meet production quotas. The style of management has become less intimate and more formal. In particular, the managers implement strict hierarchy and control and promote a climate of obeying procedures and rules, which may ultimately increase alienation on the shop floor.

For the supervisors the new system has meant a distinctive change. Their roles have been realigned and incorporated into the management. The term supervisor has deliberately been replaced by the term department manager. This change of terminology is accompanied by a complex process of learning, changing attitudes, and empowering the department managers. They are required to be more professional and exercise leadership and discipline on the shop floor. The management system has become more integrative, and the department managers have established direct communication with various functions in headquarters. Furthermore, the concern has seen the department managers as the main agents for transferring and teaching the concern's system of production, quality control requirements, and sewing systems to its plants in Egypt and Jordan. As Badhia says:

"I travel to Jordan every week. In the morning we get into a taxi, drive until the bridge, cross the border, take a Jordanian taxi, and travel to the plants in Irbid or Amaan. The plants are big and nice, very clean. They look like all the plants in the concern. We introduce new products, teach the Jordanians how to work, and check for quality. We speak the same language, and we understand their mentality. They have a lot to learn. We tell them what needs to be changed in the lines. We teach them the work procedures and check their work."

Some of the supervisors travel to Egypt and stay for a few weeks. Amal says:

"We fly to Egypt and teach the local supervisors and workers how to work. I would have never believed that my father would let me do it, but he knows that I've been working many years and he counts on me. I make a lot of money working in Egypt, since I save part of my spending allowance. In Egypt, I don't only work; I also travel. I've seen the pyramids. All of us from Israel hang out together, go to restaurants, and have a good time."

Because of the increase in variety and number of products, stringent quality standards, and more complicated sewing operations, the traditional departments of up to seventy workers are split into smaller and more specialized departments. Thus, because the number of departments in the plants has increased, the number of department managers has increased by the promotion of quality controllers. This restructuring enhances changes in a few aspects of production. For example, quality control is conducted at every stage of production, within the department as well as in specialized auditing procedures after the product is sewed.

Furthermore, a new alignment developed in the plants that expresses changes in hierarchy and control. The department managers are fully aligned with the managers and are geared toward a more systematic view of production. Delbridge and Lowe (1997), in their research of Hanwell Motors, a car assembly plant, and Nikkon CTV, a Japanese-owned electronics factory, both in southern England, show how the role of supervisors is molded. They find that weakness or the empowerment of the supervisors depends on the axis of managers-supervisors-workers. It is the identification with the management's objectives and flatter managerial structure that enables supervisors in Nikkon CTV to exercise more meaningful managerial duties. The incorporation of department managers into management ultimately empowers them and enables them to exercise more managerial authority and extend their role from predominantly mediators to managers. The department manager exercises much more control over her department and has more authority and flexibility in planning the work, which was formerly the responsibility of the production manager. As Afifa describes:

"We are out of the cage. Now we should think of the overall interest and the good of the plant, not just our department or our line. It is not routine management anymore. I constantly try to improve the process, to think forward. I have to change my 'head' through hard work. I am more responsible to my workers. The production manager doesn't interfere. Now we, the department managers, are more of a team. Look at Ramadan, for example. The seamstresses left at two, and we had a very urgent order. In the past, nobody would have done it, and we would have postponed it to the next day. This time we decided to stay. It was our initiative, not the manager's. All the department managers sat on the machines and sewed until five o'clock, until it was dark. It was fun. We laughed and shouted. One of us role-played as the supervisor and yelled at the rest of us."

Apparently the values and perceptions of the department managers became more oriented toward planning production objectives and the managerial practices to achieve them and less oriented toward personal loyalties, whether to the workers or the managers. Inclusion of department managers in planning the production of the entire plant results in better coordination and cooperation between departments. For example, two department managers decided to cooperate by "subcontracting" sewing operations for each other. One of them has seamstresses who are proficient in preliminary sewing tasks and relatively weak in dealing with elastic bands. The other has seamstresses with opposite strengths. Both department managers initiated a cooperation whereby they join forces and sew for each other those parts on which they have a relative advantage.

The changes in organizational and managerial practices have challenged senior veteran supervisors, who must give part of their departments to the quality controllers who used to be their subordinates. These changes are perceived as degrading their jobs and manifesting personal lack of trust from the managers. As Mabruka says:

"When the manager told me about the changes, taking the department from me and giving me only one line, I cried. I immediately left work and stayed home for three days. I didn't stop crying. When I returned, the manager spoke with all three of us veteran supervisors and explained the new system. He said that it is not that the old supervisors are not good, but that it's time to give others a chance. The young women should have a chance to be promoted. He also mentioned that there are new products and that there is much work in the lines. It is easier to manage smaller departments. Eventually we agreed; we didn't have much choice. We decided that we will tell the workers about the changes. I had a big party for my department and introduced them to the new supervisors. Now we call them department managers, and I, who used to be in charge of eighty women, only have twenty. But I got used to it."

The changes bring about the problems of more professional and impersonal management. The new management style is less flexible, less considerate of the personal needs of the workers and their families, and stricter about the primacy of production and goals of production. It weakens the safety net of an informal and familial work environment that emphasizes intimacy, togetherness, and personal consideration. The individual decision-making ability of the department managers, which accentuates the hierarchical gap between them and the seamstresses, ultimately reduces the workers' voice. This pattern stands in contrast to the findings of Feldman and Buechler (1998), who studied the transformation of an American textile factory under new Japanese management, in which the new collective managerial decision-making process reduced the possibility for workers to influence managerial decisions. In the Galilee sewing plants, it is the individual empowerment of the department managers that aligns them with the management, assigns them more responsibilities and authorities, and directs new managerial practices that detach them from the workers. In the Japanese-American case, the United States managers, once the sole voices of authority and individual consideration for the workers, allowed the workers to exercise more direct influence on managerial decisions.

The newly acquired individual responsibility of the department managers is accompanied by more demands, thus enhancing pressure to achieve the designated departmental objectives. Julia says:

"I have never been under so much pressure. It's not like one or two years ago. Now I have to do everything myself: train the workers, take care of my quotas, make samples, watch the quality, and run after the machinists. Today, every hour, there is something different. Every day is a new one. Yesterday I left work at five. I had today planned, but suddenly new samples came in and I had to change everything. I do it all myself. It's a lot of pressure. I dream about the work at night and I'm always worrying."

The closure of plants and the massive firings greatly shaped the work experience of the seamstresses. It spread insecurity among them and strengthened the managers' tendency to transform the familial work environment into a more impersonal and task-oriented work culture. The relative bargaining power of the management increased. They achieved more leverage in negotiating with the families and the workers regarding habits, practices, and conditions of their daughters' employment. The plant managers now limit visits by fathers and brothers of workers and have less tolerance for family and personal needs, such as helping at home at the expense of work. Furthermore, within the work itself, the managers are stricter regarding the achievement of production quotas and absenteeism.

The transformation toward more formality and business-like practices on the shop floor has eroded solidarity and loyalty. For example, there used to be an unwritten agreement in the plants that women who leave work to get married receive compensation payment as well as a letter of dismissal that enables them to receive unemployment payment from National Security. The managers stopped this custom after realizing that some of the married ex-workers used the letter of dismissal as a basis for a legal claim against the concern for not giving them notice of two weeks to a month, as required by law.

Although working relationships have altered and have become more task oriented, they still preserve their patriarchal nature. Patriarchal relationships in the plant still accentuate terms of obligation and commitment in accordance with the hierarchy. The discourse on honor, fairness, seniority, caring, and the plant as a family is still predominant. The ideology of personal commitment to your superiors also remains. The old slogan, "The seamstresses work for the supervisors, the supervisors work for the managers, and the managers work for the concern," was modified to include the added phrase, "and we all work to survive."

Closing Days Blues

In a speech to the seamstresses and families, the division manager who closed one of the oldest plants in the concern says:

"I know how much the workers depend on us. We are all family. We offer you replacement jobs in our bigger factories. You should know that we employ many Arab and Druse workers in our headquarters in Karmiel, both men and women. They work as not only seamstresses, but also in quality control and development. If we want to survive, we have to move to Egypt and Jordan, where the labor is cheap. If you want to continue to work, you should leave the village. I call on you, the families, to allow your daughters to travel to other plants."

His speech is interrupted by aggressive shouts from workers and their family members. Its patronizing and righteous tone pours salt on their wounds. One hundred and seventy workers have lost their jobs. All of them feel betrayed and deceived. A few militant workers express their rage by shouting at the division manager.

Elham, who agrees to move to another plant, later tells me, "The day they closed the plant was a day of mourning. It was our home, our family. It was really hard to leave the place. I felt that a part of me fell out, as if my son died. It was very difficult. The hardest part of moving to the new plant [in Nazareth] was leaving the village for the whole day. For us it's really hard to leave [the village]. Because I tell my mother everything that happens and I take care of myself, my parents agree to let me work here. When they told us that they were closing, we all sat together and looked at each other. They told us, 'There is no work now. We want to transfer a few women to Nazareth for two months.' We had a feeling this wasn't the truth, but we said, 'Let's try.' They transferred us in groups. They didn't tell us they were closing the plant. They just transferred a few women at a time. We cried a lot when we left. The plant was like our family. But we didn't have a choice; we had to move. The women do not want to stay at home; they want to work. They need the money."

In terms of the concern, the closings went relatively smoothly. The seamstresses tried to protest, but got little help from the General Labor Union (*Histadrut*) and the local municipality.[3] Their fight was like a call into space. Apart from a few items in the daily newspapers, the massive firing went unnoticed at the national level, another echo of the Arab women's outsider status.

The concern promised the laid-off women alternative employment in one of the remaining sewing plants. If they preferred to leave, they would receive severance compensation and three months of wages. Most of the fired seamstresses accepted the latter proposition; only about 30 percent transferred to new plants. Aliya, a fired seamstress from Kfar Tavor, says:

"I want my compensation money first. I deserve getting paid for doing nothing. Then I'll get my six months' unemployment payments. After that I'll see what happens. God is great."

Those for whom work is a necessity had to relocate and adjust to the new plant, managers, and working environment. In a few cases, the supervisors continued working in a new plant, particularly when a large group of seamstresses came with them, but in some cases they had to go back to the machines or leave the plant entirely.

"At first it was hard moving here," recalls Yasmine, "I didn't know anyone. For ten years I worked in the plant in the village, which was close to home. I didn't need a ride. Slowly but surely I got used to it, and now it really is my home. At first there were some problems, and I had a feeling of being new. Today, I'm *mabsuta* [satisfied]. The managers and the supervisors are like in the old plant. At first, when I entered through the door, I was afraid. But the manager said, 'We should be an example to all of the seamstresses in the plant.' So we try harder to show that we are better. I couldn't sit at home—it's boring. I don't just work for the money. Work gives me the feeling that I am doing something in this world. Sitting cross-legged is no life. Although the ride is difficult, the work is the same. Everyone helps us—the man-

agers, the supervisors, the mechanics. They make us feel like we belong. Eventually this became like home. The feeling is like moving,
not closing."

In closing the plants, the management of the concern gained
the best of both worlds—transferring production to places where
the cost of labor is cheap, and rationalizing and economizing the
ongoing production in the plants that remained (see also Zipp
1984; Zipp and Lane 1987).[4]

The managers handled the crisis of closing in their usual paternalistic manner. They attempted to present the situation as de-
terministic. The managers portrayed the closings as a sacrifice, as
an unavoidable crisis in the family. As one of the managers of a
plant that closed says:

"I told the laid-off workers that it is from God. Every family has its
crises. There is nothing to do but remember the good times and go on.
I promised them that they can come with me to the new plant, that I
will not abandon them, and that if they need something they should
come to me."

Conclusion

The new hi-tex plants reshuffled their organizational processes to adapt to the new demands of the concern's strategy and
the new products. The changes entailed production of small
batches of products within the smaller departments. Furthermore,
the complicated products and the higher quality requirements ne-
cessitated meticulous oversight of the shop floor. In this respect,
the department supervisors are allocated more decision-making

power and autonomy over their departments. This change, however, does not fundamentally alter production processes and the organization of work. The hi-tex flexibility is still heavily dependent on assembly line structure.

The closings themselves were traumatic and mark the breakdown of the basic tenets of the concern's clan culture. Hi-tex also modified the basic tenets of the value systems in the plants, whereby more formality and emphasis on hierarchy has generated a work culture that emphasizes personal achievement, discipline, and obedience. The image of the plant as a loving family accountable to its workers was crushed after all of the closings.

CHAPTER 9

Conclusion

You would like to live according to your own ideas . . .
and you would like to know how that can be done. But
an idea is the most paradoxical thing in the world. The
flesh combines with ideas like a fetish. It becomes
magical when there's an idea in it. An ordinary box on
the ears may, by association with the ideas of honour,
punishment, and the like, become a matter of life and
death. And yet ideas can never conserve themselves in
the state in which they are strongest. They are like
those substances that when exposed to the air instantly
transform themselves into another, more permanent, but
corrupted form of existence. You have been through it
often. For you are an idea yourself, one in a particular
state. You are touched by a breath of something, and it's
like when the quivering of strings suddenly produces a
note. And then there's something there in front of you
like a mirage, and the tangle of your soul takes on shape,
becoming an unbending cavalcade, and all the beauties of
the world seem to stand along its road. Such things are
often brought about by one single idea. But after a while
it comes to resemble all the other ideas that you have had
before, subordinating itself to them and becoming part of
your outlook and your character, your principles and your
moods. By then it has lost its wings and taken on an
unmysterious solidity.

—ROBERT MUSIL
The Man Without Qualities

THIS ORGANIZATIONAL ethnography examined the interrelationships among seamstresses, supervisors, and managers and revealed the work culture that prevails in sewing plants that are part of a leading Israeli textile concern operating in Arab communities. The various perspectives of the seamstresses, supervisors, and managers were described in order to uncover the process of creating the shared meanings that shape the work culture in the plants. The study of the sewing plants in the Galilee uncovers Arab village women's adaptation to industrial work within a pluralistic setting. The work culture in the plants, I argued, is a consequence of negotiating shared meaning within a context of patriarchal relationships, simulation of the family at work, and inherent gender and ethnic inequalities. In this chapter, I review and critically interpret the main findings concerning the work culture in the plants. First, the dynamics of creating the clan culture in the plants are presented. Second, the inherent inequalities in the plant as manifested by patriarchal relations are discussed. Finally, the chapter addresses the issue of women's employment in the context of workplace relations, the family, and global industrialization.

The Creation of the Work Culture

As shown in this study, the work culture evolving in the plants is simultaneously practical, instrumental, and effective as well as constrained by and restructured by the workers' life outside work. It is a process of creating shared meaning through a series of conflicts and renegotiations of daily events and practices, both on the shop floor and at home. It is a work environment that reflects routinization, specialization, coherent span of control, and supervision, as well as solidarity, respect, fairness, teamwork, and paternalism. Within the overall framework of the formation of shared meaning, the value systems at play are not static. There is room for maneuvering; the meanings of the work values are constantly being reformulated in light of changing conditions and events.

The organization of production in the sewing plant operates within a double context of family and work. The management must take this into account and confront the seamstresses' interpretation of various aspects of work procedures, such as quotas, quality, and absenteeism. They must understand the background and meaning of the seamstresses' interpretation of work in order to transform them and instill in them an instrumental content. Table 5 illustrates how the managers articulate production issues in the everyday life of the plant.

The work culture in the sewing plants emerged as a consequence of negotiating conflicts between the managers and the workers, each bearing an initially different set of formal values and behavioral norms. The work values of the concern exemplify the principles of textile management based on goal-oriented achievement, quality, efficiency, and authority, in which the day-to-day work is perceived as an autonomous system of rights and duties (Drori 1996; Hareven 1982).[1] The worldview, norms, and values of the workers, on the other hand, are embodied in Arab family ideology. The managers and the workers appropriate each others' codes and norms of behavior for the objectives of both. The result of these attempts is a process that restructures shared meaning in the context of the unequal power relations between the parties. For example, patriarchal relationships are part of a managerial strategy that has a Janus-faced manifestation. On one hand, it reduces alienation on the production lines. On the other hand, it serves as an effective means of control by fostering paternalism, characterized by personal obligation and the exercise of interpersonal power.

The work culture of the plants displays the characteristics of a clan organizational culture, which resembles the so-called strong organizational culture (Deal and Kennedy 1982). These organizational cultures are characterized by a system of values and behavioral norms that highlights the importance of cohesion, commitment to achieving the goals of the organization, and the willingness of the individual to identify with the organization. The superimposition of familial meaning and content, normative control, and integration of formal and informal hierarchy and authority structures creates a feeling of togetherness and common purpose. There are aspects of the plant, however, that seemingly mitigate against strong culture. Table 6 illustrates the characteristics of the work culture according to the continuum of those values that represent strong culture and those that contradict it.

TABLE 5
Interrelation between organizational aspects and managerial practices

Organizational aspects	Managerial practice
Attention and motivation	Attention to the personal problems of the workers and their families Crystallization of team spirit; managerial paternalism toward supervisors and seamstresses Control of situations in each department through staff meetings in which management ideology and the need for on the spot problem-solving is emphasized Emphasis on promoting the values of cooperation, solidarity, respect, and fairness
Responses to critical events and organizational crises	Mobilization of workers and staff for a common goal Bringing the situation of the concern to the sewing plant, i.e., "we're all in the same boat" Meeting the goals unconditionally with remuneration for attaining them Management support for the staff Dealing with problems at community level
Standards of production and quality	The manager sets a personal example by his presence on the production floor Emphasis on detailed instruction Managerial involvement at all levels of production, accompanied by feedback from all levels of management Emphasis on professionalism and excellence
Allocation of remuneration	Clear criteria for remuneration or penalties based on individual, departmental, or overall plant achievement Competitiveness, projects with an emphasis on excellence and professionalism Uncompromising penalties for breach of discipline or the flouting of work values
Recruitment of workers	The seamstresses and supervisors are given a "mandate" for interesting friends and relatives in a job Recruitment through drivers

TABLE 5
(*continued*)

Organizational aspects	Managerial practice
Training	On the job training
Working conditions and welfare	Ensuring adequate physical conditions in the plant Social activities, mainly trips
Teamwork	Indiscrimination between supervisors Providing production support on time (machinists, raw materials, accessories) Emphasis on behavioral norms of fairness
Communication	Informality Special language uniting the sewing plants, with its own vocabulary, codes, and meanings Direct communication channels between the managers and workers alongside mediation by the supervisors

TABLE 6

Organizational values of strong and weak cultures

Strong culture

Worker commitment as a central work value

"Emotional blackmail" for attaining organizational goals

Ambiguity between work and private life; using family involvement for normative control

Creating strong identification with the plant by promoting values of solidarity, cohesion, and reciprocity

Fostering paternalistic relationships

Weak culture

Perception of work as temporary

Submission to family values that do not necessarily correspond to organizational interests, such as helping at home at the expense of work

Bargaining, bartering, and "give and take" as part of the social relations of production

The absorption of familial ideologies into the plant's organizational culture creates a dynamic in which the values that characterize strong culture and the values that do not are not mutually exclusive. By incorporating them, the organization has to enter into a negotiation process and interrelationship whereby in some cases (such as the olive harvest, wedding preparations, and family duties), it must submit to the needs and wants of the family.[2]

Patriarchal Relationships

Paternalism in the plants is a behavioral manifestation of an inherent state of patriarchy. In order to assess and analyze patriarchal relationships, it is important to reveal their characteristics in Arab society. The essence of these patriarchal relations, mainly male domination over women, is accentuated in the interface of power and control in both public and private domains. As described by Moghadam (1993):

> Patriarchal societies distinguish the public arena from the private. In the public sphere, power relations overwhelmingly involved male household-heads (patriarchs), and the private sphere was usually ruled formally by a patriarch. . . . Social stratification was thus two-dimensional. One dimension comprised the two nuclei of household/family/lineage and male dominance. The second dimension comprised whatever combination of public stratification nuclei (classes, military elites, etc.) existed in a particular society. The latter dimension was connected to the former in that public power-groupings were predominantly aggregates of household/family/lineage heads. But apart from this connection, the two dimensions were segregated from each other (p. 106).

Apparently, the two dimensions of patriarchy described by Moghadam limit the option for women to exercise autonomy and self-realization at work or at home. At the workplace, the women experience both dimensions, the public and the private, because there is implicit collaboration between the managers of the concern and the fathers and brothers. The textile plants are preferred workplaces because they preserve the ideology of patriarchy, in which women are segregated from men outside the family and

Patriarchal structure
(inherent)
Derives from the dominant
position of the concern and
the unequal division of
labor between the Arab
and the Jewish sectors

↓

Double patriarchy   → *Pattern of*   →
Manifestation in the plant   *paternalism*

↑

Patriarchal structure
(household)
Stems from the traditional
structure of the Arab family
and male-female relations
in the private and public
realms

Hierarchy of gender
authority
Managerial control
over employment
condition and
wages
Mix of traditional and
company values
and norms
Simulating the home
at work
Pattern of authority
and loyalty
Linkages to family
and community
Superimposition of
private and
working life

FIGURE 4. Schematic representation of double patriarchy in the plant

there is a gender-based division of labor. Thus, women who work
in the plant experience the double types of patriarchal control—
public and private—that overlap (Hartman 1981; Westwood 1984).
This pattern is illustrated in Figure 4.

The double patriarchal relationships in the plants are internalized through the interrelationships and events governing the
shop floor. The seamstresses operate within the framework of both
their worldview and the division of labor, hierarchy, and authority.
Both of these content worlds are continuously shaped and re-
shaped through dynamic and causal negotiation for shared meaning. Thus, the work culture's main attributes derive from patriarchal relationships simultaneously linked both to the family and
the managers.

The supervisors' role as mediator exemplifies their position
within the pattern of patriarchal relations. Their relationships
with the managers are dominated by their role and status within

the authority hierarchy in the plant. The supervisors play the role of interpreter of the local values and norms of the seamstresses to the managers. In this capacity, they simultaneously exercise authority within a predetermined hierarchy and relate to their workers as fellow women and family members. Thus, the supervisors strengthen the patriarchal hold on the seamstresses by being part of the hierarchical chain of control and by contributing to the creation of familial-type patriarchal relations as a mediating tool and mechanism of creating shared meaning. Ironically, the supervisors are closest to being released from the patriarchal schemata as they pursue careers as professional junior managers and gain a degree of autonomy, particularly under hi-tex. Outside the plant, however, they pay a relatively high social price by sometimes giving up family life.

From the managers' points of view, it is imperative to employ both hierarchical and authoritative processes and systems of management, which resemble the classic model of assembly line production, and at the same time resort to paternalistic behavior and acceptance of norms and values of the family. The managers remold the patriarchal relationships in the plants to fit both their managerial outlook and the worldview of their workers in their roles at home as daughters and future wives.

The dynamic interplay of these patriarchal relationships implies a constant undercurrent of conflict in the plant. The patriarchal relationships lead to two kinds of conflicts in the plant. The first covers all aspects of work and interpersonal relationships at work. These conflicts are either circumstantial or are triggered by an event. They are varied—some of them are limited to the event itself, others are more pervasive and relate to past events, and others still are expansions of initially localized conflicts. The second kind of conflict relates to issues outside of work. These conflicts are rooted in the interrelationship between the families and the plant and in the internal affairs of the community that have an interface with the plant. The main characteristic of the interplay between these two kinds of conflicts is multiple layers of tensions, whereby deeper sentiments are disguised as arguments over the meaning and boundaries of working culture.

Workplace, Family, and Women's Self-Realization

The issue of the interrelationship between the industrial workplace and the family is a linking thread in the substantial body of research that analyzes social relations of factory work. There is no conclusive agreement on the effects of women's participation in industrial work on their positions in their families. In her work *Family Time and Industrial Time* (1982), Hareven concludes:

> Historically, however, modernization at the workplace did not automatically "modernize" family behavior. Although the family underwent significant changes in its adaptation to new work roles and urban living, and although workers adapted to "modern" work processes within the factory, family behavior did not modernize at the same pace as workers' conduct in the factory. Workers adapted to industrial schedules and work processes more rapidly, whereas changes in family life occurred more gradually. But in both cases, traditional ways of life were neither preserved in their entirety nor obliterated.
>
> The family was both a custodian of tradition and an agent of change. As a guardian of traditional culture, the family provided its members with continuity, a resource to draw upon in confronting industrial conditions. Familial and industrial adaptation processes were not merely parallel but interrelated as a part of a personal and historical continuum (pp. 369–70).

The work culture of the plant builds shared meaning that simulates the home at work. Bringing content from the home to the shop floor alleviates the tensions created by the newly extended role of the working daughters. The fathers often mentioned to me that they count on their daughters because working taught them to take more responsibilities at home, take care of the family, and understand the meaning of family responsibilities. The fathers of the working women support the simulated-family framework because it assures them that the managers will safeguard the norms regarding their daughters' behavior and honor. The managers gain the trust of the fathers by constantly reiterating that the plant preserves rules that are in accordance with familial and societal values. In this sense, the manager serves as an extension of the father. The managers, in turn, encourage this interrelationship because it facilitates normative control by ensuring the support of the family and the community, thus allowing for the smooth running of the day-to-day work of the plant and the effective promotion of the organization's aims. This unholy trust is destined to be broken in cases where the interference of the family negatively influences work.

It is important to consider the challenge that working women pose to their families, the challenge of gaining autonomy through work. The stories told in this book document the struggle of workers who seek to control the fruits of their labor, which is simultaneously a struggle over improving their status within the family and community. Despite the fact that working at the sewing plant comprises part of the seamstresses' self-identity, it is still considered a temporary condition. A career and family life are not yet seen as compatible. The choice has to be either one or the other. In a society that considers the creation of a home and family the prime means of self-fulfillment for women, combining the two would seem too heavy a price to pay. For this reason, work is perceived as temporary, relatively few married women with children work at the plant, and seamstresses are not anxious to accept the responsibility of becoming supervisors.

This book contributes to the view that industrial employment essentially strengthens women's autonomy, awareness, and self-definition. The seamstresses and supervisors who work at the plants earn salaries that enable them to exercise relative economic independence and thus weaken the hold of family patriarchal control in the economic sphere. This relative independence, the ability to fulfill their material wishes (such as buying clothes, traveling, gaining a driver's license, and buying cars), reflects also on their position within their families. They have more say and are seen as more active participants in familial decision making. This change is not revolutionary and does not usually take the form of challenging the father's authority (an exception is described in the story of the Al-Hamuda daughters in Chapter 4). This gained autonomy is careful and respectful toward the family and its basic tenets. The material support of the daughters strengthens the family by preserving its cohesion and function in a time of economic need. The change is in the identity of the provider.[3] The dictum of the ideal Arab family of the father as provider is blurred and is replaced by an ideology and practice that sees all members of the family, men and women, as responsible for the unity, well-being, and economic prosperity of the family. One basic rigid aspect of the patriarchal relationship in the Arab family remains jealously guarded—the father's exclusive right to decide upon the marriage of his daughters. This pattern reflects the unchanged strong code of family honor and chastity. Thus, patriarchy is not monolithic; it has various dimensions that are flexible and adapt to changing circumstances. This modification of patriarchal relations was also described by Cairoli (1998) in her work on women in the garment industry in Morocco:

> Despite their positions as breadwinners, factory workers retain a fierce hold on the value of the patriarchal family. Both in word and action, they revere the traditional hierarchy that establishes males as protectors and females as dependents. Garment workers speak of factory labor as a temporary aberration they must tolerate until a successful marriage places them in the position of non-working wife and mother (p. 183).

The literature on women and industrialization in East Asia and Latin America strongly emphasizes the exploitative and controlling nature of factory work.[4] It portrays women workers as captured by local gender ideology and controlled by their families and employers, discriminated against in pay, and pushed into assembly line jobs. Most studies conclude that industrialization did not fundamentally alter the position and status of women. Most of the studies recognize changes, but they are seen as piecemeal, evolutionary, and insufficient to substantially improve women's status. It is difficult not to agree with these studies. In line with previous research, this book reveals the coexistence of change and stagnation, control and autonomy, exploitation and empowerment. The context of factory work in the Arab sector in Israel, however, has its own unique qualities. The seamstresses are far from being subservient, quiet, apathetic, and fatalistic. They are passionate, active, and determined to seize opportunities when they arise for the betterment of their lives.

References

Notes

CHAPTER 1 *Introduction*

1. The issue of globalization is much debated in the literature, mainly with regard to its correlation to modernization and hegemony (Giddens 1990; Robertson 1992). Globalization describes many phenomena relating to the relationships between and within countries and societies. Many see globalization as a manifestation of an emerging "world system," the theory of which proposes to explain the development of worldwide inequalities through an analysis of the dynamics of wealth accumulation in core and peripheral regions of the world (Frank, 1967; Wallerstein 1974). Economic interdependence is increased through globalization, and the resultant integration of resources, rise of global manufacturing processes, and development of an international division of labor are facilitated by an intense flow of capital, growing availability of transportation, and spread of information systems (Spybey 1996). Other aspects of globalization include the dissemination of Western political ideas and new world orders (Schwartzman 1998) and of cultural forms (Robertson 1992). Globalization also implies greater inequalities within and between countries, dependence upon major multinational and financial conglomerates, market vulnerability, and increased participation of women from peripheral areas and traditional societies in the industrial labor force (Fuentes and Ehrenreich 1983).

2. This study describes the roles of Arab and Druse women in the workplace. Generally, Druse society has been strongly influenced by, and thus resembles, Muslim rural society, in which men's status and power are much higher than those of women (Rosenfeld 1981). The

Druse religion, however, regards men and women as equals (Dana 1980). Indeed, Druse women are seen as representing and symbolizing Druse society. In social practice, however, Druse women stand in the shadow of men. Although the man is expected to care for the woman, treat her with respect, and consult with her, the woman must be obedient to the man, control her anger, avoid contact with other men, and maintain a modest appearance. This is further discussed in the work by Layish (1976).

3. The issue of patriarchy has been extensively discussed in the feminist literature. See, for example, the works by Hartman (1976), Walby (1990) and Westwood (1984). In this book, I do not attempt to contribute to the debate on its universal political implications within the context of the feminist literature. Rather, I attempt to offer an operational definition and a model of patriarchy as a major aspect of the work culture of the sewing plants.

4. The managers often referred to their workers as "girls." Westwood (1984), in her work on a textile shop floor in England, comments on this apparently innocent use of the term *girl* as reflecting patriarchal relations:

> The term 'girls' is a diminution; it signals dependence and it undermines women which, of course, makes control easier. But the shopfloor workers also used the term 'the girls' and this was a reappropriation of the terms by the women themselves. They used the words to underline the shared nature of their lives on the shopfloor, to emphasis solidarity and strength. Nevertheless, the term was still the same, and even though it was reclaimed by the women of the shopfloor, the connotations of school and of compliance remained. (p. 25)

Referring to the workers on the shop floor, I use the term *women* throughout the book and in the direct quotes of the informants.

5. Druse society and religious institutions are not tolerant of mixed relationships between the Druse and other religions. A Druse *imam* (priest), testifying during a trial of a Druse man who had murdered his sister because she was involved with a Bedouin, said, "Such relationships can lead to uncontrollable anger" (*Ha'aretz* Sept. 21, 1997, p. 11, section Aleph).

6. The vast body of literature dedicated to the issue of organizational culture refers to the shaping of common content and meaning through socialization (Gregory 1983; Schein 1985), which affects the manner in which the organization functions (Kunda 1992; Smircich 1983; Van Maanen 1979). Researchers who have used a cultural perspective to analyze management of organizations include Ott (1989) and Trice and Beyer (1993).

7. For an analysis of how organizational environments affect an organization's structure and form, with attention to issues of diversity and uncertainty, and for a typology of various organizational environments, see Sandra Dawson (1986).

8. See for example Hijab (1988), Khoury and Moghadam (1995), and Moghadam (1993) for similar processes in other Middle Eastern countries.

9. Youssef (1974, 1978) presents an account of the factors that influence women's low labor force participation in the Middle East. She attributes this not only to economic development, but also to high marriage rates, the early age of marriage, and high birth rates. Additionally, strong social control regarding issues of chastity and honor prevents the intermingling of the sexes in the workplace.

10. On women's power in the private sphere, see for example Altorki (1986). On women's power in the public sphere, see Peterson (1989).

11. On honor in Muslim society, see Sabbah (1984), Ghoussoub (1987), Mandelbaum (1988), and Mernissi (1987).

12. Ong (1987) and Moghadam (1993) claim that the increase in women's participation in employment and education, by weakening patriarchal gender relations, has created confusion and anxiety among Muslim men.

13. Many women have joined men in opposing reforms that would lead to their equality in traditionally male realms, an equality they see as possible only at the expense of reducing their status and respect within the family. Many Muslim women aim to marry and have children in order to achieve status and respect in their communities; they do not want to forgo the only role that places them in a central position in society (Al Haj 1988).

14. On the process of Arab industrialization in Israel, see Meyer-Brodnitz and Czamanski (1986); and Schnell, Sofer, and Drori (1995).

15. There are no statistical data regarding the percentage of women employed in the industry. The plant managers and I estimate that before the three major plant closings of 1997 and 1998, about 70 percent of the workers in the industry were women.

16. These data were published by *Globes* (October 18, 1996), the main financial newspaper in Israel.

17. Dr. Neal Gandal, Program of Public Policy, Tel Aviv University, has generously supplied me with the data on the textile industry. He compiled these data from annual surveys conducted by the Central Bureau of Statistics.

18. In 1996, on average, $1 equaled 3.40 NIS (New Israeli Shekels). The 1998 data are from *Ha'Aretz* 10/29/98.

CHAPTER 2   *Methods: Reflections on the Field*

1. Helen Schwartman (1993) in *Ethnography in Organizations* reviews the history of ethnographic research in industrial settings, including the history of the integration of management consulting and research, beginning with the Hawthorne research, and the role of ethnographer as cultural broker.

2. Anthropological studies of Arab society in Israel are comprehensively reviewed by Rabinowitz (1998). Anthropological research that investigates both Jews and Arabs in a single field has been done mainly in mixed communities. For example, Rabinowitz (1997) studied the relationship between Palestinian citizens of Israel and the Jews in Upper Nazareth, describing Jewish reluctance to enable Arabs to live in the community. Shokeid (1982a, 1982b), investigating the mixed town of Jaffa, also examines ethnic tension.

3. On participant observation and its methodological attributes for organizational and social research, see the work by Goffman (1989), Schwartzman (1993), and Spradley (1980).

4. Army officers get a period of "adaptation" after their army release that includes a service vehicle for the first six months.

5. Unlike Muslim and most Christian Arabs, the Druse serve in the Israeli army.

6. Voluminous literature has been written about the complex relationship between the researcher and the informant, emphasizing mainly the implications of this unequal relationship in terms of ethical, practical, and methodological dilemmas. See, for example, Agar (1980) and Shokeid (1988).

7. In the framework of the relations between Israel and the security zone of southern Lebanon and in an attempt to alleviate the economic hardships of this war-ridden zone, it is possible for southern Lebanese women to work in Israel. The condition for their employment permit is familial relation with a South Lebanese Militia (SLM) soldier. Usually, the southern Lebanese women who work in the sewing plant travel to the border with the protection of the SLM, pass border control, and are then driven to their workplaces in Israel. Part of their salaries (approx. US$350) is paid as a tax to the SLM for granting them the right to work.

8. On the interrelationship between the self and the other, see the work by Dwyer (1982). Dwyer states that "The self's search for knowledge of the others takes the form of a personal expedition into the other's cultural and social territory, to seek a kind of understanding that has been defined by the need of Western institutions" (p. xvii). This implies an interdependence between the self and the other as the

researcher and the informant establish and develop their own content as a result of mutual interaction. Each party's content is in accordance with his or her needs and can be complementary or contradictory, accommodating or challenging (see also Atkinson 1990; Lavie 1990; Rabinow 1977).

9. Adler and Adler (1987) describe the various roles of the researcher in fieldwork situations. They present four capacities that differ in content and significance: complete observer, observer as participant, participant as observer, and complete participant. Furthermore, the researcher receives or takes for himself or herself a certain role in the field. Adler and Adler (1987) document three such roles: peripheral membership, active membership, and full membership. These distinctions express the depth of the involvement of the researcher and the extent of reciprocity of his or her relationship with the subject of the research. The role and capacity also influence many aspects of the field research, including access, depth and type of information, personal interrelationship with the members and the group, emotional involvement, biases, ethical issues, the distinction between personal life and professional life, and issues of reliability and validity. See also the work by Denzin and Lincoln (1994), and Miles and Huberman (1994).

10. Knorr-Cettina (1981) develops the concept of methodological situationalism that assumes that general social phenomena are shaped by transactions between people in specific and concrete situations.

CHAPTER 3 *On Factory Daughters and the Culture of the Workplace*

1. The title of the chapter borrows from the title of Diane Wolf's (1992) book on women factory workers in Java.

2. During my work in the textile industry, I encountered a few Arab women, who, after leaving the plant, opened up their own small businesses and became subcontractors to Israeli firms. See the case of Nohah in Schnell, Sofer, and Drori (1995, pp. 159–160).

3. Textile companies are constantly looking for relative advantages, especially with regard to labor cost. Companies relocate to areas where they can obtain a cheap and available labor force, such as areas in which unions are weak, social wage is low, and there is a plethora of unemployed people. Low social wage implies fewer alternative sources of income, resulting in workers who are willing to work for smaller salaries. See the work by Bluestone and Harrison (1982), Elson and Pearson (1981), and Harris (1983).

4. The employment of women by men has been analyzed from many perspectives. See the work by Connel (1996) for an analysis of

the influence of gender inequality on masculinity and male patterns of behavior.

5. The social relations in the textile industry can be complex because they function in a tough competitive market. Competition pressures management to cut costs while raising production levels, elevating their dependence on those workers who can quickly adapt to change and overcome unforeseen problems (Ram 1991). Doeringer (1984, 1986) claims that the paternalistic work culture is most suitable for the textile industry because it creates dependence and bonds of loyalty between the employer and the employee.

6. Social identity in organizations refers to the way in which members link their identities to the organization and its goals. Much literature deals with different levels of social identity in the organization, such as the personal, the social, and the collective. They all refer to a social context and basic characteristics such as race, religion, and ethnicity. See the work by Snow and Anderson (1987) and White (1992). Dutton and Penner (1993) and Kramer (1993) conceptualized social organizational identity as a "cognitive schema of perception" of the organization's key features, core values, culture, mode of performance, and products.

7. The strong culture paradigm claims that there is a direct link between organizational values, behavior, and success (Deal and Kennedy 1982; Denison 1984). An instrumental organizational culture promotes values conducive to those factors determined by the organization to be most relevant to its success (Meglino, Ravlin, and Atkins 1989). Strong culture is influenced by the economic environment that determines the organization's business strategy. Research on strong organizational culture demonstrates that its key values are cohesion, clear goals, and stability. These characteristics lead to a rigid organizational culture that does not easily adapt to change (Saffold 1988; Seiter 1995). Most of the research conducted on strong culture organizations supports the notion that strong cultures adhere to values and beliefs emphasizing high performance levels, motivation, loyalty, satisfaction, and participation (Gordon and Ditomaso 1992; Sathe 1983). Strong organizational culture guides the workers into normative behavior and work procedures. It is formed through "heroes" (leaders)—managers or workers who internalize the values of the organization and serve as an example to others. Strong culture also emphasizes the importance of rituals and events in the organization as essential parts of normative behavior, the organization's history, and basic assumptions.

8. The efficiency of the textile industry is based on its ability to control the flow of production. In this respect, the managerial logic matches Fordist thought in viewing the planning of the production

process and the management of the production line as encompassing almost everything. The ideal labor force is skilled and obedient. Management systems must control the labor force, operate along the lines of hierarchy, and follow strict performance indicators. The growth of mass production generated patterns of strict hierarchy and control, eventually giving them primacy. Ultimately, hierarchy and control became the leitmotiv of Fordism. On the various aspects of Fordist and post-Fordist approaches, see the works of Chandler (1977), Taplin (1995), and Wood (1993).

The Fordist concept of production usually leads to a paternalistic management system that does not encourage autonomy and initiative from the labor force. Consequently, in the textile industry, the labor force is recruited mainly from weak socioeconomic groups, and in particular, women. Burawoy (1979) and Edwards (1979) show that the social relationships between management and workers on the shop floor are designed to exercise control of the workers. This strict control can have negative implications on the workers' self-respect, autonomy, and initiative (Crozier 1964; Hodson et al. 1993).

9. Although attempts at optimization are made, the actual working conditions on the shop floor in the textile industries are often described as uncomfortable and even hazardous conditions. The work is characterized by long working days, noise, heat, humidity, and dust. Research on the subject mainly examines the implications of working in poor physical and environmental conditions on the work process, production and quality level, health, and motivation (Gullickson 1986; Hall et al. 1987).

10. The supervision of work on the textile shop floor is based on stiff managerial discipline, direct control, distinct hierarchy, and various systems of measuring the performance of the workers. Usually, remuneration and motivation techniques directly link production to reward. This approach reflects Marxist and neo-Marxist perspectives on labor processes and control. See the work by Burawoy (1979); Clawson (1980); Edwards, Gordon, and Reich (1975); Hill (1981); Rainnie (1984); and Westwood (1984).

11. For research on the role of the family on the individual at work, see the work by Grieco (1985), Harris and Morris (1986), Morris (1984, 1985a, 1985b), and Wallman (1984). Brooks and Singh (1979) and Khan (1979) report on research regarding ethnic minorities. Generally, research on the influence of family on ethnic minorities points to high involvement in the work sphere. For more on workers' strategies for maximizing autonomy and self-expression in industrial work settings, see the work by Hodson (1995).

12. For an extensive summary of various contexts of manager-

worker conflict and its relation to social structure, forms, and processes, see Morril's *The Executive Way* (1995).

CHAPTER 4   *The Sewing Plants: Scenes from the Social Arena*

1. The daily schedule of the seamstresses starts when they leave their homes to arrive at the plant. The longest travel time is about an hour, except for the southern Lebanese women who cross the border, which is at least a two-hour drive. (These women also have to pass border control, which increases the time of travel.) Work usually starts at 6:30 a.m. Between 11:30 and 12:30, the workers take one of two shifts of a half-hour lunch break. The nine-hour workday ends at 4:00 p.m.; overtime, however, is very common, though limited to two hours. For working overtime, the workers get paid 125 percent of their hourly wage. With the passing of the minimum wage law in July 1997, the working day was reduced to eight and half hours (42 hours a week; 186 hours a month). The working week is usually five days; working on Fridays, however, is routine. On Fridays, the workers get 125 percent for the first two hours and 150 percent of their hourly wage for the rest of the day.

2. The system of quality control in the sewing plants consists of three tiers. (1) The quality controller of the department, who is part of the department team, constantly checks quality during the work process. She is responsible for identifying defects during the sewing and decides upon their severity. Usually, if she finds a few defects that are considered acceptable, she returns the batch to the seamstress, who checks them herself. This is considered a penalty because the worker has to stop her work and check the batch, thus lowering her production level, and consequently, her premium. (2) The quality controller of the division takes samples from the storehouses before they are sent. If the batch does not meet adequate standards with regard to both the types of defects and their number, it is returned to the department. (3) Random periodic checks by the customers are done either in the plants or upon delivery. If a batch does not meet stringent quality demands, the consequence is RTM (return to manufacturer). Apart from the economic losses associated with it, an RTM is considered as a blow to the plant with regard to both further orders and its reputation.

Production schedule is also an important factor in the plant's work process. The system is to work according to a flow chart presenting quantities, types of products (stroke, color), inventory, both in the warehouse and in stores, and shipment schedules. In the case of shortages or not meeting the customer deadline, the division is under threat of cancellation of orders, inacceptance of the late shipments, and, in the worst cases, fines.

3. On the issue of health and work, see Chapter 5.

4. It is worth noting that the sewing plant does not operate in a vacuum, but rather under the scrutiny and magnifying glass of the community. Deviation from acceptable norms is met with a wave of protest that, if not resolved, can end in a family withdrawing its daughters from work. See also Chapters 5 and 7.

5. The issue of pay is always a reason for dispute between management and workers. Although common wisdom claims that the seamstresses are not motivated mainly by wages because the money goes to their families in any case (see Chapter 5; Kung 1983; Wolf 1992), the seamstresses are nevertheless highly aware of the pay system and the link between the amount of work accomplished, premiums, and remuneration. On the issue of women's wages in industrial organizations, see the work by Treiman and Hartman (1981).

6. According the youth labor law of 1953, the minimum age for employment in Israel is fourteen, after the ninth grade. There are specific regulations regarding wages, working hours, and after-work studies. Youth can only work eight-hour days, with no Fridays or overtime, and there are specific wages according to age.

7. The conversation took place in January 1996, and the manager is referring to the newly established sewing activities of the concern in Egypt. Apparently, the real figure for the cost of a textile worker in Egypt is approximately $100 a month.

8. The Ramadan is the holiest month for Muslims and is a time of contemplation and spiritual elation. In Ramadan, Muslims fast during the day and eat a large festive meal at night. This month represents Mohammed's delivery of the Koran to the *umma* (community of believers). Muslims consider this month as a period when one must behave in a serious, modest, and pious manner. On the Ramadan and its place in Islam, see the work by Lazarus Yafeh (1967, pp. 82–102).

9. For a discussion of marriage in rural Arab communities in Israel, see the work by Manna and Haj-Yehia (1995).

10. In Israel, Druse men must enlist in the compulsory army service along with all the Jewish Israeli citizens and can serve in almost all units. Muslim and Christian Arabs do not serve in the Israeli army. There are exceptions, such as Bedouins and a few others, who must serve either as scouts or in special designated units.

11. One of the formal management tools in the sewing plants is comparative performance reports of all the plants that are distributed among all the managers. These reports document production figures, quality rates, economic efficiency, nonproductive hours, rate of defective products, and so on. In general, the plants are measured according to various economic criteria. The most important criteria are (1) pro-

duction hours—representing the relations between standard times of producing the product multiplied by the number of products; (2) economic efficiency—production hours divided by total working hours of all workers; and (3) absolute efficiency—production hours divided by the working hours of the seamstresses.

12. The Druse consider Jethro, Moses's father-in-law (*Nebi Schoeb*), as their founding father, and his grave is the most sacred place (the main Druse holiday, *Nebi Schoeb*, which marks his birthday, takes place there). *Nebi Schoeb* is also a place where the Druse go for feasts, taking of vows, praying, and expressing gratitude. For more on Druse customs and religion, see the work by Dana (1974, 1980) and Halabi (1997).

13. After the Six-Day War in 1967, Israel conquered territory from Jordan, known as the West Bank, occupied primarily by Palestinian Arabs. This territory includes the city of Hebron, where the Grave of the Patriarchs is located. This grave is sacred for both Jews and Muslims. It is also a common prayer ground for both religions. Special arrangements exist in the grave aiming to minimize contact between Jews and Muslims during prayer time. In already extremely tense Hebron, where Jewish settlers live among the Muslims, the grave is one of the most sensitive places. It is "a barrel of gun powder" because Jews and Muslims both believe they have sole claim on a place that symbolizes the roots of their faiths. In the early morning on Friday, February 25, 1994, Baruch Goldstein, a Jewish settler from Kiryat Arbah, a Jewish neighborhood in Hebron, entered the Abraham Hall of the Patriarchs' Grave during Muslim prayer and opened automatic fire on the Muslim worshippers. He killed twenty-nine.

14. In his eulogy after Rabin's murder, United States President Bill Clinton parted from him with the words *shalom chaver* (שלום, חבר.), meaning in Hebrew "good-bye friend." These two words became a metaphor for everyone's deep shock and pain at the loss. Offices, homes, and cars were covered with a sticker bearing these words in blue against a white background.

CHAPTER 5   *The Seamstresses: In Motion Toward*
             Reconstructing Work and Life

1. Three months is the average time it takes for new workers without any sewing experience to master the sewing technology and reach the norm of 100 percent with adequate quality. The ability to reach the norm also depends on the type of workstation, the operation, and the quality of training and coaching. The goal of the managers is to raise the production rate and quality of new workers as fast as possi-

ble. New seamstresses who cannot reach 70 to 80 percent within three months are usually dismissed. However, dismissal criteria are not rigid and are subject to the plant's need for workers, type of work-stations, and forecasts of incoming orders.

2. In his work on Arab unemployment, Atrash found that that the problem is worse among Arab men than among women. Arab men, who are usually the breadwinners of their large families, are vulnerable to unemployment in times of economic recession, when the demand for workers in the Israeli economy declines. This vulnerability is accentuated by the weak economic infrastructure of the Arab sector.

3. The textile industry and the traditional family structure often function in mutually beneficial ways. One of the characteristics of the textile industry is that it pays its workers substandard wages. In her study of factory workers in Java, Wolf (1992) claims that this exploitation is in fact supported by traditional families that are interested in keeping their daughters financially dependent. Thus, the families and the factories in the rural villages benefit from each other in a system of interdependence. The factories depend on the families for providing them with workers. More importantly, according to Wolf, the families support the factories by continuing to financially support their working daughters, allowing wages to remain far below what is needed for independent survival. Although the daughters work in the factories, they remain economically dependent on their families, who provide them with the shelter, food, and other benefits they provide for all the other children (Deere and de Janvry 1979). Simultaneously, however, the working daughters contribute to their households in indirect ways by reducing the load on their family. They eat one less meal a day and earn enough for their personal spending. The families benefit from their daughters' consumption and from access to their savings.

4. Much of the current ethnographic research that has been conducted on the influence of industrialism on women, families, and communities has come from studies of factory workers in East Asia. See Arrigo (1980); Diamond (1979); Freedman, Chang, and Sun (1982); Greenhalgh (1985); Honig (1986); Hsiung (1988); Kung (1981, 1983); Salaff (1981); D. L. Wolf (1992); and M. Wolf (1972).

5. Druse society is divided into two sectors: the religious sector (*Uk'al*), who have access to the secrets of the religion, and the secular sector (*Ju'hal*), who are not allowed to read sacred documents. Their difference is expressed mainly in their dress. The relationship between the two sectors is characterized by mutual respect, although the religious sector has more social influence and the Druse usually act in accordance with their dictates (Dana 1980).

6. It is a custom that a couple does not marry until the groom has

built a house. In the villages, the marriages are usually patrilineal and patrilocal (see Keyser 1974; Manna and Haj-Yehia 1995; Rosenfeld 1957). The signing of the marriage contract (*akaad*) during the engagement ceremony usually specifies the obligation of the groom to provide his bride with a house. The bride, on the other hand, provides for her personal belongings, appliances, and other items needed for the house.

7. It is common in the Arab villages to build onto the parents' house, adding a floor for the married son. When the couple is well off and there is land available, either belonging to the family or purchased, they usually build their own separate house and establish an independent household.

8. In his research on Arab society in Israel, Al Haj (1988) found that the splitting of the woman's energy between her work and her traditional duties at home raises the potential for conflict between married couples and leads to failure in one of the two realms.

9. A diverse body of literature deals with the issue of satisfaction at work and its intersection with personal and organizational variables. Herzberg (1966) sees satisfaction as stemming from the psychological and physical conditions of the workplace. Physical factors affecting worker satisfaction include the organization's policy, administration, working conditions, and pay. Psychological or motivational factors include recognition, responsibility, achievement, and promotion. Price (1972) relates satisfaction to the worker's personal needs, treating it as an emotional orientation of the worker toward the organization. Generally, women report greater job satisfaction than men in spite of objectively inferior jobs (Glenn, Taylor, and Weaver 1977).

10. Between May and August 1995, I conducted a machine-to-machine survey on the shop floor with the help of a research assistant. During work hours, we went from one seamstress to another and asked them a set of structured questions regarding their perceptions and feelings about work. The idea was not to use the results as a survey for quantitative analysis but to get a sense of the organizational climate in the plant regarding satisfaction, working conditions, and usage of salary.

11. In Arab communities in the Galilee, women live with their families. If their parents die, they move in with their brothers or other close relatives. In some instances in the sewing plant, older seamstresses whose parents die move in with their brother and complain bitterly about friction with his wife. Living alone is still uncommon for Arab women.

12. In many cases, women from rural societies who decide to work are viewed as pursuing employment as part of a family strategy that

reflects a single collective goal reached in consensus. In this view, the woman and the household are considered identical and inseparable and the motivation for women's work is viewed as altruism. (See Arizpe 1982; Bartlett 1989; Findley 1987; Folbre 1986; Hart 1986; Morris 1990; Pahl 1984; Stern 1987; Tilly and Scott 1978). Many scholars have attacked this notion (Ben-Porath 1982; Berk 1985; Davidson 1991), claiming that this approach ignores conflicts in households and inequality and exploitation within the family and assumes that the family unit is not problematic. Research in fact shows that resources are not fairly or evenly allocated in traditional households. Because daughters have a secondary status, they receive less than their share of food, medical care, and other advantages compared with the male members (Agarwal 1991; Greenhalgh 1985).

13. A woman's control of her salary depends on her family's system of assumptions regarding their socioeconomic situation. Thus, her access to salary does not mean control of it (Blumberg 1984; Papanek 1990; Salaff 1981).

14. The work organization and process in relation to occupational health is a well-researched subject. With regard to industrial work, routinization and pressure have been demonstrated to affect health, mainly causing cardiovascular, muscular, and skeletal problems (Vinet et al. 1989). Studies also associate routinization and the stress of piecework work production with problems such as headache, fatigue, back strain, and digestion problems (Gullickson 1986; Hall et al. 1987; Robert 1983). Stressful physical work also influences family life and personal tension that expresses itself at work (Arsenault and Dolan 1983).

15. On the importance of gossip in Arab society, see the work by Ginat (1982, pp. 195–7). Gossip is usually an activity through which information is transmitted to designated groups and then to the larger community. Within the sewing plant, gossip creates a cluster of social networks. Gossip is institutionalized with regard to personal and social matters and functions as a means of social control and as an informal means of legitimizing and helping the women in delicate private matters. See Gluckman (1968) and Paine (1967).

16. Sub'hia became a *hadane* woman, the one who initiated the breakup with her fiancé (see Ginat 1981). For a few years, she fought for an official divorce. Eventually, it was given by the Kadi in Nazareth.

17. *Badal* is a form of marriage exchange where "siblings marry siblings, the unions being linked—if one union breaks up the other union automatically breaks up" (Ginat 1982, p.100).

18. Lina is referring to the situation in which, as a divorced woman,

she'll find herself at the bottom of the status hierarchy at her parents' house, where the oldest brother is the head of the family.

19. At the entrance to the sewing plant, there is a board on which are attached magnetic time cards for all the workers. Every morning each woman passes her card through an electronic device that marks her time of arrival. At the end of the day, she registers her time of departure. Her basic salary is calculated according to the hours she spent at work. Usually, when a woman comes late, her card is withdrawn by the production manager to ensure that he speaks to her before she clocks in.

CHAPTER 6 *The Supervisors: Go-Betweens*

1. Blauner (1964) and Edwards (1979) recognize the overseeing nature of the social relations of production on the shop floor, particularly between supervisors and workers. They emphasize strict control as a key for smooth operation.

2. On the double role of the supervisor as both boss and friend, sometimes with a blurred distinction between the two, see Kung (1983).

3. The notion of loyalty in the sewing plant has multiple meanings and expresses both interpersonal relations and work relations. As such, loyalty is a principal value in the sewing plant work culture. Many have claimed that loyalty to the workplace in the traditional sense (a covenant in which companies offer job security, flexibility, and rewards in exchange for adequate performance and occasional short-term sacrifices) is dead in the era of modern competitive capitalism (see Thurow 1997). Loyalty in a competitive capitalist environment may best be defined as a desire to remain an employee of the organization or as continuous commitment, as opposed to active involvement and identification with the organization. It is clear that in the sewing plants the more traditional (and more profitable) sense of loyalty to the organization prevails.

4. The characteristics of dyadic vertical relationships, such as the relationship between managers and supervisors, have been analyzed in the context of role theory and social exchange theory. According to role theory (Katz and Kahn 1978), the process of defining one's role occurs through interactions with the other member of the dyad as well as with other people in the organization who convey important role information. Social exchange theory (Emerson 1962) discusses the relevance of alternative exchange partners from whom members can gain valuable resources for the balance of power and gaining influence within the dyad.

5. In recognition of the importance of the professional contribution

of the supervisors to the sewing plant and their key role in motivating seamstresses, the division sporadically initiates professional training. These training courses concentrate on issues such as human relationships, sewing technology, production procedures, and updating on concern structure and strategy. These courses are offered to all the supervisors from the sewing plants and serve as a stage for the exchange of ideas and the making of interpersonal contacts. The supervisors see this training as a bonus because it takes place in Carmiel and includes tours of other plants, festive meals, and a break from work.

6. Research has demonstrated (Dawes 1992) that high levels of group solidarity and cohesion facilitate reciprocity. This kind of reciprocity, involving many actors and described as indirect, can be characterized as a social exchange system (Ekeh 1974). In such a system, members help each other without expecting immediate reciprocation. The reciprocation is expected at some point in the future by anyone in the organization. It is in the manager's interest to facilitate this kind of social reciprocal relationship by exhibiting solidarity and cohesion with the supervisors. See also the work by Gouldner (1960).

7. According to Kunda (1992), the organizational self is the subjective experience resulting from the balancing of the acceptance of the ideology of the work organization, in the case of the sewing plants embodied by the managers, and its rejection. On the various aspects of self-definition within work settings, see the work by Van Maanen (1976).

8. Although there are better and worse supervisors, it is a known to everyone in the plant that subjective excellence should not influence the treatment of the supervisors by the managers. Seniority is expressed in salary and in everyone's overall appreciation of the supervisor's professionalism and experience. The manager must not express his appreciation of a supervisor in terms suggesting the inferiority of another supervisor or open favoritism. This pattern recalls the concept of the "image of the limited good" (Foster 1962).

9. Perceptions of favoritism and other breaches of fairness or organizational justice are consequential because they are associated with negative emotions about the workplace (Adams 1965). Relevant research has examined perceptions of distributive and procedural justice. Distributive justice refers to the fairness of organizational outcome distribution, whereby individuals use a rule to evaluate distributions such as equity (comparing one's input and outcome relative to another), equality (all individuals should be rewarded equally regardless of input), or needs (rewards should be based on relative needs). See the work by Bierhoff, Cohen, and Grennberg (1986).

10. *Grushim* is the Hebrew equivalent to pennies.

11. Extensive literature deals with the importance and benefits of

teamwork in various organizational settings, for example, the work by Kasl, Marsick, and Dechant (1997) and LeClair (1996).

12. The incident took place in May 1994.

13. Intragroup conflict within the same organization is studied by Pinkley (1990), who found that people differentiate between two types of conflict. The first are task-based conflicts, based on disagreements about the performance of the job. The second are relationship conflicts, arising from interpersonal disagreements not related to the work itself. Jehn (1995) demonstrates negative implications of relationship conflict, including tension and animosity between the groups, lowered satisfaction, frustration, and a desire to withdraw.

CHAPTER 7 *The Managers: Embodying a Double System*

1. In Israel there is one academic institute for the textile professions. This school trains primarily fashion designers, technologists, and textile engineers.

2. According to Spybey (1984), the manager's treatment of the workers is shaped by the community of the workers. This community usually has its own cultural characteristics that may differ from those of the manager. See the work by Martin and Fryer (1973, 1975).

3. The operationalization of these management values is constantly tested; their meaning is sometimes interpreted differently by the managers, the supervisors, and the seamstresses. The challenge of the managers is to establish a common code of the content for each value.

4. A review of the literature on organizational commitment reveals many definitions, including identification of the individual with the values and goals of the organization (Buchanan 1974); feelings of belonging, pride, affection and loyalty (Steers 1977); the willingness to invest effort in the organization (Porter et al. 1974); and the desire to remain in the organization (Becker 1960). Ideological commitment results from the subjective response of the worker to characteristics of the organization such as the nature of the job, interpersonal relationships at work, the social context of the work, and the organizational structure (Steers 1977). Behavioral commitment develops gradually as a response to situational determinants (Salancik 1977). Much of the research on behavioral commitment, expressed in the degree of willingness to stay in the organization, derives from the literature on job turnover (see Iverson and Roy 1994). The identity approach conceptualizes commitment with respect to personal meaning (Burke and Reitzes 1991) as an attachment sustained by the extent to which the worker identifies with the role, behavior, and values of the institution as an alternative source of identity.

5. See also Hareven (1982), p. 133.

6. Existing research highlights the importance of interactions with organizational insiders (peers and supervisors) for the successful socialization of newcomers. Kinship ties at work also contribute to newcomer adaptation. Hareven, in her work on the Amoskeag textile industry in New England (1982), remarks that "the initial adjustment to an alien industrial environment was usually cushioned by a relative or friend" (p. 127). Successful socialization helps newcomers make sense of the new organizational setting and instills in them the ability to cope with uncertainty.

7. Murder based on the harming of family honor is still relatively common in Arab and Druse society. In 1997, there were at least three cases in the Galilee villages of brothers attempting to kill their sisters for staining family honor by having a premarital relationship. All the cases ended in arrest and trial.

8. It is the custom for an esteemed family member to take the newly engaged couple to be professionally photographed at Acre Beach during sunset. By suggesting that he take them, the manager strengthens the family tie between him and Firuz's father.

9. Studies have examined how managers manipulate female sexuality to achieve personal and organizational goals. Although in some cases women learn to use sexuality to achieve their ends, a far more common problem is the reproduction of patriarchal relationships in the workplace, creating numerous situations whereby women are expected to serve the needs of the men at work. See the work by Connel (1996) on masculine patterns in workplaces.

10. Research on sexual harassment indicates that it is a frequent problem in work organizations and has potentially harmful physical, emotional, and economic effects on its victims (Terpstra and Baker 1991). One of the main difficulties with this research is defining sexual harassment (Cohen 1987). The present use of the term in Israel is analogous with the definition of the United States Equal Employment Opportunity Commission (EEOC) (1980), whereby sexual harassment is defined as "unwelcome sexual advances, requests for sexual favors and other verbal or physical conduct of a sexual nature when submission to such conduct is made either explicitly or implicitly a term or condition of an individual's employment." This kind of sexual harassment is not characteristic of the plants. Recently, during the writing of this book, the sexual harassment law in Israel was enacted. The first phase required employers to post on a bulletin board, in plain language, the definition of sexual harassment. The workers in the Nazareth plant read the notice with curiosity. When I asked them what it meant to them, they pointed to the clause on compliments and laughed.

11. Almost all organized labor in Israel belongs to the General Labor Union, which represents them on matters such as collective work agreements, working conditions, minimum wage, and pensions.

12. The Released Soldier Organization is a local voluntary organization aimed mainly to promote housing schemes for retired soldiers.

13. Severance pay is calculated according to one month of wages for each year at the plant. Severance pay is mandatory if the worker is fired and up to the manager's discretion if she resigns.

14. The seamstress is referring to the 1993 municipal elections.

CHAPTER 8   *Out with the Old and In with the Hi-Tex*

1. The concern is following the path that began in the 1960s when American and European textile companies relocated their production to make use of cheap female labor in Central and South America, the border zone between Mexico and the United States, and the Far East. In most of its operations in Jordan and Egypt, the plants have direct ownership and partnerships with local entrepreneurs. Research on the textile industry claims that since the 1980s there has been a shift, whereby "garment companies have now begun to reverse the international sexual division of labor, to follow the strategies of 'quick response' to customer demand, and stay close to their markets" (Webster 1996, p.87). In the case of the concern, establishing production facilities in cheap labor countries and quick response are not mutually exclusive. The headquarters in Israel provides planning and logistics and relies on the production facilities in Egypt and Jordan. Apparently, the model has proved itself successful in business terms. The relative share of production of the plants in Egypt and Jordan grew from 23 percent in 1997 to 30 percent in 1998. The plants in Egypt raised their relative contribution to the turnover of the entire concern from 10 percent in 1997 to 14 percent in 1998.

2. The background of the decline of the textile industry in the Galilee, as exemplified by the closings, can be analyzed within the context of international trends of capital mobility and a struggle between labor and capital for control of the labor process. For example, see the work by Bluestone and Harrison (1982), Braverman (1974), and Edwards (1979). The common strategy for confronting shrinking profitability in industry centers is to cut labor costs and relocate production in areas where wages are low (Bluestone and Harrison 1982).

3. In the 1998 municipal elections, the closing of the plant was a heated issue on the candidates' agendas. They blamed the municipality for surrendering to the concern and not supporting the workers' fight.

4. On the economic, social, and psychological implications of closing plants, see the work by Haber, Ferman, and Hudson (1963).

CHAPTER 9 *Conclusion*

1. It is possible to describe and analyze the management system of managers in the concern according to the wide gamut of prevalent theories of organization management (see Morgan 1989). The emphasis in these theories is on understanding the various aspects of the work process and characteristics, such as organizations as machines, describing the line of authority and command, emphasizing the human relationship aspect, and issues of power, conflict, role of technology, environment, and systems (Perrow 1970). These characteristics constitute only some of the factors affecting the work culture of the sewing plants.

2. Complying with family demands and family involvement has different contents in each plant. It is common knowledge that in the sewing plants in the traditional and small Druse villages, the manager has to adhere to the demands of family and community and to be aware of the cultural values and norms of Druse and Muslim society. In sewing plants located in mixed or urban communities such as Nazareth, the work culture is more instrumental and the burden of tradition is felt less, even though some of the workers come from the rural isolated communities. This typology corresponds to the difference in levels of modernization between the villages and cities in the Arab sector in Israel (Halabi 1997).

3. Unemployment and the generally difficult economic situation in the Arab villages is liable to change the position of the man of the family from one of provider to one of victim. The unemployed man is the victim of political and economic factors, particularly government neglect of the Arab sector. In these circumstances, the work of the women is grasped as a form of defense against the system.

4. See the work by Hsiung (1996) on Taiwan, Lee (1993) on South Korea, Ong (1987) on Malasia, Wolf (1992) on Java, Salaff (1981) on Hong Kong, Tiano (1994) and Fernandez-Kelly (1983a) on Mexico, Aguiar (1976) on Brazil, and Zavella (1987) on the United States.

References

Adams, J. S. 1965. "Inequity in Social Exchange." In L. Berkowitz, ed., *Advances in Experimental Social Psychology*, vol. 2. New York: Academic, 267–99.

Adler, P. A., and P. Adler. 1987. *Membership Roles in Field Research*. Newbury Park, Calif.: Sage.

Afshar, H., ed. 1991. *Women, Development, and Survival in the Third World*. London: Longman.

Agar, M. 1980. *The Professional Stranger*. New York: Academic.

Agarwal, B. 1991. "Social Security and the Family: Coping with the Seasonality and Calamity in Rural India." In E. Ahmad, J. Dreze, J. Hills, and A. Sen, eds., *Social Security in Developing Countries*. Oxford: Clarendon, 171–244.

Aguiar, N. 1976. "The Impact of Industrialization on Women's Work Roles in Northeast Brazil." In J. Nash and H. I. Safa, *Sex and Class in Latin America*. New York: Praeger.

Al Haj, M. 1987. *Social Change and Family Process in Arab Communities in Shefara'm*. Boulder, Colo.: Westview.

———. 1988. "The Changing Arab Kinship Structure: The Effect of Modernization in an Urban Community." *Economic Development and Cultural Change* 36: 237–58.

Altorki, S. 1986. *Women in Saudi Arabia: Ideology and Behavior Among the Elite*. New York: Columbia University Press.

Amin, A. 1994. *Post-Fordism: A Reader*. Oxford: Blackwell.

Arizpe, L. 1982. "Relay Migration and the Survival of the Peasant Household." In H. I. Safa, ed., *Towards a Political Economy of Urbanization in Third World Countries*. Delhi: Oxford University Press, 19–46.

Arrigo, L. G. 1980. "The Industrial Work Force of Young Women in Taiwan." *Bulletin of Concerned Asian Scholars* 12(2): 25–38.

Arsenault, A., and S. Dolan. 1983. "The Role of Personality, Occupation, and Organization in Understanding the Relationship Between Job Stress, Performance and Absenteeism." *Journal of Occupational Psychology* 56: 227–40.

Atkinson, P. 1990. *The Ethnographic Imagination: Textual Constructions of Reality.* New York: Routledge.

Atrash, A. 1995. *Days Go By: Unemployment Among Arabs in Israel.* Kfar Saba: Institute for Israeli Arab Studies Beit Berl [Hebrew].

Bartlett, P. 1989. "Industrial Agriculture." In S. Plattner, ed., *Economic Anthrolopogy.* Stanford: Stanford University Press, 253–91.

Becker, H. 1960. "Notes on the Concept of Commitment." *American Journal of Sociology* 66: 32–40.

Belanger, J., P. K. Edwards, and L. Haiven. 1994. *Workplace Industrial Relations and the Global Challenge.* Ithaca, N.Y.: ILR.

Belussi, F. 1992. "Benetton Italy: Beyond Fordism and Flexible Specialization: The Evolution of the Network Firm Model." In S. Mitter, ed., *Computer-Aided Manufacturing and Women's Employment: The Clothing Industry in Four EC Countries.* London: Springer-Verlag.

Ben-Porath, Y. 1982. "Economics and the Family—Match or Mismatch." *Journal of Economic Literature* 20: 52–64.

Benson, S. P. 1986. *Counter Cultures: Sales: Saleswomen, Managers, and Customers in American Department Stores, 1890–1940.* Urbana: University of Illinois Press.

Berger, S., and M. J. Piore. 1980. *Dualism and Discontinuity in Industrial Societies.* Cambridge: Cambridge University Press.

Berk, S. F. 1985. *The Gender Factory.* New York: Plenum Press.

Berreman, G. D. 1972. *Hindus of the Himalayas: Ethnography and Change.* Berkeley: University of California Press.

Bierhoff, H. W., R. L. Cohen, and J. Grennberg. 1986. *Justice in Social Relations.* New York: Plenum.

Black, D. 1990. "The Elementary Forms of Conflict Management." In Arizona State University School of Justice Studies, ed., *New Directions in the Study of Justice, Law, and Social Control.* New York: Plenum, 43–69.

Blauner, R. 1964. *Alienation and Freedom: The Factory Worker and His Industry.* Chicago: University of Chicago Press.

Bluestone, B., and B. Harrison. 1982. *The Deindustrialization of America: Plant Closings, Community Abandonment, and the Dismantling of Basic Industry.* New York: Basic Books.

Blumberg, R. 1984. "A General Theory of Gender Stratification." In

R. Collins, ed., *Sociological Theory*. San Francisco: Jossey-Bass, 83–101.

Boserup, E. 1970. *Women's Role in Economic Development*. London: Allen and Unwin.

Bradley, H. 1989. *Men's Work, Women's Work*. Cambridge, Mass.: Polity.

Braverman, H. 1974. *Labor and Monopoly Capital: The Degradation of Work in the Twentieth Century*. New York: Monthly Review Press.

Brooks, D., and K. Singh. 1979. "Pivots and Presents: Asian Brokers in British Foundries." In S. Wallman, ed., *Ethnicity at Work*. London: Macmillan.

Buchanan, B. 1974. "Building Organizational Commitment: The Socialization of Managers in Work Organizations." *Administrative Science Quarterly* 19: 533–46.

Burke, P., and D. Reitzes. 1991. "An Identity Theory Approach to Commitment." *Social Psychology Quarterly* 54: 39–51

Burawoy, M. 1979. *Manufacturing Consent: Changes in the Labor Process Under Monopoly Capitalism*. Chicago: University of Chicago Press.

Cairoli, M. L. 1998. "Factory as Home and Family: Female Workers in the Moroccan Garment Industry." *Human Organization* 57(2): 181–89.

Calagione, J., and D. Nugent. 1992. "Workers' Expressions Beyond Accommodation and Resistance on the Margins of Capitalism." In J. Calagione and D. Nugent, eds., *Workers' Expressions: Beyond Accommodation and Resistance*. Albany, N.Y.: SUNY Press, 1–34.

Cameron, K. S., and S. J. Freeman. 1991. "Cultural Congruence, Strength, and Type: Relationships to Effectiveness." In R. W. Woodman and W. A. Pasmore, eds., *Research in Organizational Change and Development*. Greenwich, Conn.: JAI, 23–58

Carmi S., and H. Rosenfeld. 1992. "Israel's Political Economy and the Widening Class Gap Between Its Two National Groups." *Asian and African Studies* 26: 15–61.

Carvajal, G., and I. Drori. 1987. "La Diversidad Etnico-Cultural en la Region Atlantica y los Problemas de Integraccion Socio-Espacial al Contexto Regional Costarricense." *Revista Geographica* 106, Instituto Panamericano d' Geografia E Historia, 19–66.

Chandler, A. 1977. *The Visible Hand: The Managerial Revolution in American Business*. Cambridge, Mass.: Harvard University Press.

Chemers, M. M., S. Oskamp, and M. A. Costanzo, eds. 1995. *Diversity in Organizations: New Perspectives for a Changing Workplace*. Thousand Oaks, Calif.: Sage.

Clawson, D. 1980. *Bureaucracy and the Labor Process: The Transformation of U.S. Industry, 1860–1920.* New York: Monthly Review Press.

Clegg, S. R. 1990. *Modern Organizations: Organization Studies in the Postmodern World.* Newbury Park, Calif.: Sage.

Clifford, J., and G. E. Marcus. 1986. *Writing Culture: The Poetics and Politics of Ethnography.* Berkeley: University of California Press.

Cockburn, C. 1985. *Machinery of Dominance: Men, Women and Technological Know-how.* London: Pluto.

Collins, R. 1975. *Conflict Sociology.* New York: Academic.

Connel, R. W. 1996. "New Directions in Gender Theory, Masculinity Research and Gender Politics." *Ethnos* 61(3–4): 157–75.

Crozier, M. 1964. *The Bureaucratic Phenomenon.* Chicago: University of Chicago Press.

Daft, R. L., and K. E. Weick. 1984. "Toward a Model of Organizations and Interpretation Systems." *Academy of Management Review* 9(2): 284–95.

Dana, N. 1974. *The Druze: Community and Tradition.* Jerusalem: Ministry of Religion, Government Press [Hebrew].

———. 1980. "The Druze—A Religious Community in Transition." *Israel Economist* 24: 135–45.

Davidson, A. 1991. "Rethinking Household Livelihood Strategies." In D. Clay and H. Schwarzweller, eds., *Household Survival Strategies, Research in Rural Sociology and Development,* vol. 5. Greenwich, Conn.: JAI, 11–28.

Dawes, R. M. 1992. "Social Dilemmas, Economic Self Interest, and Evolutionary Theory." In D. R. Brown and J. E. Keith Smith, eds., *Recent Research in Psychology: Frontiers of Mathematical Psychology.* New York: Springer-Verlag, 1–27.

Dawson, S. 1986. *Analysing Organisations.* London: Macmillan.

Deal, T. E., and A. A. Kennedy 1982. *Corporate Cultures.* Reading, Mass.: Addison-Wesley.

Deere, C. D., and A. de Janvry. 1979. "A Conceptual Framework for the Empirical Analysis of Peasants." *American Journal of Agricultural Economics* 61(4): 601–11.

Delbridge, R., and J. Lowe. 1997. "Manufacturing Control: Supervisory Systems on the 'New' Shopfloor." *Sociology* 31(3): 409–26.

Denison, D. R. 1984. "Bringing Corporate Cultures to the Bottom Line." *Organizational Dynamics* 13(Autumn): 5–22.

Denzin, N. K., and Y. C. Lincoln, eds., 1994. *Handbook of Qualitative Research.* Thousand Oaks, Calif.: Sage.

Diamond, N. 1979. "Women and Industry in Taiwan." *Modern China* 5: 317–40.

Dick, B., and G. Morgan. 1987. "Textile Networks and Employment in Textiles." *Work, Employment, and Society* 1(2): 225–46.

Dicken, P. 1986. *Global Shift: Industrial Changes in a Turbulent World*. New York: Harper and Row.

Doeringer, P. B. 1984. "Internal Labour Markets and Paternalism in Rural Areas." In P. Osterman, ed., *Internal Labour Markets*. Cambridge, Mass.: MIT.

Doeringer, P. B., P. I. Moss, and D. G. Terbla. 1986. "Capitalism and Kinship: Do Institutions Matter in the Labour Market?" *Industrial and Labor Relations Review* 40(1): 48–61.

Drori, I. 1990. "Land Settlement in Jamaica: The Implementation of Socialist Experience." *Public Administration and Development* 10(1): 27–39.

———. 1996. *The Work Culture of Arab Women in the Textile Industry*. Discussion paper no. 86, Golda Meir Institute for Social and Labor Research, Tel-Aviv University [Hebrew].

Drori, I., and D. Gayle. 1990a. "Agricultural Diversification Strategy in Island States: The Case of Barbados." *Journal of Development Societies* 4(3 and 4): 219–28.

———. 1990b. "Youth Employment Strategies in Jamaican Sugar Belt Area." *Human Organization* 49(4): 264–373.

Dunlap, J. T., and D. Weil. 1996. "Diffusion and Performance of Modular Production in the U.S. Apparel Industry." *Industrial Relations* 35(3): 334–55.

Dutton, J. E., and W. J. Penner. 1993. "The Importance of Organizational Identity for Strategic Agenda Building." In J. Hendery and G. Johnson, eds., *Strategic Thinking: Leadership and the Management of Change*. New York: Strategic Management Society, Wiley, 89–113.

Dwyer, K. 1982. *Moroccan Dialogues*. Baltimore: Johns Hopkins University Press.

Ecevit, Y. 1991. "Shop Floor Control: The Ideological Construction of Turkish Women Factory Workers." In M. Redclift and M. T. Sinclair, eds., *Working Women: International Perspectives on Labour and Gender Ideology*. London: Routledge, 56–78.

Edwards, R. 1978. "The Social Relations of Production at the Point of Production." *Insurgent Sociologist* 8(2–3): 109–25.

———. 1979. *Contested Terrain: The Transformation of the Workplace in the Twentieth Century*. New York: Basic Books.

Edwards, R., D. M. Gordon, and M. Reich, eds. 1975. *Labor Market Segmentation*. Lexington, Mass.: D.C. Heath.

Eisenstadt, S. N. 1967. *Israeli Society*. London: Weidenfeld and Nicholson.

Eisenstein, Z. 1979. *Capitalist Patriarchy and the Case for Socialist Feminism.* New York: Monthly Review Press.

Ekeh, P. P. 1974. *Social Exchange Theory: The Two Traditions.* Cambridge, Mass.: Harvard University Press.

Elson, D. 1994. "Uneven Development and the Textiles and Clothing Industry." In Leslie Sklair, ed., *Capitalism and Development.* London: Routledge, 189–210.

Elson, D., and R. Pearson. 1981. "Nimble Fingers Make Cheap Workers: An Analysis of Women's Employment in Third World Export Manufacturing." *Feminist Review* 4: 87–107.

Emerson, R. 1962. "Power-Dependence Relations." *American Sociological Review* 27: 31–40.

Etzioni, A. 1961. *A Comparative Analysis of Complex Organizations.* New York: Free Press.

Feldman, S., and S. Buechler. 1998. "Negotiating Difference: Constructing Selves and Others in a Transnational Apparel Manufacturing Firm." *Sociological Quarterly* 39(4): 623–44.

Fernandez-Kelly, M. P. 1983a. *For We Are Sold, I and My People.* Albany, N.Y.: SUNY Press.

———. 1983b. "Mexican Border Industrialization, Female Labor Force Participation, and Migration." In J. Nash and M. P. Fernandez-Kelly, eds., *Women, Men, and the International Division of Labor.* Albany, N.Y.: SUNY Press, 205–23.

Fernea, E. W., ed. 1985. *Women and the Family in the Middle East: New Voices of Change.* Austin: University of Texas Press.

Findley, S. 1987. *Rural Development and Migration: A Study of Family Choices in the Philippines.* Boulder, Colo.: Westview.

Folbre, N. 1986. "Cleaning House: New Perspectives on Households and Economic Development." *Journal of Development Economics* 22: 5–40.

Foster, G. M. 1962. *Traditional Cultures and the Impact of Technological Change.* New York: Harper and Row.

Frank, A. G. 1967. *Capitalism and Underdevelopment in Latin America.* New York: Monthly Review Press.

Freedman, R., M. Chang, and T. Sun. 1982. "Household Composition, Extended Kinship, and Reproduction in Taiwan: 1973–1980." *Population Studies* 36: 395–411.

Fuentes, A., and B. Ehrenreich. 1983. *Women in the Global Factory.* Boston, Mass.: South End Press.

Galbraith, J. 1977. *Organization Design.* Reading, Mass.: Addison-Wesley.

Geertz, C. 1973. *The Interpretation of Culture.* New York: Basic Books.

———. 1983. *Local Knowledge.* New York: Basic Books.

Ghoussoub, M. 1987. "Feminism—or the Eternal Masculine—in the Arab World." *New Left Review* 161 (January-February): 3–13.

Giddens, A. 1990. *The Consequences of Modernity*. Stanford: Stanford University Press.

Ginat, J. 1982. *Women in Muslim Rural Society*. New Brunswick, N.J.: Transaction Books.

Glenn, N. D., P. A. Taylor, and C. N. Weaver. 1977. "Age and Job Satisfaction Among Males and Females: A Multivariate, Multisurvey Study." *Journal of Applied Psychology* 62: 189–93.

Gluckman, M. 1968. "Psychological, Sociological and Anthropological Explanations of Witchcraft and Gossip: A Clarification." *Man* 3(March): 20–34.

Goffman, E. 1989. "On Fieldwork." *Journal of Contemporary Ethnography* 18: 123–32.

Gordon, G. G., and N. Ditomaso. 1992. "Predicting Corporate Performance from Organizational Culture." *Journal of Management Studies* 29(6): 783–98.

Gottfried, H. 1998. "Beyond Patriarchy? Theorising Gender and Class." *Sociology* 32(3): 451–68.

Gouldner, A. W. 1960. "The Norm of Reciprocity. A Preliminary Statement." *American Sociological Review* 25: 161–78.

Gradus, Y., E. Razin, and S. Krakover. 1993. *The Industrial Geography of Israel*. London: Routledge.

Greenhalgh, S. 1985. "Sexual Stratification: The Other Side of 'Growth with Equity' in East Asia." *Population and Development Review* 11(2): 265–314.

Gregory, K. 1983. "Native-View Paradigms: Multiple Cultures and Culture Conflict in Organizations." *Administrative Science Quarterly* 28: 359–76.

Grieco, M. 1985. "Social Networks in Labour Migration." *Industrial Relations Journal* 16(4): 53–67.

Gullickson, G. L. 1986. *The Spinners and the Weavers of Auffay: Rural Industry and the Sexual Division of Labor in a French Village, 1750–1850*. New York: Cambridge University Press.

Gutman, H. 1977. *Work, Culture, and Society in Industrializing America: Essays in American Working-Class and Social History*. New York: Vintage Books.

Haber, W., L. A. Ferman, and J. P. Hudson. 1963. *The Impact of Technological Change: The American Experience*. Kalamazoo, Mich.: Upjohn.

Haidar, A. 1985. "Economic Entrepreneurial Patterns in the Arab Village in Israel." Ph.D. dissertation, Hebrew University, Jerusalem [Hebrew].

———. 1991. *The Arab Population in the Israeli Economy*. Tel Aviv: International Center for Peace in the Middle East [Hebrew].

———. 1993. *Obstacles to Economic Development in the Arab Sector in Israel*. Tel Aviv: Jewish-Arab Centre for Economic Development [Hebrew].

Halabi, R. 1997. "The Interaction Between Culture and Economics in Social Changes Affecting the Druze Community in Israel." Ph.D. dissertation, Tel Aviv University, Israel [Hebrew].

Hall, J. D., J. Leloudis, R. Korstad, M. Murphy, L. A. Jones, and C. B. Daly. 1987. *Like a Family: The Making of a Southern Cotton Mill World*. Chapel Hill: University of North Carolina Press.

Hareven, T. 1982. *Family Time and Industrial Time: The Relationship Between the Family and Work in a New England Industrial Community*. Cambridge, U.K.: Cambridge University Press.

Harris, C., and L. Morris. 1986. "Households, Labour Markets and the Position of Women." In R. Crompton and M. Mann, eds., *Gender and Stratification*. Cambridge, Mass.: Polity.

Harris, N. 1983. *Of Bread and Guns*. London: Penguin.

Hart, G. 1986. *Power, Labor, and Livelihood: Processes of Change in Rural Java*. Berkeley: University of California Press.

Hartman, H. 1976. "Capitalism, Patriarchy, and Job Segregation by Sex." *Signs* 1 (3 part 2): 137–69.

———. 1981. "The Unhappy Marriage of Marxism and Feminism: Towards a More Progressive Union." In L. Sargent, ed., *Women and Revolution*. London: Pluto.

Headland, T.N., K. L. Pike, and M. H. Harris, eds. 1990. *Emics and Etics*. Newbury Park, Calif.: Sage.

Herzberg, F. 1966. *Work and the Nature of Man*. Cleveland: World.

Hijab, N. 1988. *Womenpower: The Arab Debate on Women and Work*. Cambridge, U.K.: Cambridge University Press.

Hill, S. 1981. *Competition and Control at Work*. Cambridge, Mass.: MIT.

Hirschman, A. 1970. *Exit, Voice, and Loyalty*. Cambridge, Mass.: Harvard University Press.

Hodson, R. 1995. "Worker Resistance: An Underdeveloped Concept in the Sociology of Work." *Economic and Industrial Democracy* 16: 79–110.

Hodson, R., ed. 1997. *The Globalization of Work*. Greenwich, Conn.: JAI.

Hodson, R., S. Welsh, S. Rieble, C. S. Jamison, and S. Creighton. 1993. "Is Worker Solidarity Undermined by Autonomy and Participation? Patterns from the Ethnographic Literature." *American Sociological Review* 58: 398–416.

Hofstede, G. 1991. *Cultures and Organizations: Software of the Mind.* London: McGraw-Hill.

Honig, E. 1986. *Sisters and Strangers: Women in the Shanghai Cotton Mills, 1919–1949.* Stanford: Stanford University Press.

Hsiung, P. 1988. "Family Structure and Fertility in Taiwan." *Journal of Population Studies* 11: 103–28.

———. 1996. *Living Rooms as Factories: Class, Gender, and the Satellite Factory System in Taiwan.* Philadelphia: Temple University Press.

Iverson, R.D., and P. Roy. 1994. "A Causal Model of Behavioral Commitment: Evidence from a Study of Australian Blue-Collar Employees." *Journal of Management* 20(1): 15–41.

Jehn, K. A. 1995. "A Multimethod Examination of the Benefits and Detriments of Intragroup Conflict." *Administrative Science Quarterly* 40: 256–82.

Joseph, S. 1994. "Brother/Sister Relationships: Connectivity, Love, and Power in the Reproduction of Patriarchy in Lebanon." *American Ethnologist* 21(1): 50–73.

Joyce, P. 1980. *Work, Society and Politics.* Brighton: Wheatsheaf.

Kandiyoti, D. 1988. "Bargaining with Patriarchy." *Gender and Society* 2(3)(September): 274–89.

Kapferer, B. 1972. *Strategy and Transaction in an African Factory.* Manchester, U.K.: Manchester University Press.

Kasl, E., V. J. Marsick, and K. Dechant. 1997. "Teams as Learners: A Research Based Model of Team Learning." *Journal of Applied Behavioral Science* 33(2): 227–46.

Katz, D., and R. L. Kahn. 1978. *The Social Psychology of Organizations*, 2nd edition. New York: Wiley.

Keyser, J. M. B. 1974. "The Middle Eastern Case: Is There a Marriage Rule?" *Ethnology* 13(July): 293–309.

Khan, V. S. 1979. "Work and Network: South Asian Women in South London." In S. Wallman, ed., *Ethnicity at Work.* London: Macmillan.

Khoury, N. F., and V. M. Moghadam. 1995. *Gender and Development in the Arab World—Women's Economic Participation: Patterns and Policies.* London: Zed Books.

Knorr-Cettina, K. D. 1981. *The Manufacture of Knowledge: An Essay on the Constructivist and Contextual Nature of Science.* Oxford: Pergamon.

Kolb, D. M., and L. L. Putnam. 1992. "Introduction: The Dialectics of Disputing." In D. M. Kolb and J. M. Bartunek, eds., *Hidden Conflict in Organizations: Uncovering Behind the Scenes Disputes.* Newbury Park, Calif.: Sage, 63–91.

Kondo, D. K. 1986. "Dissolution and Reconstitution of Self: Implications for Anthropological Epistemology." *Cultural Anthropology* 1(1): 74–88.

———. 1990. *Crafting Selves: Power, Gender, and Discourses of Identity in a Japanese Workplace*. Chicago: University of Chicago Press.

Kramer, R. M. 1993. "Cooperation and Organizational Identification." In J. K. Murnighan, ed., *Social Psychology in Organizations*. Englewood Cliffs, N.J.: Prentice-Hall, 244–69.

Kunda, G. 1992. *Engineering Culture: Control and Commitment in a High-Tech Corporation*. Philadelphia: Temple University Press.

Kunda, G., and S. R. Barley. 1988. "Designing Devotion: Corporate Cultures and Ideologies of Workplace Control." Paper delivered at the 83rd Annual Meeting of the American Sociological Association, Atlanta, Georgia.

Kung, L. 1981. "Perceptions of Work Among Factory Women." In E. M. Ahern and H. Gates, eds., *The Anthropology of Taiwanese Society*. Stanford: Stanford University Press, 184–211.

———. 1983. *Factory Women in Taiwan*. Ann Arbor: University of Michigan Press.

Kurzum, G. 1995. *The Position of the Arab Labor Force in the Israeli Economy and Trends for Change*. Jerusalem: Center for Labor and Development.

Lamphere, L., and P. Zavella. 1997. "Women's Resistence in the Sunbelt: Anglos and Hispanas Respond to Managerial Control." In L. Lamphere, H. Ragone, and P. Zavella, eds., *Situated Lives: Gender and Culture in Everyday Life*. New York: Routledge.

Lavie, S. 1990. *The Poetics of Military Occupation*. Berkeley: University of California Press.

Layish, A. 1976. "Women and Succession in the Druze Family in Israel." *Asian and African Studies* 11(1): 101–19.

Lazarus Yafeh, H. 1967. *Studies in the History of the Arabs and Islam*. Tel Aviv: Reshafim Publishing House [Hebrew].

Lazonick, M. 1990. *Competitive Advantage on the Shopfloor*. Cambridge, Mass.: Harvard University Press.

LeClair, D. 1996. "Teams: Economic Theory and Managerial Applications." *American Business Review* 14(1): 60–6.

Lee, O. 1993. "Gender-Differentiated Employment Practices in the South Korean Textile Industry." *Gender and Society* 7(4): 507–28.

Leiter, J., M. D. Shulman, and R. Zingraff. 1992. *Hanging by a Thread: Social Changes in Southern Textiles*. Ithaca, N.Y.: Cornell University Press.

Leman, S. 1992. "Ethnicity, Technology and Local Labor Markets in the Clothing Industry of Northern England." *Urban Anthropology* 21: 115–36.

Lewin-Epstein, N. 1989. "Labor Market Position and Antagonism Towards Arabs in Israel." *Research in Inequality and Social Conflict* 1: 165–91.

Lewin-Epstein, N., and M. Semyonov. 1993. *The Arab Minority in Israel's Economy*. Boulder, Colo.: Westview.

Lincoln, J. R., and A. L. Kalleberg. 1990. *Culture, Control, and Commitment*. Cambridge, U.K.: Cambridge University Press.

Lustick, I. 1980. *Arabs in the Jewish State*. Austin, Tex.: University of Texas Press.

Mandelbaum, D. 1988. *Women's Seclusion and Men's Honor*. Tucson: University of Arizona Press.

Manna, A., and K. Haj-Yehia. 1995. *Mabruk: The Wedding Culture Among the Arabs in Israel*. Kfar Saba: Institute for Israeli Arab Studies Beit Berl [Hebrew].

Marcus, G., and M. J. Fisher. 1986. *Anthropology as Cultural Critique*. Chicago: University of Chicago Press.

Marcus, G. E. 1986. "Contemporary Problems of Ethnography in the Modern World System." In J. Clifford and C. E. Marcus, eds., *Writing Culture: The Poetics and Politics of Ethnography*. Berkeley: University of California Press, 165–93.

Martin, R., and R. H. Fryer. 1973. *Redundancy and Paternalist Capitalism*. London: Allen and Unwin.

———. 1975. "The Deferential Worker." In M. Bulmer, ed., *Working Class Images of Society*. London: Routledge and Kegan Paul.

Meglino, B., E. C. Ravlin, and C. L. Atkins. 1989. "A Work Values Approach to Corporate Culture: A Field Test of the Value Congruence Process and Its Relationship to Individual Outcomes." *Journal of Applied Psychology*, 74(3): 424–32.

Mernissi, F. 1987. *Beyond the Veil: Male–Female Dynamics in Modern Muslim Society*, revised edition. Bloomington, Ind.: Indiana University Press.

Meyer-Brodnitz, M. B., and D. T. Czamanski. 1986. *Economic Development in the Arab Sector in Israel*. Haifa: Technion, Center for Urban and Regional Studies [Hebrew].

Miari, S. 1986. "The Arabs in Israel: A National Minority and Cheap Labor Force, A Split Labor Market Analysis." Ph.D. dissertation, Loyola University of Chicago.

Mies, M. 1994. "'Gender' and Global Capitalism." In L. Sklair, ed., *Capitalism and Development*. London: Routledge, 107–22.

Miles, M. B., and A. M. Huberman. 1994. *Qualitative Data Analysis: An Expanded Sourcebook*, 2nd edition. Thousand Oaks, Calif.: Sage.

Moghadam, V. M. 1993. *Modernizing Women: Gender and Social Change in the Middle East*. Boulder, Colo.: Lynne Rienner.

Montgomery, D. 1979. *Workers' Control in America*. Cambridge, U.K.: Cambridge University Press.

Morgan, G. 1989. *Creative Organization Theory: A Resource Book*. Newbury Park, Calif.: Sage.

Morril, C. 1995. *The Executive Way*. Chicago: University of Chicago Press.

Morris, L. 1984. "Patterns of Social Activity and Post-Redundancy Labour Market Experience." *Sociology* 18: 339–52.

———. 1985a. "Renegotiation of the Domestic Division of Labour." In B. Roberts, R. Finnegan, and D. Gallie, eds., *New Approaches to Economic Life*. Manchester: Manchester University Press.

———. 1985b. "Local Social Networks and Domestic Organisation: A Study of Redundant Steel Workers and Their Wives." *Sociological Review* 33(2): 327–42.

———. 1990. *The Workings of the Household*. Cambridge, Mass.: Polity.

Nader, L., and H. F. Todd. 1978. *The Disputing Process—Law in Ten Societies*. New York: Columbia University Press.

Nash, J., and M. P. Fernandez-Kelly, eds. 1983. *Women, Men, and the International Division of Labor*. Albany, N.Y.: SUNY Press.

Newby, H. 1977. *The Deferential Worker: A Study of Farm Workers in East Anglia*. London: Allen Lane.

Newman, D. 1980. "Textile Workers in a Tobacco Country: A Comparison Between Yarn and Weave Mill Villages." In E. Magdol and J. L. Wakelyn, eds., *The Southern Common People: Studies in Nineteenth-Century Social History*. Westport, Conn.: Greenwood Press, 345–68.

Nichols, T., and H. Beynon. 1977. *Living with Capitalism*. London: Routledge and Kegan Paul.

Ong, A. 1987. *Spirits of Resistance and Capitalist Discipline: Factory Women in Malaysia*. Albany, N.Y.: SUNY Press.

———. 1997. "Spirits of Resistance." In L. Lamphere, H. Ragone, and P. Zavella, *Situated Lives: Gender and Culture in Everyday Life*. New York: Routledge.

Ott, J. S. 1989. *The Organizational Culture Perspective*. Pacific Grove, Calif.: Brooks/Cole.

Padavic, I., and W. R. Ernest. 1994. "Paternalism as a Component of Managerial Strategy." *Social Science Journal* 31(4): 389–405.

Pahl, R. E. 1984. *Divisions of Labour*. Oxford: Basil Blackwell.

Paine, R. 1967. "What Is Gossip About? An Alternative Hypothesis." *Man* 2 (June): 278–85.

Papanek, H. 1990. "To Each Less Than She Needs, From Each More Than She Can Do." In I. Tinker, ed., *Persistent Inequalities*. New York: Oxford University Press, 162–81.

Pasmore, W. A. 1988. *Designing Effective Organizations: The Sociotechnical Systems Perspective.* New York: Wiley.

Pateman, C. 1997. "Selection from *The Sexual Contract.*" In C. C. Gould, ed., *Gender.* New Jersey: Humanities, 317–24.

Pearson, R. 1992. "Gender Issues in Industrialization." In T. Hewitt, H. Johnson, and D. Weild, eds., *Industrialization and Development.* Oxford: Oxford University Press, 222–47.

Perrow, C. 1970. *Organizational Analysis: A Sociological View.* London: Tavistock.

———. 1986. *Complex Organizations: A Critical Essay,* 3rd edition. New York: Random House.

Peters, T. J., and R. H. Waterman. 1982. *In Search of Excellence: Lessons from America's Best-Run Companies.* New York: Harper and Row.

Peterson, J. E. 1989. "The Political Status of Women in the Arab Gulf States." *Middle East Journal* 43(1): 34–50.

Phillips, M. W. 1998. "Gendered Work: An Analysis of Work in a Fijian Garment Factory." *Australian Geographer* 29(3): 341–57.

Pinkley, R. L. 1990. "Dimensions of Conflict Frame: Disputant Interpretations of Conflict." *Journal of Applied Psychology* 75: 117–26.

Pollert, A. 1996. "Gender and Class Revisited; Or, the Poverty of 'Patriarchy.'" *Sociology* 30(4): 639–59.

Porter, L. W., R. M. Steers, R. T. Mowday, and P. V. Boulian. 1974. "Organizational Commitment, Job Satisfaction and Turnover Among Psychiatric Technicians." *Journal of Applied Psychology* 59: 603–9.

Poster, W. R. 1998. "Globalization, Gender, and the Workplace: Women and Men in an American Multinational Corporation in India." *Journal of Developing Societies* 14(1): 40–65.

Price, J. L. 1972. *Handbook of Organizational Measurement.* Lexington, Mass.: D.C. Health.

Quinn, R. E. 1988. *Beyond Rational Management.* San Francisco: Jossey-Bass.

Rabinow, P. 1977. *Reflections on Fieldwork in Morocco.* Berkeley: University of California Press.

Rabinowitz, D. 1997. *Overlooking Nazareth: The Ethnography of Exclusion in Galilee.* Cambridge: Cambridge University Press.

———. 1998. *Anthropology and the Palestinians.* Kfar Saba, Israel: Beit Berl, Institute for Israeli Arab Studies [Hebrew].

Rainnie, A. F. 1984. "Combined and Uneven Development in the Clothing Industry: The Effects of Competition on Accumulation." *Capital and Class* 22 (Spring): 141–56.

Ram, M. 1991. "Control and Autonomy of Small Firms: The Case of the West Midlands Clothing Industry." *Work, Employment, and Society* 5(4): 601–19.

Reiter, Y., and R. Aharoni. 1992. *The Political Life of Arabs in Israel*. Kfar Saba: Institute for Israeli Arabs Studies Beit Berl [Hebrew].

Rekhess, E. 1986. "The Arab Village in Israel: A Renewing National Political National Centre." *Horizons* 17–18: 145–60 [Hebrew].

Robert, A. 1983. "The Effects of the International Division of Labour on Female Workers in the Textile and Clothing Industries." *Development and Change* 14: 19–37.

Robertson, R. 1992. *Globalization: Social Theory and Global Culture*. London: Sage.

Rose, D., G. Marshall, and C. Vogler. 1987. "Goodbye to Supervision." *Work, Employment, and Society* 1(1): 7–24.

Rosenfeld, H. 1957. "An Analysis of Marriage Statistics for a Muslim and Christian Arab Village." *International Archives of Ethnography* 48(Summer): 32–62.

———. 1964. "From Peasantry to Wage Labor and Residual Peasantry: The Transformation of an Arab Village." In R. A. Manners, ed., *Process and Pattern in Culture: Essays in Honor of Julian Steward*. Chicago: Aldine, 211–34.

———. 1981. "Change and Contradiction in the Rural Family." In A. Layish, ed., *The Arabs in Israel: Continuity and Change*. Jerusalem: Magness.

Rosenhek, Z. 1995. "New Developments in the Sociology of Israel's Palestinian Citizens: An Analytical Review." *Megamot* 37(1–2): 167–90 [Hebrew].

Sabbah, F. A. 1984. *Woman in the Muslim Unconscious*. Translated by Mary Jo Lakeland. New York: Pergamon.

Sabel, C. F. 1982. *Work and Politics: The Division of Labor in Industry*. New York: Cambridge University Press.

Safa, H. I. 1983. "Women, Production, and Reproduction in Industrial Capitalism: A Comparison of Brazilian and U.S. Factory Workers." In J. Nash and M. P. Fernandez-Kelly, eds., *Women, Men, and the International Division of Labour*. Albany, N.Y.: SUNY Press, 95–116.

Saffold, G. S. 1988. "Culture Traits, Strength and Organizational Performance: Moving Beyond 'Strong' Culture." *Academy of Management Review* 13(4): 546–58.

Salaff, J. W. 1981. *Working Daughters of Hong Kong*. Cambridge: Cambridge University Press, ASA Rose Monograph Series.

Salancik, G. R. 1977. "Commitment and the Control of Organizational Behavior and Belief." In B. M. Staw and G. R. Salancik, eds., *New Directions in Organizational Behavior*. Chicago: St. Clair, 1–54.

Sathe, V. 1983. "Implications of Corporate Culture: A Manager's Guide to Action." *Organizational Dynamics* Autumn: 5–38.

Sayer, A. 1989. "Post-Fordism in Question." *International Journal of Urban and Regional Research* 13: 666–95.

Schein, E. H. 1985. *Organizational Culture and Leadership.* San Francisco: Jossey-Bass.

Schnell, I., M. Sofer, and I. Drori. 1995. *Arab Industrialization in Israel: Ethnic Entrepreneurship in the Periphery.* Westport, Conn.: Praeger.

Schwartzman, H. 1993. *Ethnography in Organizations.* Newbury Park, Calif.: Sage.

Schwartzman, K. C. 1998. "Globalization and Democracy." *Annual Review of Sociology* 24: 159–81.

Seiter, J. S. 1995. "Surviving a Turbulent Organizational Environment: A Case Examination of a Lumber Company's Internal and External Influence Attempts." *Journal of Business Communication* 32(4): 363–82.

Semyonov, M. 1988. "Bi-ethnic Labor Markets, Mono-Ethnic Labor Markets and Socioeconomic Inequality." *American Sociological Review* 53: 256–66.

Semyonov, M., N. Lewin-Epstein, and I. Brahm. 1999. "Changing Labor Force Participation and Occupational Status: Arab Women in the Israeli Labour Force." *Work, Employment and Society* 13(7): 117–31.

Sewell, G., and B. Wilkinson. 1992. "Someone to Watch Over Me: Surveillance Discipline and the Just-in-Time Labour Process." *Sociology* 26(2): 271–89.

Shokeid, M. 1982a. "Ethnicity and the Cultural Code Among Arabs in a Mixed Town: Women's Modesty and Men's Honor at Stake." In M. Shokeid and S. Deshen, eds., *Distant Relations.* New York: Praeger.

———. 1982b. "The Ordeal of Honor: Local Politics Among Urban Arabs." In M. Shokeid and S. Deshen, eds., *Distant Relations.* New York: Praeger.

———. 1988. "Anthropologists and Their Informants: Marginality Reconsidered." *Archives* 21: 31–47.

Smircich, L. 1983. "Concepts of Culture and Organizational Analysis." *Administrative Science Quarterly* 28: 339–58.

Smoocha, S. 1984. *The Orientation and Politicisation of the Arab Minority in Israel.* Monograph Series on the Middle East, no. 2. University of Haifa: Jewish Arab Center and Institute of Middle Eastern Studies [Hebrew].

———. 1990. "Minority Status in an Ethnic Democracy: The Status of the Arab Minority in Israel." *Ethnic and Racial Studies* 13: 389–413.

Snow, D. A., and Anderson, L. 1987. "Identity Work Among the

Homeless: The Verbal Construction and Avowal of Personal Identities." *American Journal of Sociology* 92: 1336–71.

Spradley, J. 1980. *Participant Observation*. New York: Holt, Reinhart and Winston.

Spybey, T. 1984. "Traditional and Professional Frames of Meaning for Managers." *Sociology* 18(4): 550–62.

———. 1996. *Globalization and World Society*. Cambridge, Mass.: Polity.

Steers, R. M. 1977. "Antecedents and Outcomes of Organizational Commitment." *Administrative Science Quarterly* 22: 46–56.

Stern, M. 1987. *Society and Family Strategy*. Albany, N.Y.: SUNY Press.

Stichter, S., and J. L. Parpart, eds., 1990. *Women, Employment and the Family in the International Division of Labour*. Philadelphia: Temple University Press.

Sundin, E. 1995. "The Social Construction of Gender and Technology: A Process with No Definitive Answer." *European Journal of Women's Studies* 2(3): 335–53.

Taplin, I. M. 1995. "Flexible Production, Rigid Jobs: Lessons from the Clothing Industry." *Work and Occupations* 22(4): 412–38.

Tentler, L. W. 1975. *Wage-Earning Women: Industrial Work and Family Life in the United States, 1900–1930*. New York: Oxford University Press.

Terpstra, D. E., and D. D. Baker. 1991. "Sexual Harassment at Work: The Psychosocial Issues." In M. J. Davidson and J. Earnshaw, eds., *Vulnerable Workers: Psychosocial and Legal Issues*. Chichester, U.K.: Wiley.

Thurley, K., and H. Wirdenius. 1973. *Supervision: A Reappraisal*. London: Heinemann.

Thurow, L. 1997. "The Rise and Fall of Brain Power." *Industry Week* 246(11): 114–17.

Tiano, S. 1987. "Gender, Work, and World Capitalism: Third World Women's Role in Development." In B. B. Hess and M. M. Ferree eds., *Analyzing Gender: A Handbook of Social Science Research*. Newbury Park, Calif.: Sage.

———. 1994. *Patriarchy on the Line: Labor, Gender, and Ideology in the Mexican Maquila Industry*. Philadelphia: Temple University Press.

Tilly, L. A., and J. W. Scott. 1978. *Women, Work, and Family*. New York: Holt, Rinehart and Winston.

Treiman, D. J., and H. I. Hartman. 1981. *Women, Work, and Wages: Equal Pay for Jobs of Equal Value*. Washington D.C.: National Academy Press.

Trice, H. M. 1984. "Rites and Ceremonials in Organizational Culture." In S. B. Bacharach and S. M. Mitchell, eds., *Perspectives on Organizational Sociology: Theory and Research*, vol. 4. Greenwich, Conn.: JAI.

Trice, H. M., and J. M. Beyer. 1994. *The Cultures of Work Organizations*. Englewood Cliffs, N.J.: Prentice Hall.

Tsuda, T. 1998. "Ethnicity and the Anthropologist: Negotiating Identities in the Field." *Anthropological Quarterly* 71(3): 107–24.

Vallas, S. P. 1999. "Rethinking Post-Fordism: The Meaning of Workplace Flexibility." *Sociological Theory* 17(1): 68–101.

Van Maanen, J. 1976. "Breaking In: Socialization to Work." In R. Dubin, ed., *Handbook of Work, Organization, and Society*. Chicago: Rand McNally.

———. 1979. "Reclaiming Qualitative Methods of Organizational Research: A Preface." *Administrative Science Quarterly* 24(4): 520–6.

Vinet, A., M. Vezina, C. Brisson, and P. M. Bernard. 1989. "Piecework, Repetitive Work and Medicine Use in the Clothing Industry." *Social Science Medicine* 12: 1283–88.

Walby, S. 1990. *Theorizing Patriarchy*. Cambridge, Mass.: Blackwell.

Wallerstein, I. 1974. *The Modern World-System*. New York: Academic Press.

Wallman, S. 1984. *Eight London Households*. London: Tavistock.

Webster, J. 1996. *Shaping Women's Work: Gender, Employment and Information Technology*. New York: Addison-Wesley Longman.

Westwood, S. 1984. *All Day, Every Day: Factory and Family in the Making of Women's Lives*. Urbana, Ill.: University of Illinois Press.

White, H. C. 1992. *Identity and Control: A Structural Theory of Social Action*. Princeton, N.J.: Princeton University Press.

Wolf, D. L. 1992. *Factory Daughters: Gender, Household Dynamics, and Rural Industrialization in Java*. Berkeley: University of California Press.

Wolf, M. 1972. *Women and the Family in Rural Taiwan*. Stanford: Stanford University Press.

Wood, S. 1993. "The Japanization of Fordism." *Economic and Industrial Democracy* 14: 535–55.

Woodward, J. 1965. *Industrial Organization: Theory and Practice*. London: Oxford University Press.

Yelvington, K. A. 1996. "Flirting in the Factory." *Journal of the Royal Anthropology Institute* 2: 313–33.

Youssef, N. H. 1974. *Women and Work in Developing Societies*. Berkeley: University of California.

———. 1978. "The Status and Fertility Patterns of Muslim Women."

In L. Beck and N. Keddie, eds., *Women in the Muslim World*. Cambridge, Mass.: Harvard University Press, 69–99.

Zavella, P. 1987. *Women's Work and Chicano Families: Cannery Workers of the Santa Clara Valley*. Ithaca, N.Y.: Cornell University Press.

Zipp, J. F. 1984. "Plant Closings and the Conflict Between Capital and Labor." In R. E. Ratclif and L. Kriesberg, eds., *Research in Social Movements, Conflict and Change*, vol. 6. Greenwich, Conn.: JAI, 225–48.

Zipp, J. F., and K. Z. E. Lane. 1987. "Plant Closings and Control over the Workplace—A Case Study." *Work and Occupations* 14(1): 62–87.

Zureik, E. 1979. *The Palestinians in Israel—A Study in Internal Colonialism*. London: Routledge and Kegan Paul.

250n2; sexuality issues in, 181–86, 249n10; types of, 15–18; working conditions in, 2, 15, 16–17, 34–36, 53–54, 56, 101, 105–8, 118–19, 189–94, 223, 237n3, 239n9, 240n1. *See also* Managers; Quality controllers; Seamstresses; Supervisors; Textile industry; Work culture
Shfaram sewing plant, 203
Shulman, Michael D., 1–2
Southeast Asia, 38
South Lebanese Militia (SLM), 236n7
supervisors: Arabs as, 1, 8; as department managers, 209–13, 217–18; Druse as, 1, 2–7, 201; equity/equality among, 156–59, 247n8; as mediators, 19, 46–47, 61, 134–35, 165, 177, 211, 223, 225–26; recruitment of, 64–67, 176, 222; relations among, 161–65, 173, 175, 212; relations with families of seamstresses, 6, 19, 22–23, 46, 135, 141–43, 177, 223; relations with managers, 6–7, 15, 19, 24, 27–29, 32–33, 46–47, 54–55, 58, 61, 64–68, 71–72, 83–84, 88, 125–27, 129–30, 134–35, 136, 137, 143–61, 162–65, 167, 173, 174–78, 184–86, 211–12, 220–24, 225–26, 246n4, 247n6, 247n8; relations with quality controllers, 60; relations with seamstresses, 3, 4, 6, 8–9, 19, 22–23, 24, 25, 28, 32–33, 46–47, 54, 55–56, 59, 61, 67–68, 73, 75–76, 93, 98, 105, 108, 110, 111, 120–21, 122–23, 125–32, 134–35, 136–43, 145–46, 147, 150, 155–56, 165, 174,

177, 201, 212–13, 225–226; religious affiliations of, 133–34; responsibilities of, 46, 55–56, 58, 59, 73, 134–38, 145, 147, 149–50, 165, 209–13, 210, 217–18; salaries of, 145, 159–61, 222, 228, 247n8; socialization of, 174–78, 249n6; as unmarried, 67, 133, 135–36

Taiwan, 40–41
Taplin, I. M., 207
Taylorism, 44–45
technology, 13, 15, 16, 44, 45, 46–47, 206–7
textile industry, 14–18, 248n1; and globalization, 1–2, 13–14, 15, 16, 38, 40, 42, 203–5; hi-tex organization in, 204–14, 217–18; relocation in, 1, 16, 18, 19, 32, 71–72, 203–6, 209–10, 214, 214–18, 250n1, 250n2; role in industrialization, 1–2, 13–14, 15, 16; technology in, 13, 15, 16, 44, 45, 46–47, 206–7; wages in, 18, 35, 71–72, 99, 107–8, 109, 113–17, 145, 159–61, 204, 208, 215, 216–17, 222, 228, 237n3, 241n7, 243n3, 250n1, 250n2; women in, 9, 12–13, 14, 34–36, 42. *See also* Sewing plants
Trinidad, 185

United States, 42, 97, 213, 249n6, 250n1
Upper Nazareth, 236n2

Van Maanen, J., 33

wage employment of women, 9, 10–11, 18, 50, 92, 235n9, 241n5;